An ATLAS and SURVEY of LATIN AMERICAN HISTORY

An ATLAS *and* SURVEY *of* LATIN AMERICAN HISTORY

MICHAEL J. LAROSA *and* GERMÁN R. MEJÍA

M.E.Sharpe
Armonk, New York
London, England

Library of Congress Cataloging-in-Publication Data

LaRosa, Michael (Michael J.)
    An atlas and survey of Latin American history / Michael J. LaRosa, Germán R. Mejía.
        p. cm.
Includes bibliographical references and index.
ISBN 10: 0-7656-1597-5 (cloth: alk. paper)—ISBN-10: 0-7656-1598-3 (pbk.: alk. paper)
ISBN 13: 978-0-7656-1597-8 (cloth: alk. paper)—ISBN-13: 978-0-7656-1598-5 (pbk.: alk. paper)
    1. Latin America—History—Maps. 2. Latin America—Historical geography—Maps.
3. Latin America—Maps. I. Mejía P., Germán. II. Title.

G1541.S1.L3 2006
911'.8—dc22   2006051197

Printed in the United States of America

The paper used in this publication meets the minimum requirements of
American National Standard for Information Sciences
Permanence of Paper for Printed Library Materials,
ANSI Z 39.48-1984.

BM (c) 10   9   8   7   6   5   4   3   2   1
BM (p) 10   9   8   7   6   5   4   3   2   1

To our parents,
Robert and Barbara LaRosa
of Braintree, Massachusetts,
and
Alfonso Mejía Restrepo and Yolanda Pavony de Mejía
of Bogotá, Colombia

CONTENTS

PREFACE AND ACKNOWLEDGMENTS

Latin America's complex history is not easy to define, quantify, or summarize, but one way to begin the process of understanding the region is to study its history as a function of physical and human geography. *An Atlas and Survey of Latin American History* offers a single-volume synthetic portrait of the interactions of physical geography and human history over a long time period in the territory commonly referred to as Latin America. We have adopted a nineteenth-century French definition of Latin America, which means that a territory is "Latin" to the extent that it was colonized by a country with a mostly Latin-derived language (for our purposes, Spanish, Portuguese, and French). By this definition, then, Haiti is Latin America but nearby Jamaica is not.

We hope this atlas is useful for students at the undergraduate and graduate levels as well as teachers who cover Latin American history/politics and geography in their courses but are not trained experts on the region. As such, this atlas helps facilitate an understanding of Latin America's history by explaining movement, patterns of development, and change throughout the region over time.

In 1967, Curtis A. Wiligus published *Historical Atlas of Latin America: Political, Geographic, Economic, Cultural.* John and Catherine Lombardi and Lynn Stoner, in 1983, published the influential *Latin American History: A Teaching Atlas,* a work found on the shelves of nearly every teacher of Latin American history and/or geography. A paperback version of that book was released in 1984. Our book is an update of these two important texts and builds on new research, theories, and realities in Latin America's ever-evolving and increasingly complex history and culture. A work that has also been of vital importance to us in preparing the current text is the 1988 *Atlas histórico-cultural de América* by Francisco Morales Padrón, a Spanish intellectual and professor in Seville. The work was published in two volumes in Las Palmas de Gran Canaria (Canary Islands).

In the work before you, the maps were drawn after the corresponding essays were written; while some information will overlap, each map/essay is designed to provide a complementary textual and visual comprehension of a specific topic. The actual map sketches are original designs by Liliana Mejía based on outline maps found at www.geography.about.com/blank/blindex/htm. All of the maps in this text use the political boundaries of "present-day" Latin America; this will provide a common point of reference for students using the atlas. Some of the statistical information used to construct the maps is found at Oxford (University's) Latin American Economic History Database, known as OxLAD and found on the Web at www.Oxlad.qeh.ox.ac.uk/. We also studied statistics produced by ECLAC, the United Nation's Economic Commission for Latin America and the Caribbean. Texts that synthesize Latin American history were especially helpful; a few such works are long out of print while others were published in the past few years. Some of the earlier, classic books include Charles Gibson's *Spain in America* (1966), Stanley and Barbara Stein's *The Colonial Heritage of Latin America* (1970), Dana Gardner Munro's *The Latin American Republics: A History* (1950), and Helen Miller Bailey and Abraham P. Nasatir's second edition of *Latin America: The Development of Its Civilization* (1968). The more recent works consulted include John Charles Chasteen's *Born in Blood and Fire* (2001) and Thomas E. Skidmore and Peter H. Smith's second edition of *Modern Latin America* (1989). Thomas Skidmore's *Brazil: Five Centuries of Change* (1999) has been particularly helpful as a synthesis of Brazil's complex history. At the end of each essay, we have cited a few of the principle sources used to construct both the essay and the map. Reflecting the reality of the times, many of our sources were found on the Internet and are cited with their complete URL.

We are fortunate to have counted on the cooperation of a number of talented individuals, without whom this project would never have been completed. In Bogotá, Mónica Hernández assisted with research. Liliana Mejía provided technical support and transferred our map designs to the appropriate computer programs. Lance Ingwersen, in Memphis, assisted with research, editing, and technical support. He also reviewed the entire manuscript in the final phase and helped with Spanish to English translations. Wesley Ingwersen, an environmental scientist in Gainesville, Florida, wrote an early draft of the essay "A Deforestation Estimate" and supplied the research for our map of the same title. Professor Tim Watkins, a musicologist at Rhodes College, wrote a first draft of the essay "Music of Latin America." Brian Shaffer, at Rhodes College, provided start-up research funds. At M.E. Sharpe, Debra Soled provided excellent technical advice and Niels Aaboe worked with us on editorial development of the project. Patricia Kolb, Angela Piliouras, and Nicole Cirino guided the project to publication. The careful copyediting of Susanna Sharpe improved this project immeasurably.

An ATLAS *and* SURVEY
of LATIN AMERICAN
HISTORY

1

THE LAND AND ITS PEOPLES

1A

Primary Geographic Features

Latin American geography is nearly impossible to define in one short essay. The vastness and complexity of "Latin America" comprises virtually all of the geographic characteristics found in the world. There are mountains, far-reaching river systems, deserts, grassy plains, high tropical plateaus (called *páramos*), jungles, even glaciers. For the purposes of this essay, Latin America will be defined as all territory south of the border that separates the United States and Mexico. The Caribbean islands conquered and colonized by countries with Latin-derivative languages will be included as well; Cuba is defined as Latin America, while Aruba is not. Climates vary from tropical to temperate. The equator bisects South America at Ecuador, Peru, Colombia, and Brazil, but climactic conditions are a function of many factors, including altitude. Thus, the city of Quito, which sits on the equator at 2,800 meters, is cold and damp while Manaus, in Brazil (at about the same latitude), sits along the Amazon River and has a more tropical climate.

Latin America consists of approximately 42 million square kilometers, but much of the Latin American continent is not populated by humans. Latin American geography—rivers, mountains, and jungles—has presented major obstacles and opportunities for the development of human civilization. Before the arrival of the European conquerors, Native Americans lived in relative isolation in diverse areas of Latin America. The nomadic Tupi in Southeast Brazil had little in common with the Aztecs of the Central Valley of Mexico, or the Caribbean Arawak peoples. These distinct civilizations were shaped, to a large degree, by the surrounding geographic and climactic factors. Europeans, upon arriving in America in 1492, were astounded by the variety of flora and fauna, and the diverse geography of the American continent. They believed that they had "discovered" a sort of Utopia that offered refuge from the wars, famines, and plagues of Europe.

Additionally, Latin America offered a vast array of natural resources that were of paramount importance to the invading Europeans. Silver and gold could be found in Mexico, Peru, Bolivia, and Colombia; sugar adapted easily to the climactic conditions of the Northeast of Brazil and the Caribbean islands; cacao became the principle export of what would become known as Venezuela. The diverse agricultural and mineral wealth reflected the wide array of climates and geography in the Latin American region.

There are three basic structural divisions that help clarify Latin America's geography. First, moving from the Atlantic toward the Pacific Ocean, there are the high eastern plains of Brazil and Guyana; the second division is generally referred to as vast interior lowlands, which extend (north–south) from Venezuela to Argentina and conform about five general geographic subdivisions: the *llanos* (or grassy plains of Venezuela and Colombia), the Amazon flatlands, the Chaco region of eastern Bolivia, the Argentine grasslands known as the Pampas, and the Patagonia plateau. This zone is comprised of the important Orinoco, Amazon, and River Plate river systems and tributaries. Finally, there are the western highlands, which extend from the south of Chile to the north of Mexico and through the Antilles. The Andes mountain range forms the spine of the Latin American continent: the mountains begin in southern Chile, divide in two places in Bolivia, run through Peru and Ecuador, divide again in Colombia, and terminate in Venezuela and Colombia at the Caribbean Sea. Mexico is characterized by vast deserts in the north, and mountains in the south, west, and central regions of the country.

This general outline of Latin American geography hardly reflects the complexity of individual areas. For example, Peru's geography alone contains a dry western coast influenced by the Pacific Ocean Humboldt current, which brings cold, moist air to the Peruvian coast. Rising up to the immediate east of the coast are the dramatic Andes, with many fertile hamlets, once home to the great Inca civilization. To the east of the Andes lies a vast tropical jungle. Peruvian geography is no more or less complex than that of other nations of Latin America, but the Peruvian case shows that human exigency has tended to overcome and adapt to complex terrain in Peru and in Latin America in general.

The geography of Latin America helps explain the history of the region. It is impossible to speak of any sort of Latin American unification, as geographic reality prevents, for all practical purposes, territorial unity. Thus, the individual personalities and characteristics of the distinct Latin American peoples were shaped by geographic factors, then reshaped by the European conquerors who arrived in the late fifteenth century.

BIBLIOGRAPHY

Clawson, David L. 1997. *Latin America and the Caribbean Lands and Peoples.* New York: McGraw-Hill.

Cunill Grau, Pedro. 1999. "La geohistoria." In *Para una historia de América Latina, I. Las estructuras,* ed. Marcello Carmagnani, Alicia Hernández Chávez, Ruggiero Romano. México, DF: FCE y El Colegio de México.

SIERRA DE JUÁREZ

VIZCAINO DESERT

GULF OF CALIFORNIA

SIERRA MADRE WESTERN

R. BRAVO (GRANDE)

SIERRA MADRE EASTERN

GULF OF MEXICO

LAKE CHAPALA

CENTRAL PLATEAU

SOUTH SIERRA MADRE

ISTHMUS OF TEHUANTEPEC

YUCATAN

YUCATAN CANAL

FLORIDA STRAITS

GULF OF HONDURAS

GREATER ANTILLES

LESSER ANTILLES

CENTRAL PLATEAU OF CHIAPAS

CARIBBEAN SEA

LAKE MANAGUA

LAKE NICARAGUA

R. SAN JUAN

PANAMA CANAL

GULF OF URABÁ

GULF OF MARACAIBO

GULF OF PANAMA

R. CAUCA

R. MAGDALENA

ORINOCO PLAINS

R. META

R. ORINOCO

R. VICHADA

GUYANAN MASSIF

R. GUAVIARE

R. VAUPEZ

R. CAQUETA

R. PUTUMAYO

R. NEGRO

R. NAPO

R. AMAZONAS

R. MARAÑÓN

JUNGLES

AMAZON PLAINS

SERTÃO

R. SÃO FRANCISCO

R. UCAYALI

R. URUBAMBA

LAKE TITICACA

MATO GROSSO

SERRA GERAL GOIÁS

SERRA DO ESPINHAÇO

YUNGAS

ATACAMA DESERT

R. PARANÁ

CENTRAL PLAIN

PRIMARY MOUNTAINS

GRAN CHACO

R. PARAGUAY

SERRA DO MAR

R. PARANÁ

PAMPAS

R. URUGUAY

RIO DE LA PLATA

PATAGONIA

1B

The Peoples and Nations

Latin America today is comprised of twenty politically independent nations, and the people who inhabit the region are as diverse as the geography that tends to separate them.[1] Two-thirds of all Latin Americans live in the three most populous countries, Brazil, Mexico, and Colombia. The political boundaries are somewhat artificial constructs, developed primarily by the Spaniards and Portuguese as a way of ordering and controlling vast territories and millions of people. During the nineteenth century, the newly independent nations of Latin America constructed territorial boundaries that roughly resembled the Spanish-Portuguese delineations. The boundaries would reflect the priorities of Europeans in America; thus, the territorial division of Latin America in the early republic period began with unfortunate consequences for the people. For example, Aymara-speaking peoples in the south of Peru were divided by a political boundary: those living to the north identified themselves as Peruvians, whereas those to the south referred to themselves as Bolivians. The same occurred with indigenous peoples living along the borders between Ecuador and Peru, Ecuador and Colombia, and Mexico and Guatemala.

Latin Americans are not a singular people, and the distinct cultures and histories of the immense Latin American region defy clear or facile definitions. It is impossible to assign a general physiognomic characterization to "Latin Americans." The people are descendents of Native Americans, Europeans, Africans, and people of Middle Eastern and Asian origin. The distribution of these peoples and their descendents varies throughout the region and reflects a dynamic sociopolitical and economic exchange over a lengthy time period. The largest concentrations of Asians in Latin America are found in Peru (mostly descendents of Chinese workers who migrated in the nineteenth century) and Brazil (mostly Japanese in origin, who migrated to Brazil and settled primarily in the city of São Paulo in the first half of the twentieth century, particularly in the interwar years). People of African descent are concentrated in the Northeast of Brazil (where they were forced to work as slaves during the sugar plantation boom of the sixteenth and seventeenth centuries), on the north coast of South America, the northern Pacific coast of South America (including the Colombian Chocó, the lowlands of Ecuador, and the northwestern region of Peru), and the Caribbean islands of Cuba, Puerto Rico, and Hispaniola (which comprises the nations of Haiti and the Dominican Republic). Large concentrations of Native Americans are found in the highlands of Guatemala, Peru, Bolivia, Ecuador, and Paraguay. Significant concentrations of Europeans are found in Uruguay, Argentina, Brazil, and the major metropolitan areas of most other Latin American countries.

The role of the Roman Catholic Church has been extraordinary in shaping Latin America's diverse culture: most people still identify themselves, nominally at least, as Catholic, though the growth of evangelical Protestantism in the region has been remarkable, especially in the past twenty years in Chile, Brazil, and Central America. Portuguese is spoken by about 185 million residents of Brazil, while Spanish is the dominant language in the rest of Latin America. However, large percentages of the populations of Peru, Bolivia, and Guatemala speak Native American languages, including Quechua, Aymara, and Quiché. The official language of Paraguay is not Spanish but Guaraní.

Latin America, it is important to note, is a remarkable melting pot—more so, perhaps, than the United States. Most Latin Americans, culturally and racially, fall somewhere "in between." Categories that are normally assigned in the United States (black or white, for example) fail to capture the reality of Latin American *mestizaje*, or race-mixing, over time. The nature of contact and conquest, the number and influence of Native American communities, and the African presence all influence the contour of *mestizaje* in Latin America and make it impossible to draw exact definitions when discussing the Latin American people. Yet, though racially mixed over time and place, social (and racial) segregation continues to pose historic challenges to Latin American citizens and societies.

NOTE

1. We are not counting the countries of Belize, Jamaica, or Guyana, Suriname, and French Guiana in our calculation of the number of Latin American countries. For the Caribbean, we include Haiti, the Dominican Republic, and Cuba as "Latin American countries."

BIBLIOGRAPHY

Asociación Latinoamericana de Estudios Afroasiáticos (ALADAA). 1983. *Asia y África en América Latina.* Tunja: Universidad Pedagógica y Tecnológica de Colombia.

Stein, Stanley, and Barbara Stein. 1970. *The Colonial Heritage of Latin America.* New York: Oxford University Press.

1B
THE PEOPLES AND NATIONS
OF LATIN AMERICA

LA HABANA
CUBA

SANTO DOMINGO
DOMINICAN REPUBLIC

MEXICO CITY
MEXICO

PORT-AU-PRINCE
HAITI

SAN JUAN
PUERTO RICO

TEGUCIGALPA
HONDURAS

GUATEMALA CITY
GUATEMALA

SAN SALVADOR
EL SALVADOR

MANAGUA
NICARAGUA

PANAMA CITY
PANAMA

CARACAS
VENEZUELA

SAN JOSÉ
COSTA RICA

BOGOTÁ
COLOMBIA

QUITO
ECUADOR

LIMA
PERU

LA PAZ
BOLIVIA

BRASÍLIA
BRAZIL

SUCRE

ASUNCIÓN
PARAGUAY

SANTIAGO
CHILE

BUENOS AIRES
ARGENTINA

MONTEVIDEO
URUGUAY

CAPITAL

NON-LATIN COUNTRY

■ COUNTRY WITH HIGH % OF BLACK POPULATION

● COUNTRY WITH HIGH % OF INDIGENOUS POPULATION

★ COUNTRY WITH HIGH % OF ASIAN POPULATION

◆ COUNTRY WITH HIGH % OF EUROPEAN IMMIGRATION, 19th AND 20th CENTURIES

● COUNTRY WITH HIGH % OF POPULATION SPEAKING INDIGENOUS LANGUAGES

▲ PORTUGUESE-SPEAKING COUNTRY

1c

Indigenous America Today

No one knows for certain how many Native Americans lived in the territory called Latin America before the arrival of the Europeans. It is known that tens of millions of natives died as a result of European disease, dislocation, excessive work, and de facto enslavement by the Spaniards and Portuguese. The colonial structure in Latin America relegated indigenous culture to a secondary plane—in fact, in many places, Native Americans were forced to adopt the culture, religion, language, and customs of their European masters and were told to forget about indigenous customs, considered (by Europeans) backward at best and barbaric in the most extreme cases.

It was not until the early twentieth century that a clear celebration of indigenous culture took shape in much of Latin America. *Indigenismo,* as the movement came to be known, was most apparent in Mexico, Peru, and some parts of Brazil. Intellectuals, particularly at the conclusion of World War I, decided to look inward at their own history and culture. The prior model, in effect since the conquest, was to assume that all that was "good" culturally (language, religion, law, government) originated in Europe. Yet the Latin American love affair with Europe changed as the savagery of World War I ground on. After about 1920 it became fashionable to celebrate indigenous culture, study native languages and traditions, and reflect on the importance of Native Americans as contributors to Latin American culture.

Today, millions of Latin Americans speak Native American languages and live in communities dominated by native customs and traditions. In Peru, Bolivia, Ecuador, and Colombia some 8.5 million people speak Quechua. In Paraguay, the official language of the republic is Guaraní, spoken by about 3 million Paraguayans. Quiché is spoken by over a million residents of Guatemala, and Náhuatl is spoken by about 1.3 million Mexicans.

Still, despite impressive gains in recognition during the twentieth century, Native American communities and cultures remain isolated, marginalized, and underappreciated throughout much of Latin America. Recently, a number of significant indigenous uprisings have taken hold, demonstrating the precarious position of millions of citizens within the region. Several important events have shaped an indigenous political agenda in key areas of Latin America. First, a new constitution in Colombia in 1991 declared the nation to be "multicultural" and acknowledged the presence of indigenous persons. This document promised to use state power to protect them. Nineteen ninety-one marked the first time in Colombian history that any such recognition was offered. Second, in 1992, the Nobel Academy in Oslo awarded the Peace Prize to Rigoberta Menchú Tum, a Quiché-speaking woman who fought to expose the genocide committed in the 1970s and 1980s against native Guatemalans. Two years later, on January 1, 1994, in Mexico, the EZLN (Zapatista Army of National Liberation) made a dramatic entrance onto the world scene by taking several towns in the south of Mexico and declaring itself against the North American Free Trade Agreement, or NAFTA. The EZLN is still fighting for the rights of the poor, mostly indigenous people, who live in southern Mexico in extreme conditions. Recent developments in Ecuador and Bolivia, where important indigenous resistance has led to the collapse of government in both places, clearly show that indigenous issues, priorities, and culture can no longer be ignored by central governments, particularly in countries with a strong Native American presence.

Table 1.1

Indigenous Latin American Languages

Language	Country	Number of Speakers
Quechua	Peru, Brazil, Bolivia, Argentina, Ecuador, Colombia	8.5 million
Guaraní	Paraguay	3 million
Quiché	Guatemala	1.3 million
Náhuatl	Mexico	1.3 million
Otomí	Mexico	261,000
Totonaco	Mexico	215,000
Miskitu	Nicaragua, Honduras	200,000
Jíbaro	Ecuador, Peru	50,000
Cuna	Panama	50,000
Emberá	Panama, Colombia	40,000
Ticuna	Peru, Colombia, Brazil	21,000

Source: Table taken and adapted from Enrique Yepes "Las otras civilizaciones precolumbinas" at www.bowdoin.edu/~eyepes/latam/civind.htm

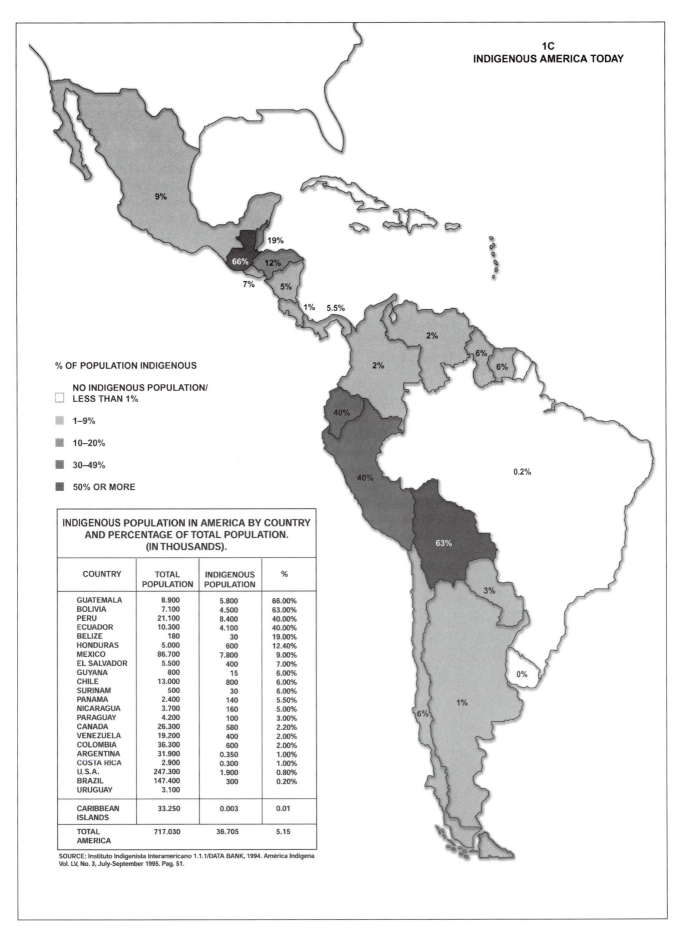

1C
INDIGENOUS AMERICA TODAY

% OF POPULATION INDIGENOUS

NO INDIGENOUS POPULATION/
LESS THAN 1%

1–9%

10–20%

30–49%

50% OR MORE

INDIGENOUS POPULATION IN AMERICA BY COUNTRY
AND PERCENTAGE OF TOTAL POPULATION.
(IN THOUSANDS).

COUNTRY	TOTAL POPULATION	INDIGENOUS POPULATION	%
GUATEMALA	8.900	5.800	66.00%
BOLIVIA	7.100	4.500	63.00%
PERU	21.100	8.400	40.00%
ECUADOR	10.300	4.100	40.00%
BELIZE	180	30	19.00%
HONDURAS	5.000	600	12.40%
MEXICO	86.700	7.800	9.00%
EL SALVADOR	5.500	400	7.00%
GUYANA	800	15	6.00%
CHILE	13.000	800	6.00%
SURINAM	500	30	6.00%
PANAMA	2.400	140	5.50%
NICARAGUA	3.700	160	5.00%
PARAGUAY	4.200	100	3.00%
CANADA	26.300	580	2.20%
VENEZUELA	19.200	400	2.00%
COLOMBIA	36.300	600	2.00%
ARGENTINA	31.900	0.350	1.00%
COSTA RICA	2.900	0.300	1.00%
U.S.A.	247.300	1.900	0.80%
BRAZIL	147.400	300	0.20%
URUGUAY	3.100		
CARIBBEAN ISLANDS	33.250	0.003	0.01
TOTAL AMERICA	717.030	36.705	5.15

SOURCE: Instituto Indigenista Interamericano 1.1.1/DATA BANK, 1994. América Indígena
Vol. LV, No. 3, July-September 1995. Pag. 51.

2

AMERICA BEFORE 1500

Theories of Arrival and Paleolithic America

There are fairly clear dates for the arrival to America of Europeans and Africans. In October 1492, the Italian Christopher Columbus—contracted by the Spanish monarchs Ferdinand and Isabelle—arrived in the Antilles and planted the Spanish flag on American soil. By 1518 the first enslaved sub-Saharan Africans arrived. Their presence had a dramatic impact on the economy and culture of Latin America, especially around the Caribbean basin and northeastern Brazil. But scholars are less clear as to when the first Native Americans arrived on the American continent, and that important issue has been the subject of a long, sometimes contentious debate.

According to the U.S. anthropologist Eric Wolf in his classic book *Sons of the Shaking Earth*, humans began arriving to the Americas about 20,000 years ago, at a time when a Siberian land-bridge existed between what is today the northeast corner of the Soviet Union and the far western edge of Alaska. The earliest Americans, then, most likely originated in Central Asia, or the territory today called Mongolia. This "one-place origin" thesis suggests that early Americans fanned out north–south and settled throughout two continents; they were the precursors of the great settled civilizations and nomadic peoples encountered by the Europeans after 1492. Anthropologists, archeologists, and biologists have considered the similarities in physiognomic type between pure Native Americans and the people who today inhabit Mongolia in Central Asia. But, it seems likely that there were successive migratory waves to America across the Bering Strait, and, given the ethnic, cultural, and linguistic diversity of the people who would come to inhabit "America," it is unlikely that only one group from Central Asia arrived and populated two continents with offspring.

The French anthropologist Paul Rivet posited a "multiple-origin" theory, which suggested that America was populated with people from many places, not just Central Asia. He theorized that migratory waves from Australia, Melanesia, Central Asia, and North Alaska (Eskimos) arrived, in the order listed, over various centuries. Rivet based his findings on similar physiognomic characteristics found among the peoples and used a linguistic categorization as well, noting that many similar words could be found between Melanesian and Native American languages. In 1947, the Norwegian anthropologist Thor Heyerdahl crossed the Pacific Ocean, starting in Peru, and arrived at the Polynesian Islands. He was thus able to show the "possibility" that such a voyage took place; his raft, called the *Kon-Tiki*, was made of materials found in Polynesia in the earliest days of Polynesian civilization.

Still another such voyage took place in 1970 when Heyerdahl crossed the Atlantic on a raft made from the papyrus used in ancient Egyptian raft-building. The voyage took the anthropologist from Morocco to Barbados. Scholars have, in the past, tried to connect ancient Egyptian society with ancient American, suggesting that similarities in architectural style (the pyramids of Egypt and the pyramids of southern Mexico and Central America) must have been transmitted from Egypt to America. However, no clear connection has ever been proven, and now, most scholars understand the American pyramids as uniquely shaped by the cultural, religious, and environmental properties of Mesoamerica.

Theories abound as to the origins of the first Americans. Yet during the Ice Age, ocean levels were lower. Thus, it is likely that the American and Asian continents were connected by some type of land-bridge that allowed passage over a ninety-kilometer distance from Asia to America. Most evidence points to a gradual, slow, successive migratory process from Central Asia to America at what is today the Bering Strait. Our map shows eight select sites in the Americas that have yielded evidence of early human habitation; we have included an approximate date of human arrival.

BIBLIOGRAPHY

Bethell, Leslie. 2001. *History of Latin America, vol. I. Colonial Latin America: Pre-Columbian America and the Conquest.* Barcelona: Crítica.

Wolf, Eric R. 1959. *Sons of the Shaking Earth.* Chicago: University of Chicago Press.

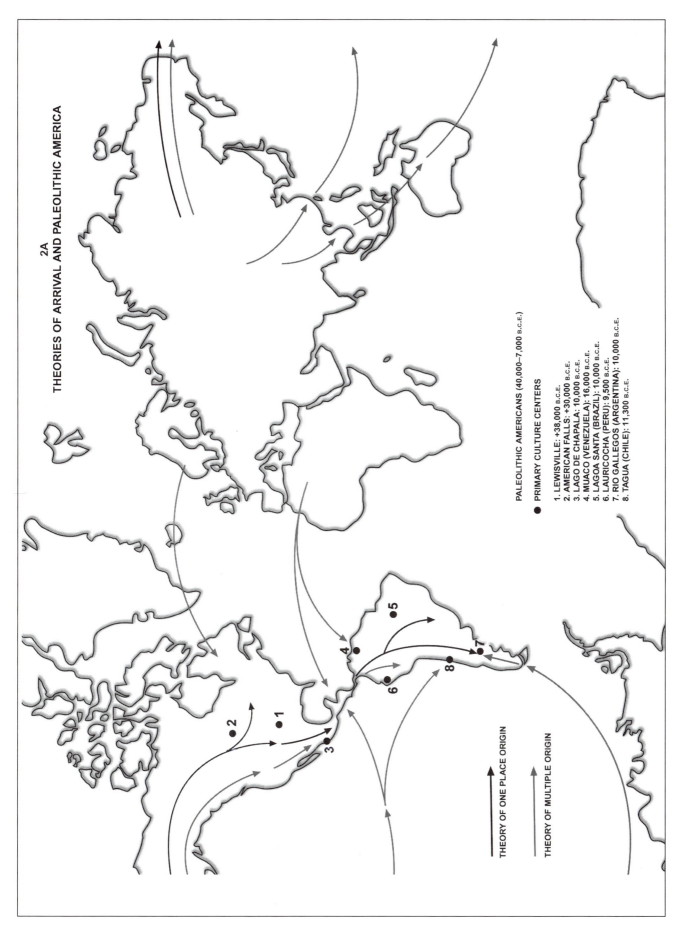

2A
THEORIES OF ARRIVAL AND PALEOLITHIC AMERICA

PALEOLITHIC AMERICANS (40,000–7,000 B.C.E.)

● PRIMARY CULTURE CENTERS

1. LEWISVILLE: +38,000 B.C.E.
2. AMERICAN FALLS: +30,000 B.C.E.
3. LAGO DE CHAPALA: 10,000 B.C.E.
4. MUACO (VENEZUELA): 16,000 B.C.E.
5. LAGOA SANTA (BRAZIL): 10,000 B.C.E.
6. LAURICOCHA (PERU): 9,500 B.C.E.
7. RIO GALLEGOS (ARGENTINA): 10,000 B.C.E.
8. TAGUA (CHILE): 11,300 B.C.E.

THEORY OF ONE PLACE ORIGIN

THEORY OF MULTIPLE ORIGIN

Mexico, Central America, and the Antilles Before 1500

The highly stratified and advanced societies of Middle America (or Mesoamerica) shocked the Europeans who arrived there about 1519. The Spaniards never imagined that a sophisticated, settled civilization could exist in America, and the cultural clash that began in 1492 in the Caribbean continued when the Spaniards fought against, and eventually defeated, the mighty Aztec civilization with its capital at Tenochtitlán. But the Aztecs were not the first people to inhabit the Central Valley of Mexico; in fact, they were relative latecomers. Many civilizations developed and collapsed in the area of Central Mexico and what is today Central America and the Yucatan Peninsula.

Sedentary and semi-sedentary peoples lived on the Caribbean islands before 1492, and the largest communities were inhabited by Arawak, Taino, and Siboney. These people lived on the islands of Hispaniola, Puerto Rico, and Cuba. The Caribs lived on scattered, smaller islands throughout the Caribbean and were considered the most hostile people in the region. One of the best sources for understanding the native peoples of the Caribbean is found in the writing of the sixteenth-century Dominican priest, Father (Fray) Bartolomé de las Casas. In *Historia de las Indias,* Las Casas rendered an extensive, surprisingly complimentary ethnographic and historical account of Caribbean natives. There were probably between 750,000 and one million people living on the Caribbean islands before the arrival of Columbus. Most of them lived on Hispaniola, the island that today is home to Haiti and the Dominican Republic.

About 5,000 B.C.E. the people of Mesoamerica created settled communities and learned to cultivate *maíz,* or corn. One of the most important groups to settle in the Central Valley of Mexico, the Toltecs, originated in the northwest (in what is today Arizona and New Mexico in the United States) and moved down into the fertile Central Valley in waves. They were great artisans and builders and fierce warriors who conquered sedentary groups that stood in their way. The Toltecs (c. 900–1100 C.E.) left impressive architectural monuments at Tula, Cholula, and Teotihuacán, the latter representing a great city, and one of the most important examples of early classical Middle American civilization, generally dated between 200–600 C.E.

The Mayan civilization spread throughout the Yucatan Peninsula in what is today southern Mexico, Guatemala, Belize, and some parts of Honduras and El Salvador. There are more than fifty important Mayan archeological sites, all of which were inhabited during the classical period, about 600–800 C.E. Settlements in Guatemala, along the Caribbean coast, defined the early period of Mayan history (to about 800 C.E.); the second period, from the ninth century to the arrival of the Europeans, was marked by a shift toward the Yucatan Peninsula and away from the coast and interior of Guatemala/southern Mexico. Many factors might have contributed to the move north, including natural disasters (earthquakes and drought), overpopulation, disease, and social conflict. But the early Mayan civilization, in full force at about the time of Christ's birth, was truly remarkable considering what remains, architecturally, today: Palenque, Tikal, and Copán (found in Mexico, Guatemala, and Honduras, respectively) were centers of great learning and artistic achievement. Mathematics and astronomy were perfected during this time, calendars were developed, and human figures were carved into friezes on Mayan temples.

The Caribbean, Mexico, and Central America were hardly unpopulated, uncultured lands before the arrival of the Europeans in the late fifteenth century. A vast array of nomadic and settled peoples lived in these territories; the Zapotec, Maya, and Toltec peoples are considered early geniuses on both American continents. They developed thriving civilizations, left behind monumental architecture, and dispelled any notion of culture as "arriving" from Europe in 1492.

BIBLIOGRAPHY

Bailey, Helen Miller, and Abraham P. Nasatir. 1968. *Latin America: The Development of Its Civilization.* 2d ed. Englewood Cliffs: Prentice Hall.

Fuentes, Carlos. 1992. *The Buried Mirror: Reflections on Spain and the New World.* Boston: Houghton Mifflin.

Las Casas, Bartolomé de. 1992. *A Short Account of the Devastation of the Indies.* London: Penguin Books.

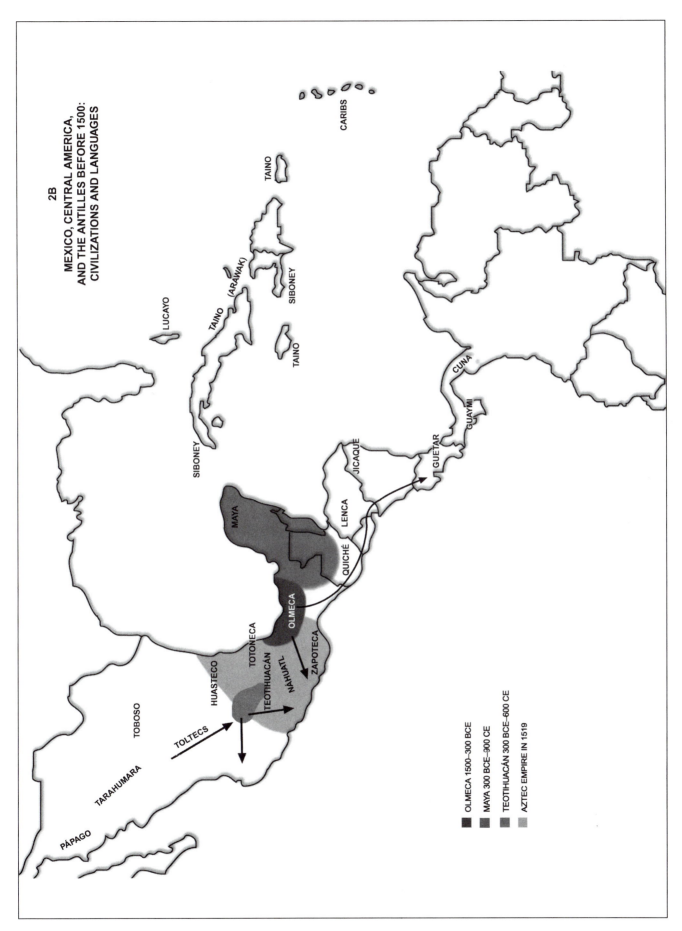

2B

MEXICO, CENTRAL AMERICA,
AND THE ANTILLES BEFORE 1500:
CIVILIZATIONS AND LANGUAGES

CARIBS

TAINO

TAINO (ARAWAK)

SIBONEY

TAINO

LUCAYO

SIBONEY

CUNA

GUAYMI

GUETAR

JICAQUE

LENCA

QUICHÉ

MAYA

OLMECA

TOTONECA

ZAPOTECA

HUASTECO

TEOTIHUACÁN

NÁHUATL

TOBOSO

TOLTECS

TARAHUMARA

PÁPAGO

OLMECA 1500–300 BCE

MAYA 300 BCE–900 CE

TEOTIHUACÁN 300 BCE–600 CE

AZTEC EMPIRE IN 1519

South America Before 1500

The great civilizations of South America, specifically the Inca Empire—which ran from Bolivia and northern Chile, through Ecuador and Peru, to present-day Colombia—were hardly the first important civilizations to inhabit the South American continent. Ancient Peruvian civilization was characterized by extensive coastal and highland communities to the north, east, and south of present-day Lima. One of the most impressive coastal cities, Chan Chan, was home to the Chimus, skilled craftspeople who perfected the art of pottery making. Coastal civilization developed once people learned to grow cotton, from which nets could be woven to catch fish. Water was transported using gourds, and later clay pots, and a vast economic exchange developed between specialized peoples on the coast and the interior civilizations.

One of the earliest Peruvian highland civilizations, Chavín, existed at an altitude of about 3,000 meters (above 10,000 feet) in the eastern Andes and flourished from 1000 to 300 B.C.E. In Peru, people living in the highlands depended on coastal peoples for salt, pottery, and cotton, while the highlands provided wool, potatoes, and corn. In the southern area of Peru, around Lake Titicaca, the primary language group was Aymara; further north, the people spoke Quechua.

By the fifteenth century, Tawantinsuyu, or the Inca state, came to dominate much of western South America. The *camino real* represented a network of roads extending out from and through the city of Cuzco—the capital of the Inca Empire located in southern Peru. The earliest accounts of the Inca Empire are from "The Inca" Garcilaso de la Vega, son of a Spaniard and an Inca princess, born in 1539 in Cuzco. De la Vega, a mestizo, wrote *Historia general del Perú* in 1617, in which he emphasized the contributions of the Inca civilization, de-emphasized the contributions of their forefathers, and suggested that Andean civilization began with the Inca peoples.

In what is today Colombia, the Muisca peoples (generally referred to as Chibchas) established an important civilization based on a fertile, high plateau, or savannah, called Bacatá (today, Bogotá). They also dominated the land north of Bogotá, and it is estimated that their civilization had reached a population of just over one million at the time of Spanish conquest in the early sixteenth century. The Muiscas developed advanced social structures, an elaborate trade network, and organized religious identity. They traded salt from an important mine at nearby Zipaquirá.

People belonging to the Arawak linguistic family occupied the eastern plains of Colombia, extending into Venezuela. Carib-speaking peoples lived on the northern coast of South America. Another impressive civilization established itself around the present-day city of Santa Marta (Colombia); the Tairona are Chibcha-speaking peoples whose descendents still live in and around the Sierra Nevada mountains of Santa Marta.

In present-day Paraguay, the Guaraní established an important civilization and their language is spoken by millions of Paraguayans. The Guaraní settled in small communities where they farmed and traded with Aymara-speaking peoples from Bolivia. Their relatives, the Tupi-Guaraní, lived in contemporary Brazil, along the coast. The Tupi were semi-sedentary peoples who lived off of fish and cultivated manioc root, or cassava.

Thus, a vast matrix of indigenous civilizations existed throughout South America at the time of the Spanish conquest. The Native Americans produced, traded, lived in complex societies, and left behind impressive architectural monuments and hand-crafted evidence, all of which shed light on the development of important civilizations in South America prior to 1500.

BIBLIOGRAPHY

Moseley, Michael. 1992. *The Incas and Their Ancestors*. New York: Thames and Hudson.

Rojas Rabiela, Teresa (dir.), and John V. Murra (co-dir.). 1999. *Historia general de América Latina*. Vol. 1, *Las sociedades originarias*. Madrid: Editorial Trotta.

Safford Frank, and Marco Palacios. 2002. *Colombia: Fragmented Land, Divided Society*. New York: Oxford University Press.

2C
SOUTH AMERICA BEFORE 1500:
CIVILIZATIONS AND LANGUAGES

CARIBS

ARAWAK

CHIBCHA

TUCANO

CARIBS

CHIMU
1200–1400 C.E.

QUECHUA

CHAVÍN
1000–300 B.C.E.

MOCHICA
300 B.C.E.–700 C.E.

TUPI

CUZCO

NAZCA
300 B.C.E.–700 C.E.

TIAHUANACO
700–1200 C.E.

GE

TUPI

AYMARA

GUARANÍ

TUPI

INCA EMPIRE IN 1500

ARAUCANOS

PATAGONES

3

SCIENCE, EXPLORATION, AND EXPANSION

3A

Exploration of the Atlantic and the West African Coast

The Italian navigator Christopher Columbus was not the first European to contemplate and study the Atlantic Ocean. The Italians, Spanish, and Portuguese were the principal sea-faring southern Europeans in the fifteenth century, but the Portuguese clearly led the way.

Technological advances, including Portuguese perfection of the astrolabe and compass, greatly assisted Portuguese pilots in the fourteenth century. Other factors facilitated Portugal's rise as early world sea power: first, geography—Portugal's western boundary is the Atlantic Ocean; second, the port city of Lisbon helped the territory referred to by the Romans as Lusitania emerge as a major sea power; third, compared to the neighboring kingdoms in Spain, the Portuguese unified earlier, and expelled the Moors more efficiently. Thus, by the early fifteenth century, Portugal was a strong, independent kingdom under the rule of King John the Great (r. 1385–1433) and managed to remain independent from the surrounding Spanish kingdoms. King John opened up an early entrance into Africa by capturing the port of Ceuta, situated on the African side of Gibraltar.

Prince Henry the Navigator (1394–1460), son of King John, is generally credited with advancing the Portuguese seaborne empire. Henry's motivations were religious and commerical; like many devout Christians of his day, he believed that the best way to definitively beat the Muslim forces and their influence was through an "encircling" strategy, whereby Christian Europe would engulf Muslim Africa and Constantinople. To accomplish this, the Portuguese would sail out into the Atlantic and down the West African coast. At Sagres, in southwest Portugal, Henry presided over a naval institute where he surrounded himself with naval experts and "built an observatory, made maps and charts, built ships, trained pilots, and received reports from his captains who were year by year working farther down the shoulder of Africa."[1]

Commercial interests also motivated the Portuguese. Slaves, gold, ivory, cotton, and spices could be taken from Africa. The Portuguese sailed to Madeira and the Azore islands, and from there to Africa in search of riches; with the support of the papacy, they laid claim to a large portion of West Africa, including Ghana, Benin, Gabon, and Mali. Much of the wealth generated was in human cargo: In 1441, people from sub-Saharan Africa were brought back to Portugal as slaves. At Arguin Bay, Africa, a slave-trading post was set up through which enslaved Africans were transported to Lisbon, the primary slave port in Europe at this time. Some African leaders were interested in exchanging slaves for European products, such as weapons and horses. In 1443, one horse, for example, could be exchanged for 25 to 30 African slaves. Though other Europeans would become involved in the overseas slave trade after 1441 (including the Dutch, Spanish, Belgians, British, and French), the Portuguese have the dubious distinction of setting the template, in modern times, for the removal of Africans from their homelands and their enslavement in other parts of the world.

Christian Europe panicked when Constantinople fell to the forces of Islam in 1453. That event pushed Europeans to search for a westward sea route to the fabled riches of the East (India); logically, the Portuguese would take the lead in this venture given the decades of seaborne experience accumulated during the early part of the fifteenth century.

NOTE

1. Helen Miller Bailey and Abraham P. Nasatir, *Latin America: The Development of Its Civilization,* 2d ed. (Englewood Cliffs, NJ: Prentice Hall, 1968), p. 29.

BIBLIOGRAPHY

Gibson, Charles. 1966. *Spain in America.* New York: Harper and Row.
Stein, Stanley, and Barbara Stein. 1970. *The Colonial Heritage of Latin America.* New York: Oxford University Press.

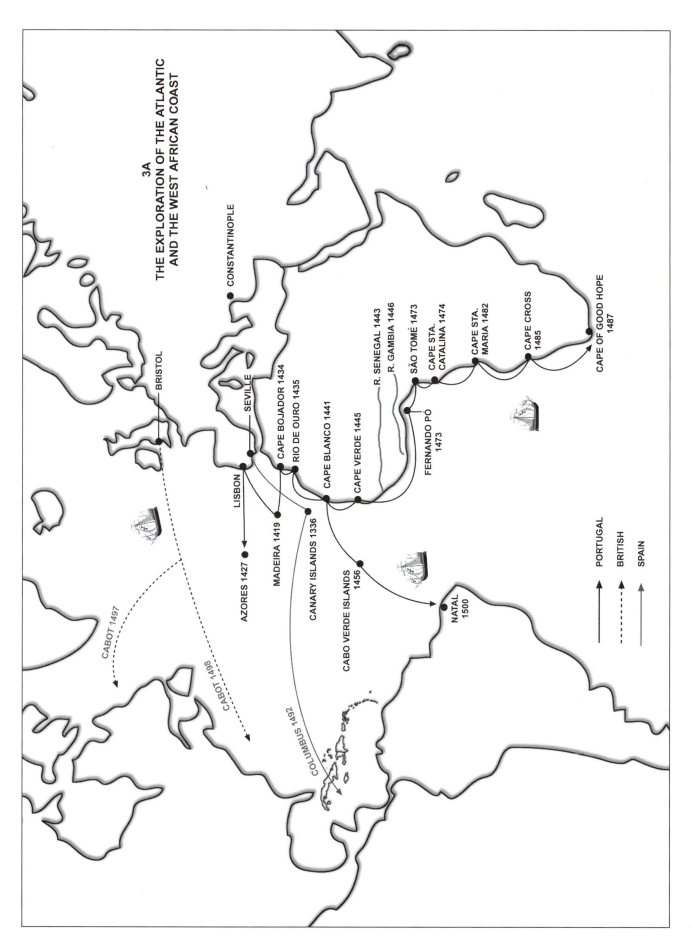

3A
THE EXPLORATION OF THE ATLANTIC
AND THE WEST AFRICAN COAST

CONSTANTINOPLE

BRISTOL

SEVILLE

LISBON

CAPE BOJADOR 1434
RIO DE OURO 1435

CAPE BLANCO 1441

CAPE VERDE 1445

R. SENEGAL 1443
R. GAMBIA 1446

SÃO TOMÉ 1473
CAPE STA.
CATALINA 1474
CAPE STA.
MARIA 1482
CAPE CROSS
1485
CAPE OF GOOD HOPE
1487

FERNANDO PÓ
1473

AZORES 1427

MADEIRA 1419

CANARY ISLANDS 1336

CABO VERDE ISLANDS
1456

NATAL
1500

CABOT 1497

CABOT 1498

COLUMBUS 1492

PORTUGAL

BRITISH

SPAIN

3B

The Four Voyages of Columbus

Christopher Columbus, son of a Genovese wool merchant, sailed for Spain in 1492 and is credited with "discovering" America. Neither Italian nor Portuguese merchants/nobility were interested in contracting the young, brash navigator who proposed sailing straight out into the Atlantic to arrive at India. The Portuguese were well on their way, by 1492, to establishing important trading colonies along the African coast, which brought great riches to Portuguese merchants and noblemen. By contrast, the Italians had a well-established trade network throughout the Mediterranean world. By Columbus's own calculations, thirty to forty days' sailing from the Canary Islands, due west, would put him in India. Columbus knew the earth was round; what he did not know about was the presence of two significant obstacles that would prevent him from achieving his objective—the American landmass and the Pacific Ocean.

One reason Spain accepted Columbus's plan and financed his voyage involved the luck of timing. In 1492, the kingdoms of Aragon and Castile, unified in the arranged marriage of Ferdinand and Isabelle in 1469, finally defeated the forces of Islam at the Battle of Granada. The wars of reconquest—*la reconquista*—had lasted since the year 711, when the Iberian Peninsula was quickly and dramatically overrun by Muslims from the north of Africa. With Spain firmly in the hands of the Catholic monarchs for the first time in 800 years, the king and queen could contemplate a more expansive role for Spain in the world, and so they contracted Columbus in 1492.

In September 1492, Columbus left the Spanish mainland and headed for the Canary Islands. From there, he headed east, and after about a month at sea, Rodrigo de Triana sighted land and the island encountered was named San Salvador: Columbus and his crew explored the Caribbean islands of Cuba, and Hispaniola. They returned to Spain having left some crew members behind at Hispaniola and they took some Native Americans with them as evidence that they had, in fact, been somewhere that was unmistakably not Europe. The second voyage took place immediately after the first. This journey (1493), which comprised seventeen ships, took Columbus and his crew to the Lesser Antilles, Hispaniola, and other minor islands in the Caribbean. The third voyage, in 1498, took Columbus to the mainland of South America at the Orinoco River, and from there he headed to Santo Domingo, the capital of what is today the Dominican Republic. The final voyage lasted from 1502 to 1504 and was fraught with difficulties. Columbus returned to Spain a broken man, unsure of his legacy, and confounded by a Caribbean that refused to yield India.

Columbus's own log reveals the real motivation behind his journey: fortune and fame. The word *oro*, or gold, is used about seventy-five times in the Admiral's own writings, and at the time of his death in 1506, he insisted that he had been to the Far East. Others were not so certain, and all the evidence brought back by Columbus, as well as the trajectories of his four voyages, suggested that some other place lay between Europe and India. But Columbus's contribution to world history is singular: he was bold and daring, stubborn and superior, and the legacy he brought to America—the notion that Europeans were superior beings compared to the Native American peoples who resided in America—lasted for centuries.

BIBLIOGRAPHY

Carpentier, Alejo. 1990. *The Harp and the Shadow.* San Francisco: Mercury House.

Gibson, Charles. 1966. *Spain in America.* New York: Harper Torchbooks.

Phillips, William D., and Carla Rhan Phillips. 1992. *The Worlds of Christopher Columbus.* New York: Cambridge University Press.

1st TRIP: LEAVES PALOS AUG. 3, 1492
    RETURNS TO PALOS MARCH 15, 1493
2nd TRIP: LEAVES CÁDIZ SEPT. 25, 1493
    RETURNS TO CÁDIZ JUNE 11, 1496

3rd TRIP: LEAVES SAN LUCAR MAY 30, 1498
    RETURNS TO CÁDIZ NOV. 20, 1500
4th TRIP: LEAVES SEVILLE/CÁDIZ MAY 2, 1502
    RETURNS TO SEVILLE/CÁDIZ NOV. 7, 1504

3c

America: The Name

What is America, and where does the name come from? Who is American? These are questions that seem simple enough to answer, but in reality, the answers are complex and far from clear.

In contemporary days, many citizens of the United States of America assume that they are "Americans" and that the word "American" distinguishes them from other peoples of other nations. However, America is both a geographic and cultural term. It has linguistic implications and a long historic significance.

Geographically speaking, there are two continents that carry the name America: One is South America, which refers to all the territory south of Panama, and the other is North America, comprising three countries—Mexico, the United States, and Canada. In between, there are the seven Central American republics. The residents of any of these countries can call themselves Americans; they all are Americans in the sense that they live on one or two of the American continents, or the lands in between.

In all of the Americas, there are only three countries named for a specific historic person. Bolivia is named for the hero of Latin American independence, Simón Bolívar. Colombia is named for Cristóbal Colón (Spanish for Christopher Columbus), and the United States of America is named after the Italian explorer, commercial trader, and mapmaker Amerigo Vespucci.

Most accounts of Vespucci's voyage are unclear, though we know he made at least one voyage to the territories that bear his name in the late 1490s or 1502. Vespucci was a vivid and dedicated letter writer; some of his letters were published in Florence. In those letters, Vespucci claimed that a "New World" had been found, at the same time Columbus was still insisting that the Caribbean was some sort of eastern shelf of India. Vespucci, of course, was right, and the proper name for the "New World" gradually became America. This occurred thanks to a German geographer: the idea of naming all of the lands of the "New World" America is attributed to Martin Waldseemüller, who added Vespucci's letters to a textbook he published in 1507. One source states that the geographer, in explaining the four parts of the world (Europe, Asia, Africa, and the "New World") wrote, "and the fourth part of the globe, which, since Amerigo discovered it, may be called Amerigo's land."[1]

A few years before Vespucci's voyage, and only two years after Columbus's first voyage, a line of demarcation was drawn by the pope that separated Spanish and Portuguese claims in the New World. The Treaty of Tordesillas (1494) essentially set the boundaries between Portuguese America and Spanish America.

Still, though, Spain referred to its overseas New World holdings with Spanish place names: Mexico was New Spain, or "Nueva España"; Colombia was the New Kingdom of Granada or "El Nuevo Reino de Granada." It was not until the period of independence that the republic names, as we know many of them today, were registered—political independence created artificial borders that separated peoples into distinct nations.

The term "Latin America" originated in nineteenth-century France: the French, trying to increase their world profile, especially after 1848, applied a linguistic categorization to America and referred to all territories in the Americas with Latin-derivative languages as "Latin America." This way their claim to the region (however small in the nineteenth century) would be valid. By the French definition, the United States is not part of Latin America, but Brazil is. Belize is not part of Latin America but Colombia is. Haiti is also considered part of Latin America.

The Spanish, in the twentieth century, devised yet another way to distinguish the Americas in a manner that gave Spain the linguistic advantage: they used the term Ibero-América to refer to those countries where Spanish was the primary language spoken, or where Spain was the primary colonizing nation.

While America has many meanings to different people, all people who live on the two American continents and in the seven countries between those continents are correct in referring to themselves as Americans.

NOTE

1. Helen Miller Bailey and Abraham P. Nasatir, *Latin America: The Development of Its Civilization,* 2d ed. (Englewood Cliffs, NJ: Prentice Hall, 1968), p. 88.

BIBLIOGRAPHY

Gibson, Charles. 1966. *Spain in America.* New York: Harper Torchbooks.
Lambert, Jacques. 1967. *Latin America: Social Structures and Political Institutions.* Berkeley: University of California Press.
Langley, Lester D. 1989. *America and the Americas.* Athens: University of Georgia Press.

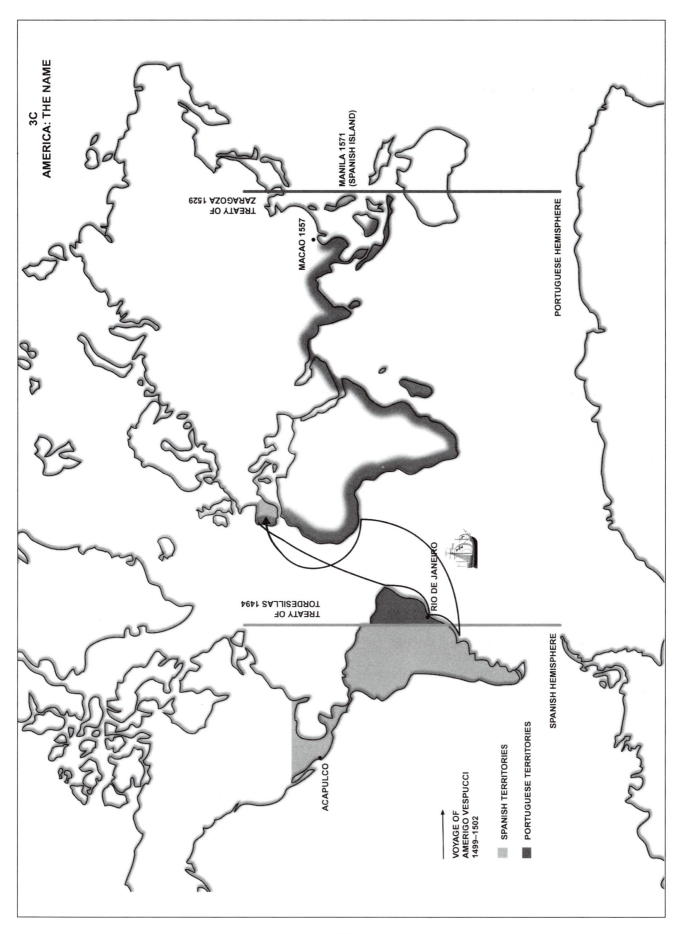

3C
AMERICA: THE NAME

TREATY OF
ZARAGOZA 1529

MANILA 1571
(SPANISH ISLAND)

MACAO 1557

PORTUGUESE HEMISPHERE

TREATY OF
TORDESILLAS 1494

RIO DE JANEIRO

ACAPULCO

SPANISH HEMISPHERE

VOYAGE OF
AMERIGO VESPUCCI
1499–1502

SPANISH TERRITORIES

PORTUGUESE TERRITORIES

3D

The First Voyages Around the Globe

The Portuguese, with an established record of maritime travel along the African coast during the fifteenth century, would be the first European power to arrive at India, land at Brazil, and circumnavigate the world. The riches accumulated and experience gained during their century of exploration made them the likely contenders to develop a trade network that was, for that time, worldwide.

With overland trade virtually cut off after 1453, the Portuguese were especially motivated and eager to reach the Far East by sea. In 1488, Bartolemeu Dias was the first European to make it around the Cape of Good Hope in a ship, but a mutiny by his crew ended his voyage earlier than planned. In 1498, Vasco da Gama, a Portuguese sailor, followed the route established by Dias and arrived at India. He returned to Lisbon with precious silks, spices, and other products native to the region. Two years later, in 1500, Pedro Álvares Cabral landed at the northeast tip of Brazil. The territory was named for a type of wood found there (brazilwood), which was made into a rich, red dye. Legend has it that Cabral's fleet was blown off course by fierce winds, but some scholars suggest that his off-course jog into the heart of the expanding Spanish overseas empire was actually intentional. In any event, Cabral claimed the territory of Brazil for Portugal, and then left to continue his voyage to the Far East. The Portuguese overseas empire, by the earliest days of the sixteenth century, extended from Africa to India, through Java, and onward to China and Japan.

Not surprisingly, the first voyage around the globe was undertaken by a Portuguese sailor, Ferdinand Magellan (Fernando de Magalhães). Magellan, though, sailed under the Spanish flag and his voyage was intended to further Spanish claims in the Far East. The Portuguese attempted to squelch his voyage, as they were deriving enormous profit from the Spice Islands in the Far East and were pleased with maintenance of the status quo.

The world, dominated by Portuguese and Spanish ships, grew much larger—at least in the imaginations of Europeans—when in 1513 Vasco Núñez de Balboa saw the Pacific Ocean at Panama. Magellan's plan, which was put into effect five years after this "discovery," involved sailing around the tip of South America at the strait later named for him and proceeding to India via the Pacific Ocean. Magellan, killed in the Philippines, never actually made it around the world, but the expedition he directed continued without him, led by the second in command, Juan Sebastián del Cano. Cano stopped at the Spice Islands, headed around the Cape of Good Hope, and returned to Spain. The journey took three years. According to Charles Gibson, "the Magellan–del Cano expedition demonstrated empirically [the earth's] approximate size and above all indicated that an enormous expanse of water separated the western coast of America from the Far East."[1]

In a relatively short period of time, tiny Portugal came to dominate trade in much of the world. Technological innovation, careful planning, outright exploitation, and the perfection of overseas transportation were keys to Portuguese success. But Portuguese dominance of the seas would be short-lived, for the Spanish, Dutch, French, and English would all participate in this expanding and profitable venture during the sixteenth, seventeenth, and eighteenth centuries.

NOTE

1. Charles Gibson, *Spain in America* (New York: Harper and Row, 1966), p. 19.

BIBLIOGRAPHY

Burns, E. Bradford. 1970. *A History of Brazil*. New York: Columbia University Press.
Levine, Robert M. 1997. *Brazilian Legacies*. Armonk, NY: M.E. Sharpe.
Worcester, Donald. 1973. *Brazil: From Colony to World Power*. New York: Charles Scribner's Sons.

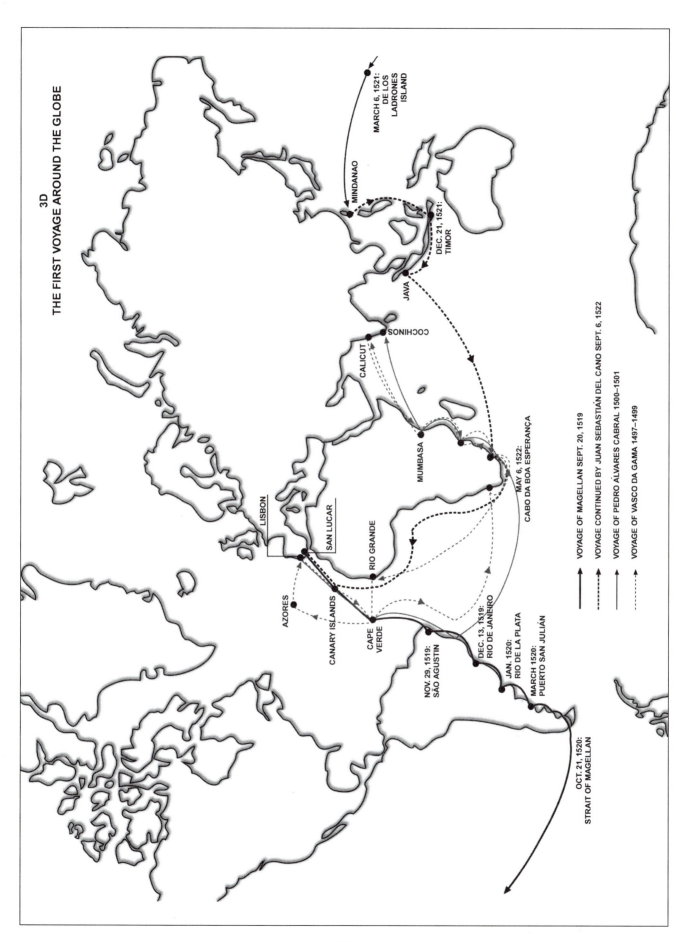

3D

THE FIRST VOYAGE AROUND THE GLOBE

MARCH 6, 1521:
DE LOS
LADRONES
ISLAND

MINDANAO

DEC. 21, 1521: TIMOR

JAVA

COCHINOS

CALICUT

MUMBASA

MAY 6, 1522:
CABO DA BOA ESPERANÇA

LISBON

SAN LUCAR

RIO GRANDE

AZORES

CANARY ISLANDS

CAPE VERDE

NOV. 29, 1519: SÃO AGUSTIN

DEC. 13, 1519: RIO DE JANEIRO

JAN. 1520: RIO DE LA PLATA

MARCH 1520: PUERTO SAN JULIÁN

OCT. 21, 1520: STRAIT OF MAGELLAN

VOYAGE OF MAGELLAN SEPT. 20, 1519

VOYAGE CONTINUED BY JUAN SEBASTIÁN DEL CANO SEPT. 6, 1522

VOYAGE OF PEDRO ÁLVARES CABRAL 1500–1501

VOYAGE OF VASCO DA GAMA 1497–1499

4

THE IBERIAN CONQUEST OF AMERICA

From Trading Post to Colonies: The Creation of the Grand Antilles

Columbus's voyages led to a new understanding of world geography, the flora and fauna present on earth, and of course, the human societies that populated the planet.

The "discovery" of America touched off a debate in Europe on the nature of the people who lived in the New World. Native Americans had never before been seen by Europeans, so they were thought—at first—to be related to, perhaps, one of the lost tribes of Israel. In fact, it was not until 1537 that the Roman Catholic Church, via the papal bull *Sublimus Deus,* promulgated in 1537 by Pope Paul III, officially recognized the humanity of Native Americans, deeming them fit and equipped, as men, to receive the Catholic faith (and thus, salvation).

Unfortunately, the Caribbean became a sort of "test case" for construction of a Spanish overseas empire and the results were mostly disastrous. Nearly all of the Native Americans living in the Caribbean died of European disease and dislocation during the first forty years of the Spaniards' arrival in the Caribbean. The treatment of Native Americans by Spaniards generated intense debate over the nature of Spanish rule in the Americas. Would the church priorities dominate, or would the priorities of the crown and the men who conquered on its behalf be followed? In December 1511, the Dominican Father Antonio de Montesinos addressed this issue with a stinging attack against his fellow Spaniards for their cruel treatment of Native Americans. Montesinos's denunciation probably influenced the passing of the so-called "Leyes de Burgos" in 1512–13. The Burgos Laws attempted, for the first time, to systematically govern the conquest of the Americas. They stipulated that the *repartimiento,* or unsystematic division of Native Americans into Spanish-controlled work groups and towns, be outlawed. It would be replaced with the medieval institution known as the *encomienda,* which put Spaniards directly in charge of Native Americans but implied and assigned duty and privilege to each party.

Of course, the Burgos Laws were unenforceable and were not obeyed by Spaniards living in America. The Spaniards' penchant for legalism is clearly evident in the 1514 ordinance requiring Spaniards to read a medieval document known as "the requirement," *el requirimiento,* before engaging in any conquest in the Americas. The statement, read to natives in Latin, invited the opposing group to lay down their weapons and accept the one true faith (the Catholic faith) and the Spanish monarchy. If they failed to acquiesce, then Spaniards could wage a "just war" against them and all resulting death/destruction would be the fault of those who failed to yield to Spanish virtue. Father Bartolomé de las Casas, responding to the requirement, once said, "I don't know whether to laugh, or cry."

In 1522, Las Casas published a work that is still in print today, entitled *The Devastation of the Indies.* The book is a graphic, systematic account of Spanish cruelty in the Caribbean. Las Casas published widely, during a long career, on native customs and traditions, and his ethnographic work is important in helping contemporary students understand Caribbean traditions and cultures during the early years of the sixteenth century.

The Greater Antilles—the large islands of Cuba, Hispaniola (shared by Haiti and the Dominican Republic), Puerto Rico, and Jamaica—were fortified by Spaniards as they began their conquest of America. When the majority of the Native Americans died, and as the Spaniards realized that there were no precious metals in the Caribbean, they largely abandoned the area and moved toward the American mainland.

BIBLIOGRAPHY

Gutiérrez, Gustavo. 1993. *Las Casas: In Search of the Poor of Jesus Christ.* New York: Orbis.

Knight, Franklin W. 1990. *The Caribbean.* 2d ed. New York: Oxford University Press.

Las Casas, Bartolomé de. 1992. *The Devastation of the Indies: A Brief Account.* Baltimore: Johns Hopkins University Press.

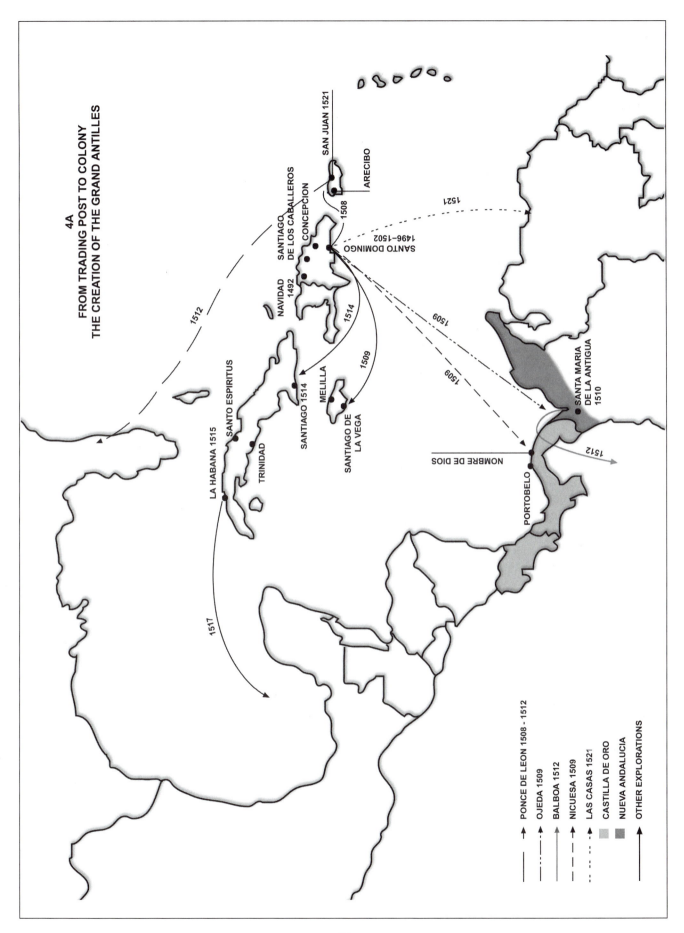

4A
FROM TRADING POST TO COLONY
THE CREATION OF THE GRAND ANTILLES

SAN JUAN 1521

ARECIBO

SANTIAGO
DE LOS CABALLEROS
CONCEPCION

1508

1521

SANTO DOMINGO
1496–1502

NAVIDAD
1492

1512

1514

1509

1509

1509

SANTIAGO 1514

MELILLA

SANTIAGO DE
LA VEGA

SANTA MARIA
DE LA ANTIGUA
1510

SANTO ESPIRITUS

TRINIDAD

NOMBRE DE DIOS

1512

LA HABANA 1515

PORTOBELO

1517

PONCE DE LEON 1508 - 1512

OJEDA 1509

BALBOA 1512

NICUESA 1509

LAS CASAS 1521

CASTILLA DE ORO

NUEVA ANDALUCIA

OTHER EXPLORATIONS

31

4B

Toward the Interior:
The Aztec Empire and Its Dominion

The conquest of the Aztec Empire was a singular event in world history, and marked a new beginning for European colonization projects in America. The Spaniards, after twenty-seven years of searching, found the fabled city of riches, and both Spanish and American history changed forever with the "discovery" of Tenochtitlán in 1519. The destruction of the Aztec Empire meant the end of a young, creative, growing civilization; the massive clash of civilizations from 1519 to 1521 left a legacy that is still seen today in the racial/social tensions that mark Mexican and Central American societies.

The leader of the expedition into the heart of the Aztec Empire was a man from Medellín, Spain. Hernán Cortés did not want to repeat his father's destiny—that of a poor farmer in Spain—and his determination and audacity set the tone for the invasion of Mexico. Moctezuma II, who became leader of the Aztecs in 1502, was a man steeped in tradition, myth, legend, and philosophy. According to Aztec myth, Quetzalcóatl, the god of community—the life-giver in Mesoamerican tradition —would return to Mexico by sea, from the east, signifying the end of an era, that of the Fifth Sun. He was always depicted as a "fair-skinned" deity, and Moctezuma's power lay in his ability to predict, via reading natural portents, the date of Quetzalcóatl's return. When Spanish ships—"floating houses" according to Aztec spotters—were seen moving from the east toward the coast, Moctezuma's training led to one conclusion: the return of Quetzalcóatl was at hand.

Thus, when the Spaniards arrived to Tenochtitlán, Moctezuma welcomed the invaders as long-awaited guests. "Welcome," he said, "we have been waiting for you. This is your home."

Rather than focusing on Spanish heroics in the battle for Tenochtitlán, it is more appropriate to consider the cultural differences separating Aztecs and Spaniards in 1519. The Aztecs were a people steeped in myth and they adhered rigidly to their tradition. Their lives centered on interpreting the will of the gods and pleasing them, even though the deities were thought to be somewhat whimsical and vindictive. The Spaniards were, in 1519, certain of the righteousness of their project, believing that history and God were on their side. This had been "demonstrated" by the successful expulsion of Muslim forces from Spain in 1492. Aztec skepticism and doubt ran headlong into Spanish certainty and confidence.

Disease is another critical factor that helps explain the rapid decline of the mighty Aztec Empire. European diseases took a toll on the Aztecs, and the vast majority of the millions of people who died in the Central Valley of Mexico died of measles, smallpox, and whooping cough—European infirmities to which they lacked natural immunities. Also, the Spaniards were assisted in their march from Veracruz to the Aztec capital through the forging of linkages with Aztec enemies, most notably at Tlaxcala, on the way to the capital. One person—known to the Aztecs as Malintzin, to the Spaniards as Doña Marina, and to contemporary Mexicans as La Malinche—figured prominently in the conquest of Mexico. She was the translator for Spanish invaders, and bore Cortés's son. Mexicans view her as a traitor. More generous accounts refer to her as victim, but the fact is, her understanding of Náhuatl and rudimentary Spanish assisted the Spaniards in their march toward Tenochtitlán in 1519.

BIBLIOGRAPHY

Keen, Benjamin. 1971. *The Aztec Image in Western Thought.* New Brunswick: Rutgers University Press.
León-Portilla, Miguel. 1962. *The Broken Spears.* Boston: Beacon Press.
Paz, Octavio. 1961. *The Labyrinth of Solitude.* New York: Grove Press.

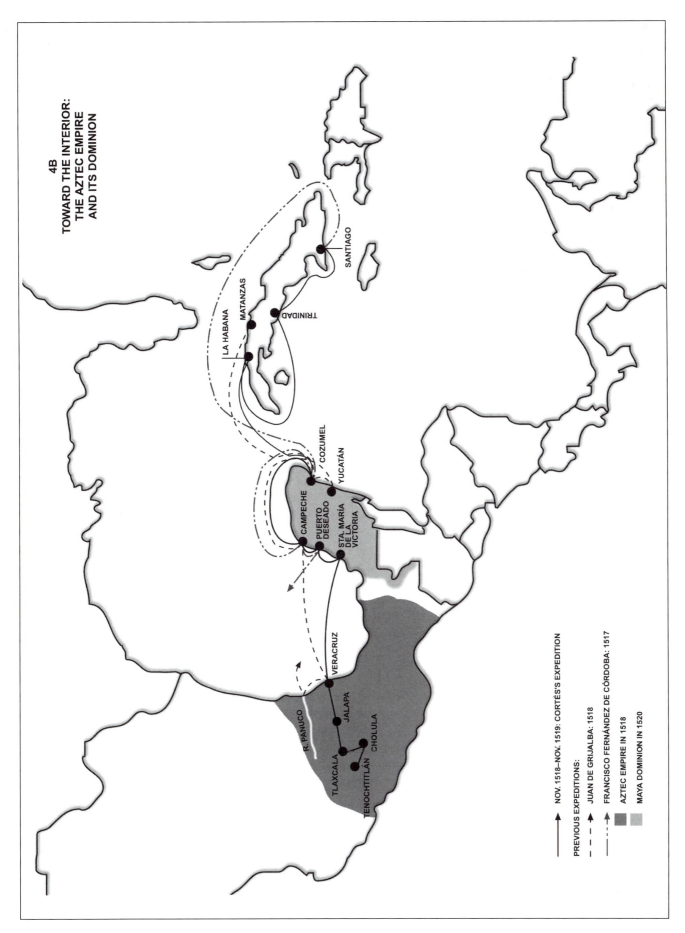

4B
TOWARD THE INTERIOR:
THE AZTEC EMPIRE
AND ITS DOMINION

SANTIAGO

MATANZAS

TRINIDAD

LA HABANA

COZUMEL

YUCATÁN

CAMPECHE

PUERTO
DESEADO

STA. MARÍA
DE LA
VICTORIA

VERACRUZ

R. PÁNUCO

JALAPA

TLAXCALA

CHOLULA

TENOCHTITLÁN

NOV. 1518–NOV. 1519: CORTÉS'S EXPEDITION

PREVIOUS EXPEDITIONS:

JUAN DE GRIJALBA: 1518

FRANCISCO FERNÁNDEZ DE CÓRDOBA: 1517

AZTEC EMPIRE IN 1518

MAYA DOMINION IN 1520

33

4c

Toward the Interior: The Spanish Territories in North America

With the fall of Tenochtitlán in 1521, Spaniards moved out over the once mighty Aztec Empire in all directions. They were especially eager to move north of the city, toward the principle mine regions of Mexico—Zacatecas and Guanajuato.

Spaniards, motivated by riches, assumed that other great, settled civilizations existed north of the Aztec capital. This prompted further exploration in the north, in what is today New Mexico, Arizona, and Texas. Missionaries and miners headed north with equal zeal, but the primary city in North America at that time, Tenochtitlán (later renamed Mexico City), would dominate the entire region for several centuries.

Spanish policy in America, formulated during the 800-year *reconquista* of Spain, required Native Americans to settle under Spanish dominion. The great northern desert of Mexico, extending into what is today the southwestern United States, was sparsely inhabited. Spaniards established *presidios,* or military outposts, in addition to Catholic churches. Normally, exploratory parties moved in, claimed the land, and wrote reports or surveys of what they had found. These reports, often fanciful, unsystematic, and/or politically motivated, encouraged others to commit to a journey. Spanish missionaries were usually the first to arrive, to begin the difficult work of spreading the faith to people whose worldview was radically different from their own. Of course, propagation of the faith had political and economic consequences, as priests and friars came into de facto control of the subdued native groups. Jesuit missionaries arrived to Mexico in 1572; disciplined and decisive, they settled in Guanajuato by 1582 and San Luis Potosí ten years later. Motivated by a spirit of conversion, education, and enterprise, it is not surprising that Jesuits succeeded in areas where great natural wealth was readily available.

About sixty years after the conquest of Tenochtitlán, Franciscan missionaries made their way to the territory that is today New Mexico in the United States. Father Agustín Rodríguez moved into New Mexico to establish missions, and this led to the establishment of the city of Santa Fe in 1610.[1] Spaniards also settled what is today Baja California, Arizona, and California in search of souls to convert. During the late eighteenth century, a series of missions was founded from San Diego to San Francisco along the California coast. Santa Barbara, San Juan de Capistrano, and San Jose are among the cities that originated as missions. The mission system, established by the Franciscan Father Junipero Serra, essentially co-opted the land and labor of Native Americans who lived in the region, forcing the natives into semi-servitude in support of the economic goals of the missions and priests.

During the early eighteenth century, French incursions into Spanish-held territories created tensions, and realigned the pace and pattern of settlement. The French settlements in Louisiana, with its capital New Orleans, threatened Spanish settlements in east Texas and Mexico, and for this reason, the city of San Antonio was established in 1718. French and Spanish territorial disputes in the region reached a climax in the mid-eighteenth century. In 1762, France ceded Louisiana to Spain via the Treaty of San Ildefonso at the conclusion of the French and Indian War.

Spanish-French tensions in the region would change, about a century later, to American-Mexican tensions when the United States, in 1846, invaded Mexico, taking all of its land north of the Rio Grande. The Treaty of Guadalupe Hidalgo of 1848 and the Gadsden Purchase of 1853 effectively set the present border between the United States and Mexico.

NOTE

1. Charles Gibson, *Spain in America* (New York: Harper Torchbooks, 1966), chapter 9, "The Borderlands."

BIBLIOGRAPHY

González, Juan. 2000. *Harvest of Empire: A History of Latinos in America.* New York: Penguin.

Jackson, Robert H. 1994. *Indian Population Decline: The Missions of Northwest New Spain, 1687–1840.* Albuquerque: University of New Mexico Press.

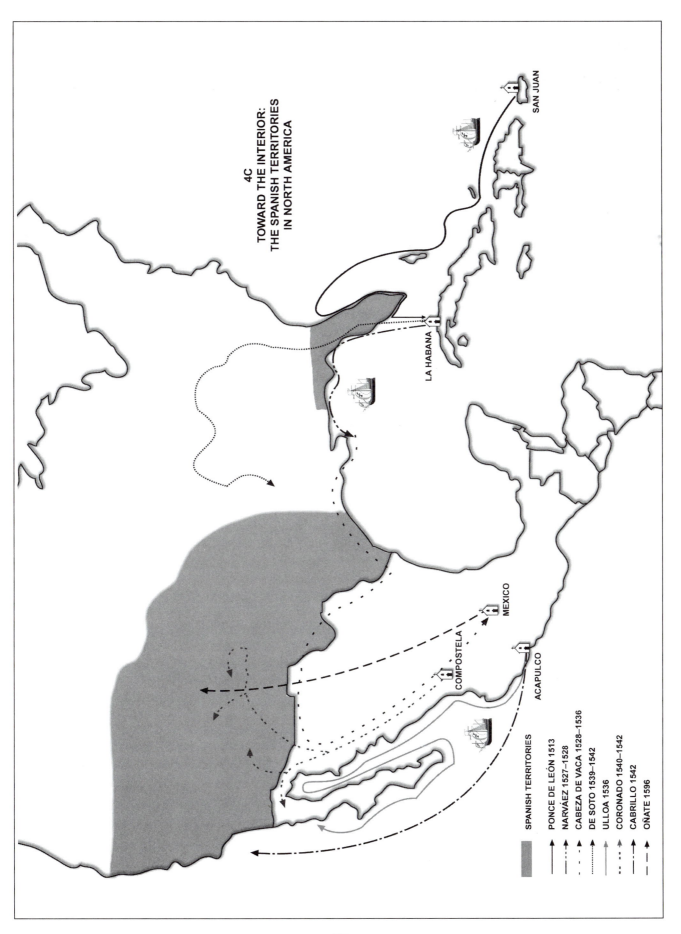

4C

**TOWARD THE INTERIOR:
THE SPANISH TERRITORIES
IN NORTH AMERICA**

SAN JUAN

LA HABANA

MEXICO

COMPOSTELA

ACAPULCO

SPANISH TERRITORIES

PONCE DE LEÓN 1513

NARVÁEZ 1527–1528

CABEZA DE VACA 1528–1536

DE SOTO 1539–1542

ULLOA 1536

CORONADO 1540–1542

CABRILLO 1542

OÑATE 1596

4D

Toward the Interior: The Inca Empire and Its Dominion

About ten years after the fall of the Aztec Empire in Mexico, the Spaniard Francisco Pizarro sacked the once mighty Inca Empire in Peru. The Incas had established a significant world empire that extended from the northern section of Chile to what is today the southernmost point of Colombia. The empire dominated over 1,500 miles of territory and was held together by a common language (Quechua), an impressive system of roads, and a system of taxation and forced work projects (*mita*) for the benefit of the state. The empire, though, was essentially in a state of civil war in the early 1530s over the question of dynastic succession, and the Spaniards were able to benefit from this situation when they arrived in 1532.

Pizarro, an illiterate swineherd, organized his adventure into the heart of the Inca Empire at Panama and sailed down the Pacific coast in 1532. He and his men, arriving in Peru, climbed for about forty-five days from the coast to Cajamarca, where they met the Inca ruler, Atahualpa. Atahualpa had just consolidated the empire from his base at Quito and was making his way to Cuzco, having stopped to set up a capital at Cajamarca, which sat roughly halfway between the northern and southern axes of the Inca dominion. Atahualpa, with about 40,000 soldiers by his side, was "invited" by Pizarro to accept King Charles V as king and the Christian god as the one true God. When the Inca ruler inspected, then tossed the Holy Book to the ground, the slaughter began. The Inca leader was held captive and was forced to fill two rooms with gold and silver as a ransom. He was then killed by strangulation at the main plaza at Cajamarca, having been given the opportunity to convert to Christianity (and die by strangulation), or remain a pagan and die by burning at the stake.

The duplicity, cruelty, and hypocrisy of the Spaniards knew no limits, especially given the fact that, according to one source, "It has been estimated that the ransom [Atahualpa's] amounted to about 13,265 pounds of gold and 26,000 pounds of silver."[1] Pizarro next marched on to Cuzco, where a Spanish municipality was set up in 1534; one year later, the city of Lima was founded at the mouth of the Rimac River on the coast. Low-level rebellions continued to break out for another forty years until 1572, when the Inca Tupac Amaru I was captured and killed. After his death, the Spaniards consolidated their power in Peru as Tupac Amaru I was the last legitimate heir to the throne of the Inca Empire; however, the country would never be completely under Spanish control, and a marked system of "apartheid" would emerge in Peru that remains to this day: Native Americans live in highland villages and communities, generally in inferior social and economic conditions to those of the ruling elites, most of whom are of European descent. A large number of *mestizos* (people of mixed blood) conforms the middle part of this structure and their economic and social status varies. The current president of Peru as of this writing, Alejandro Toledo, is a person of mixed ancestry. His tenure in office has been marked by cruel and derisive comments from Peruvians (and others) concerning his heritage, and by extension, questions regarding his fitness to serve as president of the Peruvian Republic.

NOTE

1. Helen Miller Bailey and Abraham P. Nasatir, *Latin America,* 2d ed. (Englewood Cliffs, NJ: Prentice Hall, 1968), p. 124.

BIBLIOGRAPHY

Macera, Pablo. 1988. *Trabajo de historia.* Tomo 1, 2d ed. Lima: G. Herrera Editores.

Vargas Llosa, Mario. 1990. "Questions of Conquest." *Harpers,* December.

Wachtel, Nathan. 1977. *The Vision of the Vanquished.* Brighton: Harvester Press.

PANAMA

PUERTO DEL HAMBRE

PUERTO QUEMADO

GORGONA

PUNTA CHARANBIRA

GALLO ISLAND

TUMACO

ATACAMES

PUNA ISLAND

TUMBES

PIURA

MOTUPE

SAÑA

CAJAMARCA

SANTA

OYÓN

JAUJA

HUARAS

PUCARA

LIMA

AYACUCHO

CUZCO

FRANCISCO PIZARRO: 1524–1525

FRANCISCO PIZARRO: 1526–1527

FRANCISCO PIZARRO: 1531–1534

HERNANDO PIZARRO

INCA EMPIRE

4E

Toward the Deep Continental Conquest

The three major conquests in Latin America—that of the Caribbean islands, the Aztec Empire, and the Inca Empire—resulted in an important process of consolidation for Spanish imperial ambitions. The Spaniards sought control over the entire South American landmass (save Brazil). After 1532, new Spanish incursions would center on northern South America, focusing primarily on the Muisca civilization in what is today Colombia. The Spaniards would also advance on the Guaraní peoples of Paraguay and Brazil, and the Native Americans living in the central valley of Chile.

The earliest contact and exploration along the Colombian coast probably occurred in 1499 by Alonso de Ojeda, and two years later by Juan de la Cosa; however, it was not until about 1510 that permanent settlements were established in the Darién region, just west of the Gulf of Urabá. Three main expeditions headed into the Colombian mainland after the conquest of Peru. First, Sebastián de Belalcázar and his forces, entering from Peru, marched into Pasto and the Cauca Valley in 1535. In a separate journey, Gonzalo Jiménez de Quesada made an eleven-month voyage up the Magdalena River, arriving at a vast, grassy, fertile, cool savannah called, by the Muisca who inhabited the region, Bacatá. Another expedition, led by a German, Nicolas Federmann, traveled over the eastern plains from what is today Venezuela and arrived at Bogotá after scaling the eastern cordillera. Thus, the three separate expeditions arrived at the Muisca capital at about the same time, leading historians Frank Safford and Marco Palacios to quip that this meeting "must . . . have been quite picturesque."[1] The reality, however, was less than picturesque, as the Muisca peoples were quickly subdued by the Europeans, and their culture was forever changed. The Europeans exacted tribute in the form of food, clothing, land, labor, salt, and emeralds from this civilization.

Present-day Chile was settled after the Spaniards had established rule over much of Peru. Pedro de Valdivia left, from Cuzco, with orders to settle the southern extreme of what would become the massive Spanish overseas empire. The city of Santiago was founded in 1540, and later, the city of Concepción—established as a frontier post designed to protect the rich, fertile Chilean central valley from hostile Araucanian Indians. The Araucanians never accepted Spanish dominance; rather, they fought tirelessly against Spanish incursions into their territories and are known to this day for their struggle to maintain an independent, distinct culture separate from Spanish rule and authority.

The Guaraní of present-day Paraguay (and some sections of Brazil) came under the dominion of the Spaniards in the mid-sixteenth century when Domingo Martínez de Irala set up a fort at Asunción in 1537. The Guaraní were immediately transformed into agricultural laborers, providing food, clothing, and other forms of tribute to the Spaniards. However, the Guaraní did manage to preserve many of their customs, including their language, which to this day is spoken widely as the official language of Paraguay. The Jesuits, during the seventeenth century, would come to have a profound impact on the Guaraní, establishing some thirty missions that thrived for many years—until the Jesuits were expelled from the Americas in 1767. The Jesuits did learn and record the Guaraní language and helped ensure its survival as a written Native American language in South America.

NOTE

1. Frank Safford and Marco Palacios, *Colombia: Fragmented Land, Divided Society* (New York: Oxford University Press, 2002), p. 33.

BIBLIOGRAPHY

Ganson, Barbara. 2003. *The Guaraní Under Spanish Rule in the Rio de la Plata*. Stanford: Stanford University Press.
Loveman, Brian. 1979. *Chile: The Legacy of Hispanic Capitalism*. New York: Oxford University Press.

MÉXICO
1519

GUATEMALA
1524

LEÓN 1527

PANAMÁ
1519

CARTAGENA
1533

SANTA MARTA
1525

CORO 1529

CARACAS 1567

BOGOTÁ 1538

POPAYÁN 1536

QUITO 1534

TO THE AMAZON
1541–1542

LIMA 1535

LA PAZ 1548

ASUNCIÓN
1537

RIO DE JANEIRO
1502

SANTIAGO 1541

BUENOS AIRES
1536/1580

Brazil in the Sixteenth and Seventeenth Centuries

The Portuguese colonial project in America differed dramatically from that of the Spaniards. First, Portugal could afford, in 1500, to neglect its American colony because its established trade network extended from Africa to Japan. After 1531, however, when French pirates began exploring off the coast of Brazil, the Portuguese decided that the time had come to permanently settle and occupy Brazil. The church presence in Brazil was less significant than in Spanish America, and the enormous Brazilian landmass (larger than the United States, excluding Alaska) made total territorial occupation impossible.

To entice Portuguese settlers to Brazil, the crown developed a semi-feudal, semi-capitalist structure called the captaincy system, whereby huge tracts of land were divided into territories. Each territory was about 130 miles wide and extended from the coast into the interior at the imaginary border with Spain. Thus was established the initial European landholding pattern in Brazil. The king would donate the land, but the *donatário*—the man to whom the land was granted—had to make the land profitable by encouraging settlement, economic activity, taming the Native Americans, establishing towns, and so on. Only two of the fifteen captaincies succeeded, the most successful in the northern state of Pernambuco with its capital Recife.

Sugar became the fundamental product sustaining Brazil in the sixteenth and seventeenth centuries. The Portuguese had perfected sugar cultivation and processing on the tropical Atlantic islands (the Madeiras) over which they held dominion, and sugar cane adapted ideally to the warm, moist tropical climate of northeast Brazil. The labor problem was solved via the importation of African slaves. Since 1441, the Portuguese had accumulated ample experience in trading Africans from the African coast to Europe. Now, the slave ships would make the Middle Passage and deposit human cargo at the Brazilian Northeast coastal cities of Olinda, Recife, and Salvador (Bahia). As many as 4 to 5 million slaves arrived in Brazil during a slave trade that extended from 1538 to the mid-nineteenth century; not only did enslaved Africans allow Portuguese planters to become fabulously wealthy during the sugar boom, but they also contributed to the rich cultural development of Brazil. Slaves were not granted freedom in Brazil until 1888.

From the northeast quadrant of Brazil, the economic activity shifted during the early eighteenth century to the southeast segment of the country, especially when diamonds and gold were discovered at an interior state called Minas Gerais. The Brazilian *bandeirantes,* rugged explorers, were the ones responsible for helping open up the interior during the seventeenth and eighteenth centuries. The Brazilian sugar economy, though still profitable during the eighteenth century, was forced to compete with the Caribbean islands, which had a natural comparative advantage—proximity to market. Technologically, the Caribbean islands' sugar-refining process was more efficient than the Brazilian system.

From Minas Gerais, the Brazilian economy shifted, during the nineteenth century, further south to the area between Rio de Janeiro and São Paulo. Here, the coffee boom provided enormous wealth for the "coffee barons," and the development of infrastructure to support the coffee economy (railroads, port works, insurance companies, and banking) became the basis of twentieth-century industrialization. The Brazilian industrial boom, which really began in the 1960s, occurred around the city of São Paulo at an impressive pace, and Brazil is today the world's eighth- or ninth-leading industrial power.

BIBLIOGRAPHY

Moreno Fraginals, Manuel, ed. 1977. *Africa en América Latina.* Mexico: Siglo Veintiuno Editores.

Skidmore, Thomas. 1999. *Brazil: Five Centuries of Change.* New York: Oxford University Press.

Smith, T. Lynn. 1963. *Brazil: People and Institutions.* Rev. ed. Baton Rouge: Louisiana State University Press.

4F
BRAZIL IN THE SIXTEENTH AND SEVENTEENTH CENTURIES

PARAÍBA 1585

OLINDA 1537

BAHIA 1549

SANTA CRUZ 1536

ESPÍRITU SANTO 1535

RIO DE JANEIRO 1565

SÃO PAULO 1554

COLONIZED ZONE, 16th CENTURY

ZONE OCCUPIED BY FRENCH
AND DUTCH, 17th CENTURY

17th CENTURY *BANDEIRANTES*

DONATÁRIO DIVISION

IMPORTANT CITY AND YEAR FOUNDED

5

AMERICA UNDER HAPSBURG RULE

5A

Cities Founded in Hispanic America Before 1600

From 1516 to 1700 Spain and the Spanish Empire were ruled by the European Hapsburg monarchy. King Charles I (r. 1516–1556) created the Spanish Empire, and Charles II, the last Hapsburg king to rule Spain, died childless in 1700. The essential infrastructure of Spain's overseas empire was set down during Hapsburg rule.

One central characteristic of Spaniards is their affinity for cities and city life. This tradition dates back to the period when Spain was occupied by the Romans, and later by Muslims. Both civilizations imparted the idea of the city as center of civilization, and the great cities of Spain are architectural and cultural monuments that express fundamental elements of Spanish character.

During the Spanish *reconquista,* which lasted from about 711 to 1492, Spain was "retaken" from the Muslims gradually, and cities were built and occupied as symbols of Spanish, Catholic primacy. When the Spanish entered America in 1492, their very first task was to organize, charter, and build cities. "Citizens" were those who lived inside the city walls, those outside were, according to Spanish thinking, literally uncivilized. Spanish cities were uniform in structure and design, with a central plaza occupied by governmental offices, the church and church officials, and the most important (Spanish) citizens of the city. This pattern is still seen today, and the central plazas of Mexico City, Lima, Bogotá, Quito, and others still reflect this design.

The early Latin American city was a center of culture, religion, government, education, and Spanish values. A wave of city construction by Spaniards in America occurred from 1492 to about 1570. The earliest of these cities were founded in the Caribbean, the first being the city of Santo Domingo (present-day Dominican Republic), founded in 1496; shortly after that, in 1503, Vera Paz was founded in what is today Haiti. Trinidad and La Habana (Havana) followed in 1514. From the Caribbean, the Spaniards moved inland to Mexico and conquered the great city of Tenochtitlán in 1521, eventually renaming it Mexico City. Guanajuato, the important mining center north of Mexico City, was founded shortly thereafter in 1554, as the Spaniards generally established cities at sites where native communities were settled and where resources were abundant. Bogotá (1538), Quito (1534), Trujillo (1535), Cuzco (1554), and Potosí (1545) all followed this basic premise and pattern of city construction. The cities of what is known today as the Southern Cone were founded a few years after the primary Mexican and Peruvian cities, reflecting, of course, the contour and rhythm of Spanish conquest and colonization. Thus, Santiago (Chile) was founded in 1541, Asunción (Paraguay) in 1537, and the interior cities of Argentina—Mendoza and Córdoba—were founded in 1561 and 1573 respectively.

Of course, there were significant differences between the coastal cities and the cities in the interior. The coastal cities, such as Havana, Santo Domingo, Cartagena, Veracruz, and Portobelo, were integrated into the world economy; slaves entered at Cartagena, Veracruz, Rio de Janeiro, and Salvador (Bahia). Those cities had direct contact with European and African trading centers, and the cities—particularly Portobelo and Cartagena—transformed from sleepy towns to vibrant metropolitan centers when the ships arrived. The interior cities, like Bogotá, Cuzco, and Mendoza, were tied in to local economies and had far less direct contact with Europe or Africa.

It is important to note that, by the time Jamestown was founded in 1607, or when Plymouth was settled in 1620, vibrant, culturally active, and wealthy cities in the Caribbean, Mexico, and in South America already conformed a dynamic and expanding Spanish and Portuguese overseas colonial structure.

BIBLIOGRAPHY

Hoberman, Louisa Schell, and Susan M. Socolow, eds. 1991. *Cities and Society in Colonial Latin America.* Albuquerque: University of New Mexico Press.
Morales Padrón, Francisco. 1988. *Atlas histórico-cultural de América.* Tomo 1. Las Palmas de Gran Canaria: Gobierno de Canarias.

5A
CITIES FOUNDED IN HISPANIC AMERICA
BEFORE 1600

ST. AUGUSTINE 1512/1565

GUANAJUATO 1554
ZACATECAS 1548
SAN LUIS POTOSÍ 1576
GUADALAJARA 1529
QUERÉTARO 1550
MÉXICO 1521
VERACRUZ 1519
PUEBLA 1530
OAXACA 1521

MÉRIDA 1542

LA HABANA 1514
SANCTI SPIRITUS 1514
TRINIDAD 1514
BARACOA 1512
SANTIAGO 1515
PTO. PLATA 1502
SAN JUAN 1521
SANTIAGO DE LA VEGA 1527
STO. DOMINGO 1496
VERA PAZ 1503

SAN PEDRO SULA

ANTIGUA (GUATEMALA) 1542
SAN SALVADOR 1536
LEÓN 1527
GRANADA 1524
CARTAGO 1563

CARTAGENA 1533
SANTA MARTA 1525
CORO 1529
CARACAS 1567

MÉRIDA 1558

PANAMÁ 1519

TUNJA 1538
BOGOTÁ 1538

POPAYÁN 1536
PASTO 1536
QUITO 1534
GUAYAQUIL 1535

TRUJILLO 1535

LIMA 1535

CUZCO 1534
LA PAZ 1548
AREQUIPA 1540
STA. CRUZ 1561
POTOSÍ 1545

JUJUY 1561
SALTA 1582
TUCUMÁN 1565
ASUNCIÓN 1537

CORRIENTES 1588

LA SERENA 1544

VALPARAÍSO 1544
CÓRDOBA 1573
SANTIAGO 1541
MENDOZA 1561
BUENOS AIRES 1536/1580

VALDIVIA 1552

45

5B

Hapsburg Territorial and Administrative Organization

The Hapsburg administrative organization in the Americas was based on a clear division of authority and power, centered at the two most important sites of conquest, Mexico and Peru. These places, from the earliest days of the conquest, provided everything that the Spaniards hoped to find in America: plentiful supplies of natural resources (especially silver), large numbers of Native Americans who could serve as a work force, fertile land, and a moderate climate.

In the sixteenth century, the Spaniards organized their colonial possessions in America into two major divisions called viceroyalties (*virreinatos*)—centers that were second in authority only to the king of Spain. The first was called the Virreinato de Nueva España (with its capital at Mexico City), and the second was the Virreinato del Perú, based at Lima. New Spain covered all of Mexico and Central America (north of Panama) and the territories that extended into the southwest section of what is today the United States of America. The Viceroyalty of Peru covered a massive amount of territory, from Panama down to Chile, over to the treaty line of Tordesillas separating Portuguese territorial claims from those of Spain. Venezuela fell under the Audiencia of Santo Domingo.

The *audiencia* was the second level of political division under the *virreinato*. Under Hapsburg rule there were ten *audiencias*, including the Audiencias of Santo Domingo (which governed the Caribbean), Guatemala (based at Guatemala City), Mexico City, Nueva Galicia (for the northern Mexican provinces), Santa Fe (Nueva Granada), Quito, Lima, Panama, Charcas and Chile. The *audiencias* held broad advisory and judicial authority, and they varied in size and power. At a lower level, *corregidores* presided over municipal councils that oversaw local, mundane, day-to-day affairs of individual towns, such as crime prevention, maintaining order, tax collection, and prison upkeep.

Contrary to popular belief, church–state relations were difficult in the colonies. First, by virtue of the Patronato Royal (Royal Patronage) of 1501, the Spanish kings were given the extraordinary ability to appoint ecclesiastic authorities in the Indies (the Americas). This power was handed over as "payback" for the Spanish monarchy's loyalty to the church during an 800-year struggle against the forces of Islam in Spain. By virtue of this mandate, the Spanish monarchs held de facto power over the church in America: high church officials such as archbishops and bishops were loyal, by necessity, to the crown (except, of course, in the case of the Jesuits, a group of priests that would be expelled from America in 1767 by the Spanish crown for their excessive loyalty to the pope, their disobedience, and their many successful enterprises in the Americas).

Catholic priests in America were generally either "regulars" or "seculars." The regular clergy were members of European orders (they lived via the *regla,* or rule of the order); they were known as Franciscans, Augustinians, Jesuits, Dominicans, and so forth. The regular clergy were more loyal to European orders than to local American bishops. The secular clergy (the local parish priest), on the other hand, were loyal to the local bishop who distributed salary and benefits; in reality, regular clergy also depended on local economic structures for survival. Infighting and bickering were constant in the Catholic Church—between European and local orders, regular and secular priests, and between bishops and archbishops.

The Inquisition came to America and was installed at Lima, Mexico City, and Cartagena; however, it never rose to the same level of prominence as its European counterpart. For the most part, Native Americans and African slaves (pagans in need of Christian instruction) were exempt from the Inquisition. Heretics, Jews, and enemies of politically and ecclesiastically connected Christians in America were sometimes dragged before the Inquisition: they could spend years or decades defending themselves, and they generally had their property seized as part of the process. In the case of Cartagena, a dozen or so individuals were sentenced to death by the Inquisition.

The Latin American Inquisition was a formidable church bureaucracy that employed a lot of people and maintained surveillance over society to protect good Catholics from foreign ideas—ideas that generally arrived by ship, from Europe.

BIBLIOGRAPHY

Greenleaf, Richard E. 1969. *The Mexican Inquisition of the Sixteenth Century.* Albuquerque: University of New Mexico Press.

Splendiani, Ana María. 1997. *Cincuenta años de inquisición en el tribunal de Cartagena de Indias, 1610–1660.* Bogotá: Instituto Colombiano de Cultura Hispánica.

Zea, Leopoldo. 1957. *América en la historia.* Madrid: Ed. Revista de Occidente.

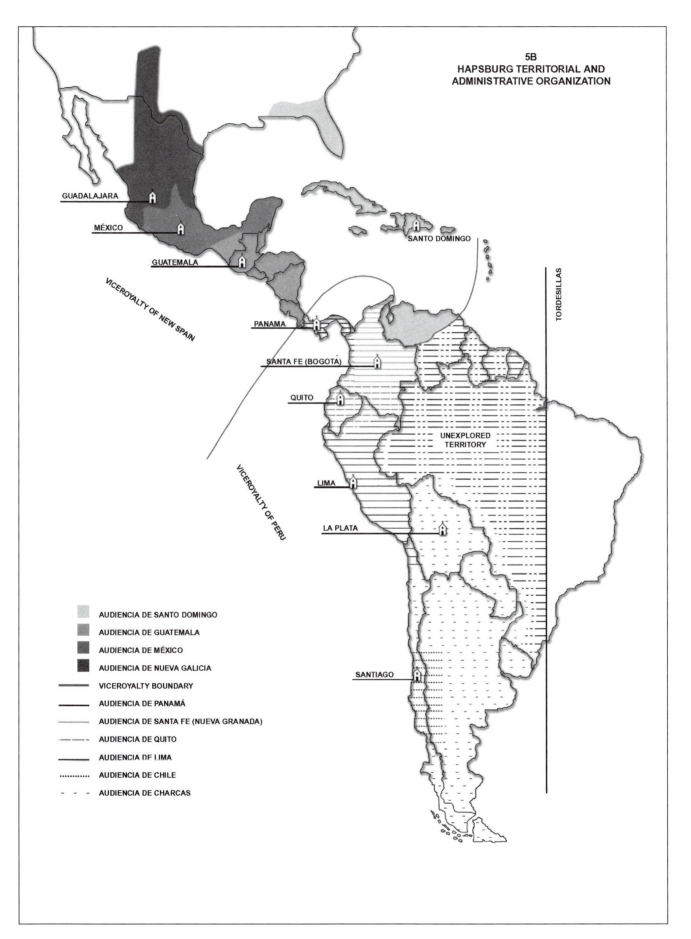

5B
HAPSBURG TERRITORIAL AND
ADMINISTRATIVE ORGANIZATION

GUADALAJARA

MÉXICO

GUATEMALA

SANTO DOMINGO

VICEROYALTY OF NEW SPAIN

TORDESILLAS

PANAMA

SANTA FE (BOGOTÁ)

QUITO

UNEXPLORED
TERRITORY

VICEROYALTY OF PERU

LIMA

LA PLATA

SANTIAGO

AUDIENCIA DE SANTO DOMINGO
AUDIENCIA DE GUATEMALA
AUDIENCIA DE MÉXICO
AUDIENCIA DE NUEVA GALICIA
VICEROYALTY BOUNDARY
AUDIENCIA DE PANAMÁ
AUDIENCIA DE SANTA FE (NUEVA GRANADA)
AUDIENCIA DE QUITO
AUDIENCIA DE LIMA
AUDIENCIA DE CHILE
AUDIENCIA DE CHARCAS

Republics of Citizens (Spaniards) and Indians

Spaniards, from the first day they arrived to the Caribbean, never thought of Native Americans as their social or racial equals. In fact, their policies in the Caribbean and elsewhere throughout the empire tended to accentuate the differences between themselves and the native residents of America. Spaniards who aspired to the historic conception of the Spanish gentleman—the *hidalgo*—had no intention of toiling in fields or mines once in America. Such work was deemed appropriate only for those they perceived as their social inferiors—Native Americans (Indians) or enslaved Africans.

Even city construction in the Americas separated Spaniards from Indians, and, in fact, the central section of the city could only legally be inhabited by Spaniards. Indians lived outside the city, close to the mines or fields where they worked. Indians were forbidden from wearing clothing worn by Spaniards, and when passing a Spaniard on the street, they were ordered to bow down in an appropriate gesture of servitude and submission.

Some—but very few—Spaniards complained publicly about the mistreatment of Native Americans: Father Antonio de Montesinos, Father Francisco de Vitoria (in Spain), and Father Bartolomé de Las Casas, the so-called Defender of the Indians, all challenged Spanish treatment of natives in America. Sometimes the priests' motives were self-serving and selective; for example, Father Las Casas had little to say about the actual enslavement of Africans in America. But the criticism of Spanish policies during the early phase of the conquest resulted in actual legislation: the New Laws of 1542 were promulgated to bring some needed "order" to the process of colonization. These laws offered clear protection to Native Americans, defined as the king's colonial subjects, but were often ignored by Spaniards in America who responded to much Spanish legislation with the phrase *obedezco pero no cumplo* (I obey the law—and the king—but I don't comply). Under the New Laws, natives were guaranteed protected lands (called *resguardos*), they were offered Catholic religious instruction via regular visits from a *doctrinero,* and Spaniards were legally forbidden from enslaving Native Americans or treating them cruelly. In exchange, Native Americans were forced to obey Spanish authorities in America, especially the designated *corregidores de indios* (regional administrators/overseers). Most importantly perhaps, natives were forced to pay tribute in exchange for the crown's protection. Tribute to Spaniards took essentially three forms: *concierto agrario* (work in the fields), *minería* (work in the mines), and *obraje* (city labor in workshops), where essential items for the city were manufactured such as horseshoes, candles, textiles, bricks, and so forth. Via this arrangement, well-connected Spaniards became wealthy, the king took 20 percent (in theory, anyway) off the top, natives were not enslaved (again, in theory), and the system was functional.

However, great abuse occurred throughout the Americas despite the sermons of some progressive clerics or the weight of Spanish law. "America" was simply too far away from Spain, and too big, to be carefully administered. Moreover, Spanish officials in America were motivated, more often than not, by greed, quick profit, and pretense. For most, representing the king in America and treating the natives with dignity were second-tier objectives.

One place that offers a different model is Paraguay during the late seventeenth and eighteenth centuries (up to the expulsion of the Jesuits in 1767). Jesuit missions in Paraguay were extraordinarily powerful, wealthy, highly stratified, and self-contained economic and social units. The success of the missions worried local landowners (who were deprived of a native labor force) and the crown, which always felt it was being "cheated" by Jesuits who, historically, pledged absolute loyalty to the pope in Rome. Mounting tensions between church and state, between Spaniards and Portuguese, and even within the church itself led to war in Paraguay in the 1750s. After 1767, the missions were taken over by civil administrators, resulting in a gradual decline of the Guaraní population at these locations.

BIBLIOGRAPHY

Carmagnani, Marcello, Alicia Hernández Chávez, and Ruggiero Romano. 1999. *Para una historia de América. I. Las estructuras.* México, DF: El Colegio de México.

Mörner, Magnus. 1953. *The Political and Economic Activity of the Jesuits in the La Plata Region: The Hapsburg Era.* Stockholm: Victor Pettersons Bookindustri.

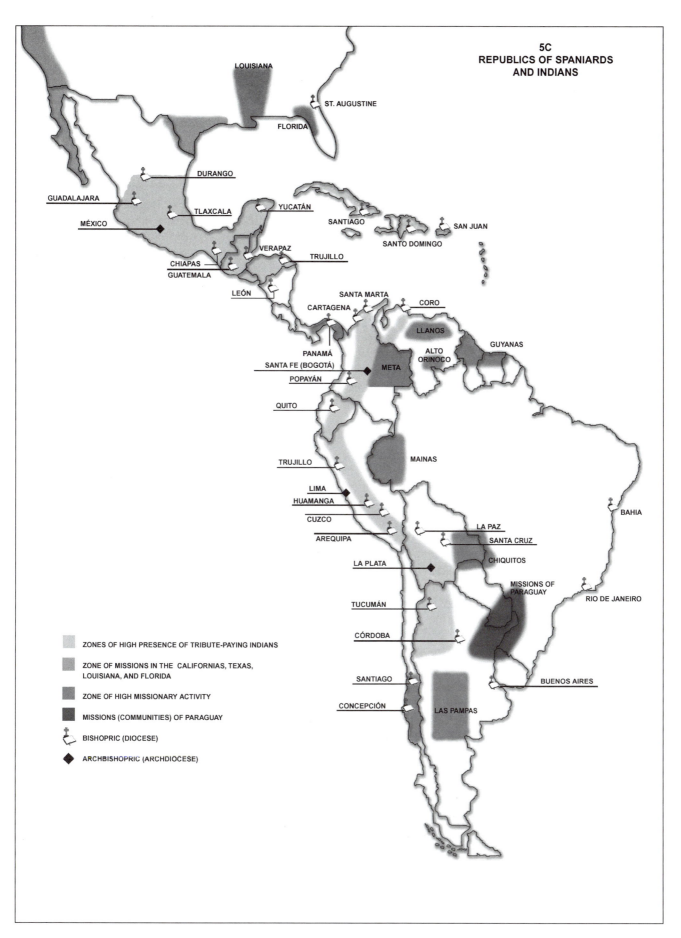

5C
REPUBLICS OF SPANIARDS
AND INDIANS

LOUISIANA

ST. AUGUSTINE

FLORIDA

DURANGO

GUADALAJARA

TLAXCALA

MÉXICO

YUCATÁN

SANTIAGO

SANTO DOMINGO

SAN JUAN

VERAPAZ

CHIAPAS

GUATEMALA

TRUJILLO

LEÓN

SANTA MARTA

CARTAGENA

CORO

LLANOS

GUYANAS

PANAMÁ

ALTO
ORINOCO

SANTA FE (BOGOTÁ)

META

POPAYÁN

QUITO

MAINAS

TRUJILLO

LIMA

BAHIA

HUAMANGA

CUZCO

LA PAZ

AREQUIPA

SANTA CRUZ

CHIQUITOS

LA PLATA

MISSIONS OF
PARAGUAY

RIO DE JANEIRO

TUCUMÁN

CÓRDOBA

SANTIAGO

BUENOS AIRES

CONCEPCIÓN

LAS PAMPAS

ZONES OF HIGH PRESENCE OF TRIBUTE-PAYING INDIANS

ZONE OF MISSIONS IN THE CALIFORNIAS, TEXAS,
LOUISIANA, AND FLORIDA

ZONE OF HIGH MISSIONARY ACTIVITY

MISSIONS (COMMUNITIES) OF PARAGUAY

BISHOPRIC (DIOCESE)

ARCHBISHOPRIC (ARCHDIOCESE)

5D

Slave Centers During the Sixteenth and Seventeenth Centuries

Slavery was an accepted practice during the colonial period in Latin America. In fact, it was not until the eighteenth-century European Enlightenment that Western thinkers began reconsidering slavery by applying "universal" declarations of the rights of all men. Simply put, slavery, after 1789, did not fit with modern Western political or social philosophy. It did, however, make economic sense for plantation owners in the Caribbean, South America, and the U.S. South to hold slaves. Thus, the institution was only gradually dissolved during the nineteenth century. The largest slave-owning states —Brazil, Cuba, and the United States—were the last to end the institution. Brazil did so in 1888, Cuba in 1878 (after a ten-year bloody conflict), and the United States, via the Thirteenth Amendment to the Constitution, in 1865, after a civil war that resulted in about 620,000 deaths.

In the Spanish Empire, those who benefited from African slavery viewed the status of enslaved Africans in a totally different light from that of "subjugated" Native Americans. Native Americans were subject to Spanish law, and there were certain clear rights and obligations associated with their status. No such rights protected Africans, who were treated as mere chattel —property. In fact, in some slave centers of the Americas, Spaniards justified enslaving Africans by arguing that in America, at least, they were free from pagan Africa and could enjoy the sacraments of the church together with some Catholic instruction and Hispanic acculturation. A clear "social hierarchy" drove the development of the Spanish and Portuguese overseas empire, and enslaved Africans were at the bottom of that hierarchy. They were seen as humans, but certainly not equals in relation to their Spanish and Portuguese masters.

A total of about 9 million Africans were transported to America, the vast majority destined for the Caribbean basin and Brazil. In the Caribbean, enslaved Africans arrived to four central slave markets: Havana, Cartagena, Portobelo, and Veracruz. Slaves would be sold and distributed throughout the Caribbean from Havana; at Cartagena, slaves would be distributed throughout northern South America.

One of the most important figures in the religious history of Cartagena is the Spanish Jesuit priest Pedro Claver (1580–1654), elevated to sainthood in 1888 by Pope Leon XIII and commonly known as the "slave to the slaves." His chief concern was "the defense and protection of the poor slaves that arrived from Africa to America."[1] Claver never denounced the institution of slavery. He did, however, physically embrace the slaves and treated them with kindness upon their arrival to the city of Cartagena.

From Portobelo, Panama, the slaves crossed the isthmus to what is today Panama City and began the long journey down the Pacific, arriving at Guayaquil and Peru, particularly along the north coast (Trujillo), where slaves worked on sugar and cotton plantations. Brazil, the Portuguese colony, became a slave center in the early 1540s. As many as 4 million slaves came to Brazil during a 320-year period, and the majority worked during the sixteenth and seventeenth centuries in the thriving northeastern sugar plantations. Salvador (Bahia), Recife (Pernambuco), and Rio de Janeiro were important slave centers in Brazil, and Afro-Brazilian culture today thrives in those places and throughout much of the rest of Brazil. Four hundred forty-seven years transpired from the day the first slaves arrived in Lisbon to the ending of the institution in Brazil (1888). Slavery thus transformed the history and culture of Latin American society and continues to do so to this day.

NOTE

1. From www.cartagena.com/sanpedroclaver/ (our translation from the Spanish).

BIBLIOGRAPHY

Conrad, Robert E. 1994. *Children of God's Fire.* University Park: Penn State Press.

Wade, Peter. 1993. *Blackness and Race Mixture: The Dynamics of Racial Identity in Colombia.* Baltimore: Johns Hopkins University Press.

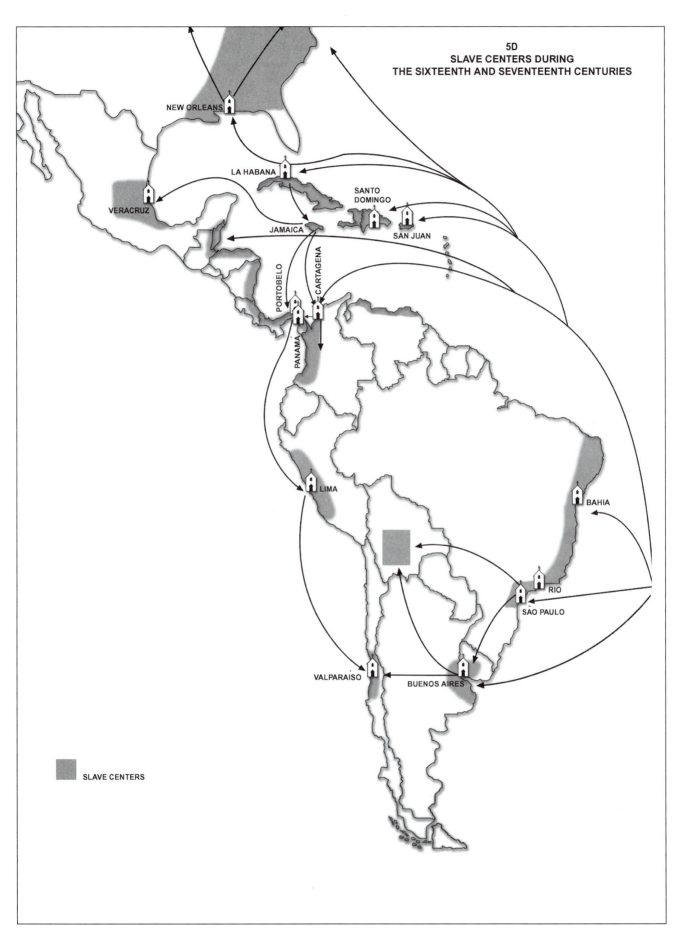

5D
SLAVE CENTERS DURING
THE SIXTEENTH AND SEVENTEENTH CENTURIES

NEW ORLEANS

LA HABANA

VERACRUZ

SANTO
DOMINGO

SAN JUAN

JAMAICA

PORTOBELO

CARTAGENA

PANAMA

LIMA

BAHIA

RIO

SAO PAULO

VALPARAISO

BUENOS AIRES

SLAVE CENTERS

The Spanish Flotilla

Much of the mineral wealth found in the Americas made its way back to Europe during the sixteenth and seventeenth centuries. Silver from South America (Peru) moved up the west coast and crossed over Panama to Portobelo, where it was reloaded onto ships and moved out through the Caribbean to Spain. Because of the enormous amount of wealth moving through it, the Caribbean became one of the most contested regions of the world during the sixteenth and seventeenth centuries, and, as such, the Spaniards fortified the main cities with impressive walls and military forts (which still exist today, in varying degrees of disrepair). The fortified cities—including Veracruz, Cartagena, Havana, Santo Domingo, and San Juan—served a pivotal function in moving silver and other precious metals from America to Europe. The most intense period of silver production occurred early in the colonial period, from about 1550 to 1650.

Essentially, the flotilla was a tightly controlled system for shipping precious cargo to and from Spain. The *flota* constituted at least fifty ships, some of which were provided exclusively for the defense of the cargo. Normally, the ships from Spain (carrying weapons, European manufactured goods, slaves, books, and other luxury items from Europe unavailable in the Americas) would arrive to the island of Dominica, and from there the ships would divide into four separate paths. One set of ships would head to San Juan, the other to Santo Domingo; another group of ships would go to Santiago de Cuba and then on to Veracruz, while the final portion of the flotilla would head to Cartagena, then Portobelo. From Cartagena, goods would make their way into what is today the Colombian interior. The products sent to Portobelo would be transported across the isthmus of Panama, be reloaded on the Pacific side of Panama, and move down the west coast of South America to Peru, with stops at Guayaquil and other port cities along the way.

The Spanish ships, upon unloading their cargo, would remain in port for about a month before beginning the return journey to Spain. The return route for the flotilla reunited the ships at Havana from Portobelo (via the west coast of South America), Cartagena and Veracruz. Upon arrival at Havana, the ships would take on additional supplies, and depart the Caribbean through the Straits of Florida to the open sea. Twice a year the flotilla returned to Spain loaded with silver, and, according to Charles Gibson, between 1550 and 1650, "approximately two-fifths of the precious metals received in Spain constituted direct royal income, derived from the *quinto* or 20 percent tax on mine yields, and from other royal taxes."[1]

Spain became wealthy with the influx of American silver and the tight control over its production and shipping, but there were many problems with Spanish economic development during this time. First, the complete monopoly of American ports held by Spain resulted in the ports' economic stagnation and encouraged illicit trade. Second, Spain's absolute monopoly over the silver trade made the country vulnerable to outsiders (the French, British, and Dutch) who wanted a share in the wealth. Finally, and perhaps most important, Spain took in a great deal of bullion in the early colonial period, but most of it "left" Spain and migrated to the manufacturing centers of Europe, such as England, Scotland, the Netherlands, and France. The Spaniards' ability to buy anything they wanted meant that American silver, flowing through Spain, would finance Northern European industrial development and leave Spain, by the eighteenth century, with beautiful architecture and artwork, but little in terms of industry. This reality would come to haunt Spain, particularly during the nineteenth and twentieth centuries.

NOTE

1. Charles Gibson, *Spain in America* (New York: Harper Torchbooks, 1966), p. 103.

BIBLIOGRAPHY

Kamen, Henry. 2004. *Empire: How Spain Became a World Power.* New York: HarperCollins.

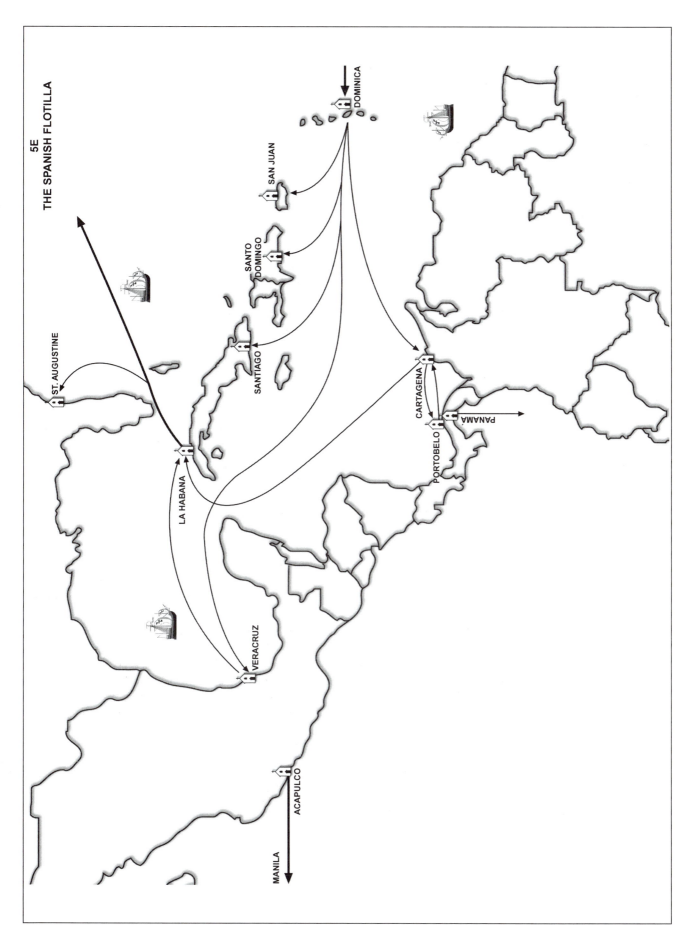

DOMINICA

SAN JUAN

SANTO
DOMINGO

SANTIAGO

ST. AUGUSTINE

LA HABANA

VERACRUZ

CARTAGENA

PORTOBELO

PANAMA

ACAPULCO

MANILA

5F

Exploiting Mining Centers

During the 1970s and early 1980s, prominent economic historians and political scientists researched mining and its impact on the Latin American colonial economy. Peter Bakewell and Theodore H. Moran studied mining in colonial Mexico and contemporary Chile, while other studies have focused on Peruvian and Bolivian mining, especially the creation and collapse of the city of Potosí (Bolivia) in the seventeenth century.

Spaniards, in the earliest days of the conquest and throughout much of the sixteenth, seventeenth, and eighteenth centuries, were motivated by a mercantilist mentality. They believed, in a strictly precapitalist sense, that wealth was finite and mostly confined to subsoil mineral holdings. Land, of course, was valuable to Spaniards, but it could not be "moved" as easily as gold and silver, which was melted down, shaped into bars, and transported across the ocean. This was "bullionism," another term used to describe Spanish economic policy in the early days of the empire. The idea of "creating wealth" through trade and comparative advantage emerged later in the eighteenth century with the thinking of Adam Smith in *The Wealth of Nations,* published in 1776. The Spaniards' belief in the finite nature of resources affected the pace and rhythm of the conquest, the placement of cities, and the construction of walls around cities in the Caribbean basin. This network of walled cities served as a defense against marauding English, French, and Dutch pirates.

The early mining centers in America were found primarily in Mexico. Zacatecas, San Luis Potosí, and Guanajuato produced silver, gold, platinum, iron, and copper. Thus, Mexico became one of the most important centers of wealth in the Spanish Empire. Another site of extraordinary mineral wealth was found in Peru; the Cerro de Pasco mining region, in the mountains west of Lima, produced silver; mercury was found at Huancavelica. Mercury was a critically important product in the silver smelting process, and Spaniards in America made significant advances in mining/smelting technology and procedures. Huancavelica, Peru, became the most important mercury deposit outside of Spain.

By 1545, some of the richest silver veins in the Americas were found in present-day Bolivia in a town called Potosí; by the end of the sixteenth century, this city would be one of the most populous in the Americas. La Paz and Oruro were other important mining centers in Bolivia.

Colombia's mining boom centered in the western province of Antioquia, where gold deposits were discovered during the second half of the sixteenth century. Much of the gold in this region was mined in rivers. The deposits and mining activities produced a steady stream of gold and other minerals—most notably emeralds from the central highlands—but the Colombian experience never paralleled the magnitude of the silver booms in Mexico, Peru, and Bolivia. Colombian economic history is defined by gradual, moderate growth, rather than the boom–bust cycles characteristic of economies with massive mineral deposits.

By about 1700, precious metals began to play an important role in the economy of Brazil. The interior state of Minas Gerais (General Mines) grew in importance during the eighteenth century as a center of diamonds and gold. Economic activity in Brazil gradually shifted south and southwest to reflect the newfound wealth at Minas Gerais. One of the most beautiful cities in all of the Americas, Ouro Preto (Black Gold), located in Minas Gerais, started out as a rough-and-tumble mining town. By the late eighteenth century, Ouro Preto had become an important American center of baroque culture and architecture.

BIBLIOGRAPHY
Bakewell, Peter. 1971. *Silver Mining and Society in Colonial Mexico: Zacatecas, 1546–1700.* Cambridge: Cambridge University Press.
Lockhart, James. 1968. *Spanish Peru: 1532–1560: A Colonial Society.* Madison: University of Wisconsin Press.
Twinam, Ann. 1982. *Miners, Merchants and Farmers in Colonial Colombia.* Austin: University of Texas Press.

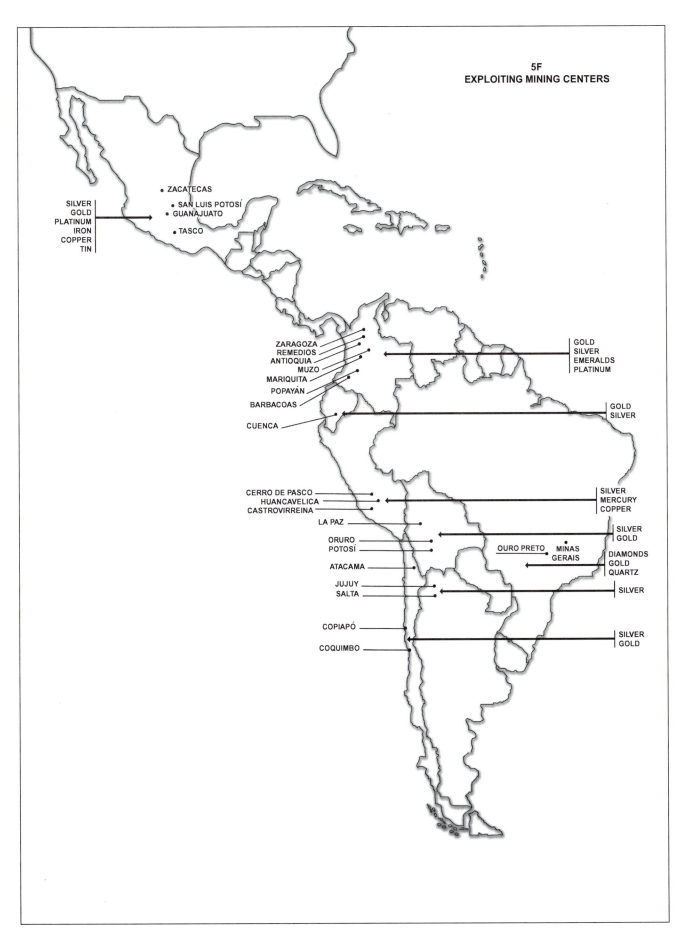

5F
EXPLOITING MINING CENTERS

SILVER
GOLD
PLATINUM
IRON
COPPER
TIN

• ZACATECAS
• SAN LUIS POTOSÍ
• GUANAJUATO
• TASCO

ZARAGOZA
REMEDIOS
ANTIOQUIA
MUZO
MARIQUITA
POPAYÁN
BARBACOAS

CUENCA

GOLD
SILVER
EMERALDS
PLATINUM

GOLD
SILVER

CERRO DE PASCO
HUANCAVELICA
CASTROVIRREINA

LA PAZ

ORURO
POTOSÍ

ATACAMA

JUJUY
SALTA

COPIAPÓ

COQUIMBO

SILVER
MERCURY
COPPER

SILVER
GOLD

OURO PRETO • MINAS
GERAIS

DIAMONDS
GOLD
QUARTZ

SILVER

SILVER
GOLD

5G

Intra- and Interregional Circulations in the Americas

The Spanish overseas empire—with its vast network of coastal and interior cities—depended on the wide circulation of commercial activity: this included locally produced manufactured goods, mineral and other primary products, and goods produced in Europe. Early in the formation of the Spanish overseas empire, the Caribbean region served as an axis for the movement of goods; this made perfect sense considering the limitations on transportation imposed by the Andes Mountains and other geographic barriers in places like Colombia, Ecuador, Bolivia, and the interior of Peru.

When contemplating the complex trade networks and circulation of products in the Spanish Empire, several factors must be considered: First, the Spanish flotilla hardly supplied all of the goods needed in the Americas. It arrived only twice a year and supplied the goods used by the upper classes—that is, the Spaniards. Slaves, books, fancy clothing, furniture, musical instruments, and such were all unloaded at the port cities of Havana, Cartagena, Veracruz, and Portobelo. The majority of goods needed in the Americas were produced in the Americas and circulated around the Caribbean and throughout the primary cities of the interior of South America. Second, Spaniards used established indigenous trade routes and networks to advance their own trade interests. Thus, what were largely functional for the Aztecs, or Incas, became trade networks for the Spaniards in the interior of Mexico or Peru/Bolivia.

Another important consideration when thinking about internal Latin American trade in the sixteenth and seventeenth centuries is the difference between and among coastal and interior trade. In the Caribbean, the cities of the coastal network—as explicated in essay 5A—traded with one another, and they were the first to receive up-to-date information from Europe, the latest gossip, and the most advanced scholarship. Thus, Cartagena—literally—faced Europe and North America, but turned its back on the interior Colombian cities, such as Bogotá, Tunja, or Medellín. Knowledge from Europe arrived to the Caribbean cities months before the same information arrived to the interior, and this lent an air of sophistication, openness, and cosmopolitanism to the coastal cities.

Along the Pacific coast, a vast and established trade network existed between Acapulco (which received the flotilla from Manila, with a wide assortment of goods from the Far East) and Panama, Guayaquil, Trujillo, Callao (Lima), and finally Valparaíso.

In the interior, several important trade networks existed, moving products such as wheat, cattle, corn, minerals, and mules throughout the cities and towns in the plains and mountainous regions of South America. One such network extended westward from the Argentine *pampas,* north through the interior cities of Tucumán and Córdoba, up to Potosí, and on through Peru to Callao. Another significant network extended southwest from Bogotá to Popayán and Pasto (in present-day Colombia) down to Quito, Ecuador, and eventually led to the coastal city of Guayaquil. From Bogotá northeastward, a trading route extended up to Mérida in Venezuela and onward toward the coast at Caracas. Along this route, tobacco, *aguardiente* (cane liquor), cattle, wheat, salt, and other primary agricultural products were exchanged.

Intra- and interregional trade made up the vast majority of trade during the early colonial period in Latin America. Spaniards tried to control all trade and production in the Americas, but this proved impossible given the vast distances and difficult terrain in South America. Early Spanish policy (before the eighteenth century), which only allowed official trade from select American ports (including Acapulco, Cartagena, Callao, Veracruz, Panama, Havana, and Santo Domingo), inadvertently encouraged illicit trade, contraband, and smuggling—characteristics of Latin America's economic reality seen to this day.

BIBLIOGRAPHY

Fisher, John R. 1997. *The Economic Aspects of Spanish Imperialism in America, 1492–1820.* Liverpool: University of Liverpool Press.
Lane, Kris F. 1998. *Pillaging the Empire: Piracy in the Americas, 1500–1759.* Armonk, NY: M.E. Sharpe.

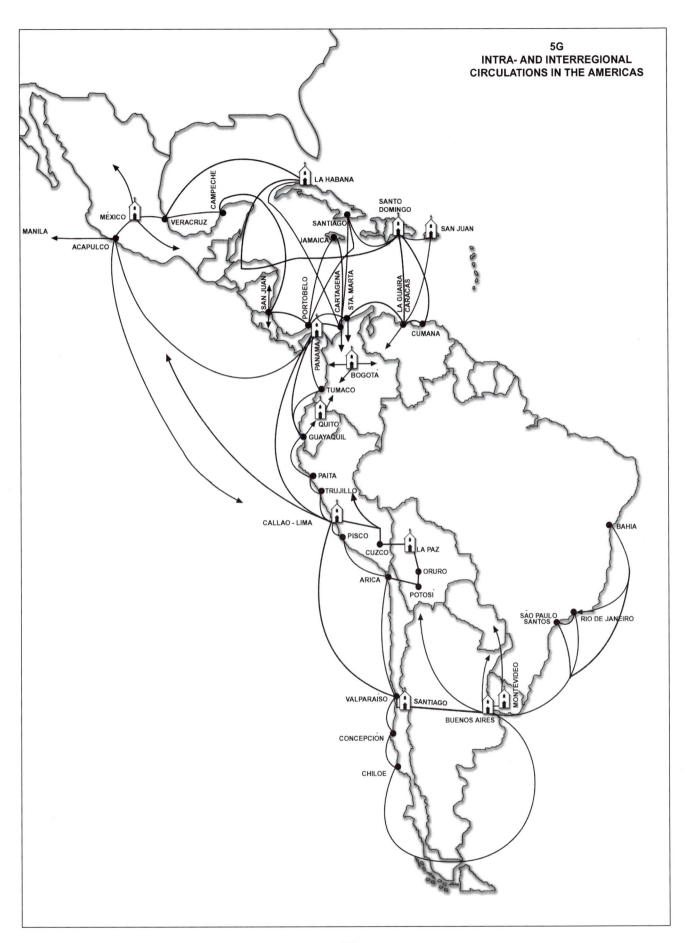

MANILA

ACAPULCO

MÉXICO

VERACRUZ

CAMPECHE

LA HABANA

SANTIAGO

JAMAICA

SANTO
DOMINGO

SAN JUAN

SAN JUAN

PORTOBELO

CARTAGENA

STA. MARTA

LA GUAIRA
CARACAS

CUMANA

PANAMA

BOGOTA

TUMACO

QUITO

GUAYAQUIL

PAITA

TRUJILLO

CALLAO - LIMA

PISCO

CUZCO

LA PAZ

ORURO

ARICA

POTOSÍ

BAHIA

SÃO PAULO
SANTOS

RIO DE JANEIRO

MONTEVIDEO

VALPARAÍSO

SANTIAGO

BUENOS AIRES

CONCEPCIÓN

CHILOE

6

AMERICA UNDER BOURBON RULE

6A

The Intendancy System and Other Administrative Reforms

The ascendance of the Bourbons to the Spanish throne—a primary outcome of the War of the Spanish Succession (1700–1713)—meant that the eighteenth century in America would be a century of reform. The Bourbons were modern, enlightened Frenchmen; they had new ideas about running an overseas empire that created, over a long period of time, significant change in the colonies. Collectively, the changes are referred to as the Bourbon Reforms.

The administrative reforms were begun under King Philip V (1700–1746) and continued through the rule of his successors, Ferdinand VI (1746–1759) and Charles III (1759–1788). The Bourbon kings realized that America was virtually ungovernable from across the Atlantic, in Spain, and they grew distrustful of American administrators. They felt the colonies needed stricter rule, better, more modern administrative structuring, and more enlightened, less monopolistic economic policies. The Bourbon kings feared they were not collecting their "fair share" of American revenues (or royal *quinto*—20 percent) and understood that tremendous graft, corruption, smuggling, and fraud defined economic relations in America. Though they understood they could never stop all fraud, they implemented policies designed to curtail it.

First, the Bourbons broke down the massive, somewhat illogical structure of a two-kingdom administrative system in America. They created two new viceroyalties: one for New Granada in 1717 (based in Bogotá), which would have jurisdiction over Venezuela, Panama, Colombia, and Ecuador, and the other, in 1776 for La Plata (based in Buenos Aires), which would have jurisdiction over Argentina, Paraguay, what is today Uruguay, and Bolivia. The reforms meant more administrators, and the Bourbons preferred that important posts be staffed by "trustworthy" Europeans rather than "dishonest" creoles (persons of Spanish descent born in the New World). One such administrator was the intendant, the primary figure at the head of a new intendancy system. The intendancy was French in concept, and the intendant held wide administrative and fiscal powers; this person worked to curb corruption, encourage trade and industry, and facilitate the honest collection of taxes and other royal revenues. The intendant would be sent over from Spain, and thus would (in theory) be free from corrupt practices that defined "business" in the American colonies. Whereas previous officeholders in the Americas purchased their offices and used their position to shake down locals, the intendant was a modern, salaried employee who viewed his position as "service to the crown." This novel concept of office holding emerged, largely, during the European Enlightenment.

One of the most significant reforms of the Bourbon kings, especially during the reign of Charles III, involved changes in economic thinking. The Bourbons realized that chaneling all trade through one Spanish port (Cádiz) and five American ports (Havana, Callao, Portobelo, Veracruz, Cartagena) stifled trade and encouraged piracy. By 1789 all American ports were opened to Spanish trade, and the flotilla system—which was costly to operate, cumbersome, and inefficient—was eliminated during this time period.

Other manifestations of reform involved replacing *criollos* (creoles) with *peninsulares* (Spaniards) in senior military posts and on the town councils, or *cabildos*. These reforms accentuated the differences between American-born Hispanics (whites) and Spaniards, and created tensions between the two groups. Those tensions eventually erupted in independence movements during the early nineteenth century. Before independence, though, a series of significant rebellions in Colombia (Comuneros, 1780) and Peru (Tupac Amaru, 1781–1783) foreshadowed the future. Both rebellions demonstrated the peoples' aversion to the new, "efficient" reforms that translated into higher taxes for the people, more efficient collection of tribute, and less ability to "negotiate" with incorruptible intendants.

The administrative, economic, and political changes ushered in during the eighteenth century created widespread discontent in the Americas—at all levels and among all classes—and led many creoles to ask a simple question by the late eighteenth century: Could we not handle our own administrative, political, and economic affairs without the "help" of the Spaniards?

BIBLIOGRAPHY

Andrien, Kenneth J., and Lyman L. Johnson, eds. 1994. *The Political Economy of Spanish America in the Age of Revolution, 1750–1850.* Albuquerque: University of New Mexico Press.

Lynch, John L. 1989. *Bourbon Spain, 1700–1808.* Oxford: Basil Blackwell.

GOVERNORSHIP
OF NEW CALIFORNIA

GOVERNORSHIP
OF NEW MEXICO

GOVERNORSHIP
OF SONORA

GOVERNORSHIP
OF TEXAS

FLORIDA

AUDIENCIA OF
SANTO DOMINGO

GOVERNORSHIP
OF OLD CALIFORNIA

ARIZPE

GOVERNORSHIP
OF NEW VIZCAYA

GOVERNORSHIP OF COAHUILA

GOVERNORSHIP OF THE NEW KINGDOM OF LEÓN

GOVERNORSHIP OF NEW SANTANDER

DURANGO
ZACATECAS
GUADALAJARA

SAN LUIS POTOSÍ
GUANAJUATO
VERACRUZ   MÉRIDA

CAMAGÜEY
(FROM 1795)

SANTO DOMINGO
(UNTIL 1795)

VALLADOLID

MEXICO CITY
PUEBLA
OAXACA

COMAYAGUA

CHIAPAS

GUATEMALA CITY

SAN SALVADOR   LEÓN

SAN JOSÉ

AUDIENCIA AND CAPTAINCY
GENERAL OF GUATEMALA

CAPTAINCY GENERAL
OF CARACAS

UNDER NEW GRANADA UNTIL 1777
LATER, MILITARY ZONE CONNECTED TO THE
CAPTAINCY GENERAL OF VENEZUELA
AND A JUDICIAL AREA UNDER THE CONTROL
OF SANTO DOMINGO (UNTIL 1786)

AUDIENCIA OF PANAMÁ

AUDIENCIA OF SANTA FE

SANTA FE
(BOGOTÁ)

AUDIENCIA OF QUITO

QUITO

CUENCA

TRUJILLO

HUANCAVELICA
AUDIENCIA OF LIMA
LIMA
PUNO

HUAMANGA

AUDIENCIA OF CUZCO

LA PAZ

AREQUIPA

COCHABAMBA

AUDIENCIA OF CHARCAS

CHUQUISACA

ASUNCIÓN

SALTA

CAPTAINCY GENERAL OF CHILE
(AUTONOMOUS FROM 1778)

CÓRDOBA

VICEROYALTY OF NUEVA GRANADA

VICEROYALTY OF PERU

VICEROYALTY OF RIO DE LA PLATA

VICEROYALTY OF BRAZIL

VICEROYALTY OF NUEVA ESPAÑA

AUDIENCIA OF SANTIAGO DE CHILE
SANTIAGO

AUDIENCIA OF BUENOS AIRES
BUENOS AIRES

CONCEPCIÓN

BOUNDARY, AUDIENCIAS AND CAPTAINCIES

NON-HISPANIC TERRITORIES OTHER THAN BRAZIL

● VICEROYALTY CAPITAL

▲ AUDIENCIA HEADQUARTERS

▮ CAPTAINCY GENERAL HEADQUARTERS

★ INTENDANCY HEADQUARTERS

Non-Iberian European Territories in the Caribbean and Central, South, and North America

Spain and Portugal, the two most important colonizers in what is today Latin America, were not alone in their pursuits of profit and colonies. Other European powers, including France, Denmark, Holland, and England, all managed to hold colonies during the height of Spanish/Portuguese power and domination. Important centers of non-Iberian power exist today in what is considered "Latin American" territory.

Before independence, Belize (called British Honduras) belonged to the British, as did Jamaica, Trinidad, and Tobago. The small islands of Martinique and Guadeloupe were taken by the French, as was Haiti (in 1679); Haiti remained a French possession until the bloody independence revolution of the late eighteenth and early nineteenth centuries. The Dutch colonized some of the islands of the Lesser Antilles, including Aruba, Curaçao, and Suriname. Guyana was colonized by the British, and French Guiana still belongs to the French. For many years, the British colonized the Caribbean coast of Nicaragua—the so-called Mosquito Coast—and still, today, the region's culture is more closely associated with the Caribbean basin than the interior Hispanic cities of Managua, León, and Granada.

Though Spain attempted to control the entire Caribbean basin, it simply could not—the area was too large. There were too many islands and tremendous fortunes to be made via sugar production. So, during the late sixteenth and especially the seventeenth century, the Dutch, British, and French moved in, and the legendary English pirates of the day, Francis Drake, John Hawkins, and Henry Morgan, "all became knights of the English realm."[1]

As the demand for sugar grew and as profits from its cultivation increased, the Caribbean became a center of contention. It was already the primary "pathway" for the shipment of gold and silver to Spain, yet sugar became almost as profitable as gold during the seventeenth century. Thus, the English took control of Jamaica in 1655 (and held it until 1962), and the French took a number of islands, as did the Dutch. These islands were characterized by slave labor, easy transportation to sugar markets on the east coast of North America and in Europe, and they provided huge profit margins to the European countries and companies that organized the sugar trade. A blessing and a curse, sugar left the Caribbean economies dependent on one or two agricultural products and created an ugly social structure in which wealthy Europeans and their administrators lived in regal tropical splendor on the same islands where the other people, mostly African slaves, barely survived.

Florida and New Orleans belonged to the economies and culture of the Caribbean basin. San Agustín (Florida) was settled in 1565 by the Spaniards, and the site is distinguished as the earliest city of continuous settlement in the present-day United States. Spain held Florida, as well as territory north of Mexico City and into Texas, up through present-day Arizona, New Mexico, California, Utah, and Colorado. The area between Florida and Texas was controlled by the French until the Seven Years' War (1756–1763), at which point all of Louisiana became Spanish territory. In 1800, though, Spain ceded the Louisiana Territory to France, and France sold it to the United States in 1803 as the Louisiana Purchase. With the Louisiana Purchase, incursions into Florida (by the United States) became commonplace; the interior of Florida had long been a sort of colony for runaway slaves from plantations of the U.S. South—escaped slaves intermingled with native Floridians and were referred to as "Seminoles," which is probably an attempted English pronunciation of the Spanish word *cimarrón,* referring to runaway slaves. By 1819, Florida was "sold" by Spain to the United States, but only after war was waged in the territory by Andrew Jackson. Jackson would become president of the United States in 1828.

NOTE

1. Thomas E. Skidmore and Peter H. Smith, *Modern Latin America,* 2d ed. (New York: Oxford University Press, 1989), p. 280.

BIBLIOGRAPHY

Liss, Peggy K. 1982. *Atlantic Empires: The Network of Trade and Revolution, 1713–1826.* Baltimore: Johns Hopkins University Press.

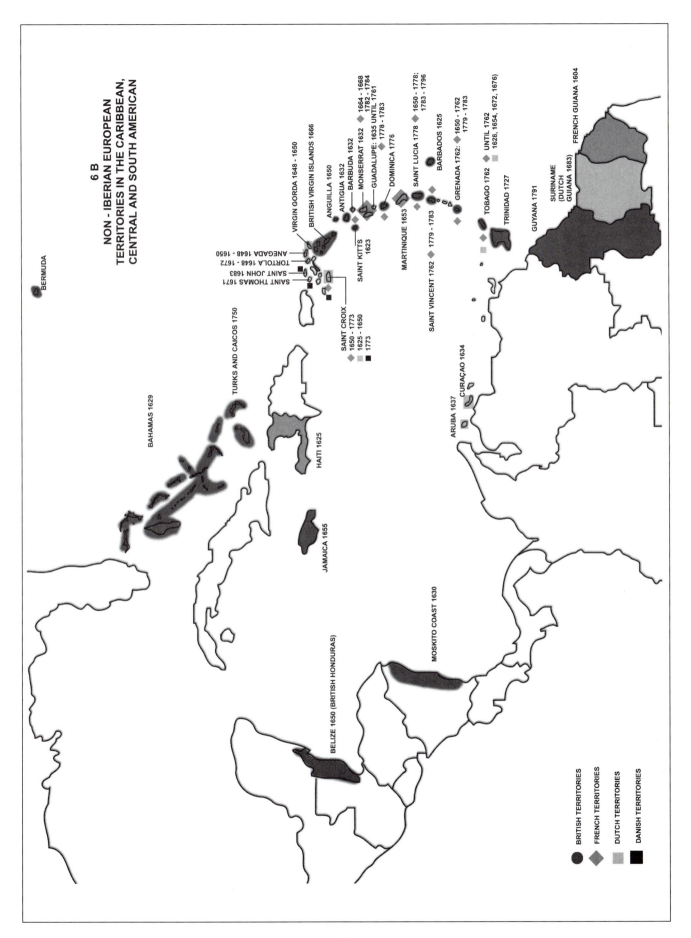

6 B
NON - IBERIAN EUROPEAN
TERRITORIES IN THE CARIBBEAN,
CENTRAL AND SOUTH AMERICAN

BERMUDA

VIRGIN GORDA 1648 - 1650
BRITISH VIRGIN ISLANDS 1666
ANGUILLA 1650
ANTIGUA 1632
BARBUDA 1632
MONSERRAT 1632
GUADALUPE: 1635 UNTIL 1761
1778 - 1783
DOMINICA 1776
SAINT LUCIA 1778
1664 - 1668
1782 - 1784
1650 - 1778;
1783 - 1796
BARBADOS 1625
GRENADA 1762:
1779 - 1783
1650 - 1762
1779 - 1783
TOBAGO 1762
TRINIDAD 1727
UNTIL 1762
1628, 1654, 1672, 1676)
MARTINIQUE 1653
SAINT VINCENT 1762
1779 - 1783
SAINT KITTS
1623
GUYANA 1791
SURINAME
(DUTCH
GUIANA 1683)
FRENCH GUIANA 1604

ANEGADA 1648 - 1650
TORTOLA 1648 - 1672
SAINT JOHN 1683
SAINT THOMAS 1671

SAINT CROIX
1650 - 1773
1625 - 1650
1773

CURAÇAO 1634
ARUBA 1637

TURKS AND CAICOS 1750

BAHAMAS 1629

HAITI 1625

JAMAICA 1655

MOSKITO COAST 1630

BELIZE 1650 (BRITISH HONDURAS)

BRITISH TERRITORIES
FRENCH TERRITORIES
DUTCH TERRITORIES
DANISH TERRITORIES

63

Universities, Science, and Culture

Latin American intellectual life developed over a long period of time, and was shaped, almost exclusively, by European trends, traditions, and intellectual currents. The Roman Catholic Church, during much of the sixteenth and seventeenth centuries, was the principle arbiter of academic life in the colonies. The early church adopted a mentality that can only be described as "under siege," especially in the period after the Council of Trent in the mid-sixteenth century. Thus, the church's central academic and cultural mission for the overseas colonies involved keeping foreign (i.e., non-Catholic) ideas out of the colonies. The Inquisition was designated as the institution responsible for maintaining intellectual uniformity and purity.

However, by the mid-sixteenth century, the first university opened in the Americas, the Universidad de San Marcos, in Lima. San Marcos, which predates Harvard College by about one hundred years, still operates today as Peru's premier public institution of higher learning. The pontifical Universidad de Mexico opened in 1553, and the Universidad de San Carlos (Guatemala City) opened about a century later, in 1676. These three universities educated the creole elite in America. Indian children, *mestizos,* and women were not invited to attend schools or universities.

Students at these traditional universities were rewarded for the degree to which they could recite approved texts, teachings, and lectures. Independent, critical thinking was discouraged, and scientific investigation was considered subversive and dangerous. Intellectual pursuit was purely scholastic. Students memorized, and via summaries written in embellished language and rhetorical devices, gained academic standing. They were educated to the extent that they could digest (almost literally) and debate previously published texts of grammar, theology, history, and languages—especially Latin and Greek. Discovery of new knowledge was not the goal of the early Latin American university.

The situation changed by the eighteenth century, when the Enlightenment hit Europe and the new research conducted at the great European universities arrived in America, despite the best efforts of the church to keep it out. Botany was studied in America, and given the comparative advantage held by the New World in terms of diversity of tropical plants and vegetation, it was only natural that plant life would be studied scientifically and systematically. José Celestino Mutis, a Spanish physician, spent twenty-five years in Bogotá studying, organizing, and categorizing plant life in what is today Colombia. The founding of the astronomical observatory in Bogotá (which stands today on the grounds of the presidential palace in the Colombian capital city) occurred in 1802, as Colombians and others began looking to the heavens for scientific, rather than religious, explanations of natural phenomena such as comets, meteorites, and eclipses.

The most important late eighteenth, early nineteenth-century explorer, geographer, and scientist to visit America was Alexander von Humboldt. His stay in America lasted five years, from 1799 to 1804, and his maps, visits, lectures, and teachings were embraced by people throughout Latin America. His work had wide political implications: Humboldt suggested, in his writings published as *Voyage to the Equinoctial Regions of the New Continent,* that Latin America was grossly mismanaged, overtaxed, burdened by outmoded political and economic structures, and in need of widespread political and social change. For the creole elite—growing increasingly dissatisfied with Spanish rule in the late eighteenth century—this was exactly the sort of encouragement needed. Of course, it is a stretch to suggest that von Humboldt's writings led to the Latin American independence movements, but clearly, his work and the scientific thinking emerging in Latin American universities suggested new possibilities for major change in the not-too-distant future.

BIBLIOGRAPHY

Lanning, John Tate. 1956. *The Eighteenth Century Enlightenment in the University of San Carlos de Guatemala.* Ithaca, NY: Cornell University Press.

Nieto Olarte, Mauricio. 2000. *Remedios para el Imperio: Historia natural y la apropiación del nuevo mundo.* Bogotá: Instituto Colombiano de Antropología e Historia.

6C
UNIVERSITIES, SCIENCE,
AND CULTURE

1553

MINING SCHOOL
1792
BOTANICAL GARDEN
1788

1721

1676

NATURAL HISTORY
MUSEUM 1796

1749

1721

BOTANICAL EXPEDITION 1783
ASTRONOMICAL OBSERVATORY
1803

1608

1586

1551

SCHOOL OF MEDICINE
SCIENTIFIC ACADEMY
1772

SCHOOL OF METALURGY
1779

SCHOOL OF
MEDICINE

ASTRONOMICAL
OBSERVATORY 1789

● UNIVERSITY

▲ SEMINARY

■ IMPORTANT CENTERS
OF HIGHER EDUCATION

◆ FINE ARTS ACADEMY

★ ART SCHOOLS

⬢ SCIENTIFIC CENTERS

The Birth of Public Opinion:
The Printing Press, Newspapers, and Literary Salons

During much of the sixteenth century, books were sent to the colonies from Spain and Portugal. The printing press arrived in Mexico first, and later in Peru, but printing of books in America was strictly limited to works deemed "pleasing" to Spanish royal and church authorities. One seventeenth-century woman who ran afoul of the church, the Mexican Sister (Sor) Juana Inés de la Cruz, is considered today an important baroque poet, perhaps one of the greatest in the world. Her poetry and writing were learned, daring, and political. She criticized Hispanic hypocrisy regarding gender relations and wondered why women were punished for prostitution while men were congratulated (or envied) for their sexual lasciviousness. Mexican church authorities turned against her when she criticized a prominent Portuguese theologian, Father Antonio Vieira: Sor Juana was forced to give up her library (about 5,000 books) and take care of the sick during the epidemics of the early 1690s. She died in 1695.

The Enlightenment arrived in Latin America about 100 years after the death of Sor Juana. The church tried to suppress the Enlightenment, but had to grudgingly accept the fact that, though they might be able to control publication of some books, man's mind was free and the Enlightenment offered a totally new way of viewing the world. The post-Enlightenment world stressed scientific research over outdated church theories; John Locke wrote of popular sovereignty, which, as a concept, clearly undermined the authority of the monarchy and church; Voltaire brazenly criticized the authority of the Roman Catholic Church with the phrase *Écrasez l'infâme,* or destroy the infamous one (the church).[1]

Newspapers appeared late in Latin America due to a scarcity of paper in the colonies, but during the late eighteenth, and especially early nineteenth centuries, newspapers, literary societies, and libraries were organized in the Americas. Newspapers and scientific journals produced in America were seen as dangerous, particularly by royal officials who feared change, openness, and dialogue. Thus, *Seminario del Nuevo Reino de Granada,* a weekly scientific journal, lasted for only four years (1808–1811). The editor, Francisco José de Caldas, an American intellectual and scientist, was executed by royalist forces—as were many of the contributors to the *Seminario.*

After the independence period, newspapers, magazines, and intellectual salons began to play important roles in constructing national identity and culture throughout Latin America. Scientific expeditions grew in prominence in the new republics because the very creoles who had fought for the liberation of Latin America did not know exactly what they had liberated. Just as Lewis and Clark in the United States traveled to the northwest corner of the Louisiana Territory on an expedition of discovery for President Jefferson, scientific and literary clubs were established to promote, encourage, finance, and publish the scientific, geographic, and naturalist expeditions of learned men in the Americas.

The lofty ideas of the Enlightenment, newspaper publication, and scientific journals hardly reached the majority of citizens in Latin America, before or after independence. Public opinion in Latin America *was* the opinion of a select group of educated men from prominent creole families. The concept of public education did not exist at the time of independence and would arrive later in the century to much of Latin America. Hierarchical thinking and action, which left an indelible stamp on Latin American society, suggested that only the "better" classes should be educated, and that the poor (Native Americans, enslaved Africans, most *mestizos*) should work for the elites. Circulation of newspapers and journals was limited to a very small number of citizens, but those were the citizens who made critical decisions in society—the decisions that the rest of society had to live with.

NOTE

1. Carlos Fuentes, *The Buried Mirror: Reflections on Spain in the New World* (Boston: Houghton Mifflin, 1992), p. 241.

BIBLIOGRAPHY

Del Castillo Senn, Lina María. 2005. "Science and Scientists." In *Iberia and the Americas,* ed. J. Michael Francis. Santa Barbara, CA: ABC-Clio.

Lynch, John. 1965. *Origins of the Latin American Revolutions, 1808–1826.* New York: Alfred A. Knopf.

6D
THE BIRTH OF PUBLIC OPINION:
THE PRINTING PRESS, NEWSPAPERS,
AND LITERARY SALONS

1723
1764 1791

SINCE XVI
CENTURY
1722 1796

1660
1729
1795

1820

1808
1808

1737
1785 1802

1741
1792
1791

1583
1743

1705

1807
1748 1780
1787 1764

● PRESS

■ NEWSPAPERS

▲ LITERARY SALONS

◆ SOCIEDAD ECONÓMICA
DE AMIGOS DEL PAIS
(SCIENTIFIC SOCIETIES)

7

FROM AUTONOMY
TO INDEPENDENCE

7A

Haiti: The Forgotten Revolution

The events of 1789 really did change the Western world. The French Revolution of that year collapsed the French monarchy, brought down the power of the Roman Catholic Church in France, and reordered the agrarian structure of the country. That same year the Universal Declaration of the Rights of Man was promulgated in Paris: the concept of *liberté, egalité,* and *fraternité* became a hallmark of Western political and philosophic thought.

Haiti, the western part of the island of Hispaniola, was taken by the French in 1679 and proved to be an extraordinarily successful sugar-producing region for more than a hundred years. The work force consisted of enslaved Africans, and France grew rich, thanks—in good measure—to the overseas sugar economy. When the Universal Declaration was announced, the people in Haiti (a French colony, after all) assumed that the Declaration referred to them. And while the French *philosophes* might have intended it to be that way, the French planter elite had no intention of giving up their labor force, or their way of life.

Understanding clearly the contradiction of the Universal Declaration, the self-educated slave Toussaint l'Ouverture organized and fought in a massive slave rebellion in Haiti that dramatically changed the history of that land. The Haitian Revolution, begun by l'Ouverture and concluded by one of his lieutenants, Jean-Jacques Dessalines, lasted for about thirteen years and resulted in death or exile for the entire planter aristocracy and its supporters. In 1822, Haiti annexed the Dominican Republic, an arrangement that lasted until 1844. Haitian-Dominican relations have been strained ever since. In 1937, thousands of Haitian agricultural workers were killed by Rafael Trujillo, the murderous dictator of the neighboring Dominican Republic.

The Haitian Revolution provides some important lessons and "firsts" for Latin American history. It was the first successful independence revolution in the region, and Haiti became the first independent black republic in the world. But the Haitian situation frightened property owners, church officials, monarchists, and creole elites—just about everyone in power throughout the Americas due to its intensity, level of violence, and the extent to which it changed Haitian society. Latin American creoles (i.e., American-born whites), had watched, with great enthusiasm, the American Revolution for independence in the thirteen English colonies, and, later, the French Revolution. These two revolutions suggested that they too might one day extract themselves from royal rule and govern their own affairs in a republican form of government. But two years after the Universal Declaration of the Rights of Man, the violent situation in Haiti and the potential reverberations in the region caused excited creoles to pause. For what if, in their own countries—say in Mexico, Peru, or Guatemala—poor, de facto enslaved Native Americans and/or enslaved Africans reacted with the same verve, efficiency, and determination as the slaves of Haiti? What if a revolution for independence, once initiated in Latin America, grew out of control, as it had in Haiti? Would the overworked, landless poor in Latin America distinguish between Spaniards and creoles? These were important questions, and, not surprisingly, the actual fighting to achieve independence from Spain in Latin America would not begin until about twenty years after the start of the Haitian Revolution. Many factors contributed to this delay, but everyone who held power, land, and slaves in Latin America understood what had happened in Haiti beginning in 1791. This reality dampened the revolutionary impulse among the Latin American creoles generated during the summer of 1789.

BIBLIOGRAPHY

James, C.L.R. 1989. *The Black Jacobins.* 2d ed. New York: Random House.

Williams, Eric. 1970. *From Columbus to Castro: The History of the Caribbean, 1492–1969.* New York: Random House.

1801: TOUSSAINT L'OUVERTURE
TAKES POWER AND DECLARES
A CONSTITUTION

1804–1805: DESSALINES
PROCLAIMS INDEPENDENCE
AND CROWNS HIMSELF EMPEROR

1805–1820: DIVISION BETWEEN THE SOUTH (PETION)
AND THE NORTH (CRISTOPHE)

1820: BOYER UNIFIES THE COUNTRY

1822–1844: HAITI ANNEXES THE
DOMINICAN REPUBLIC

KINGDOM OF HAITI

REPUBLIC OF HAITI

NORTH (KINGDOM OF HAITI)
UNDER CONTROL OF CRISTOPHE 1805–1823

SOUTH (REPUBLIC OF HAITI)
UNDER CONTROL OF PETION 1805–1817

1822–1844 DOMINICAN REPUBLIC
ANNEXED BY HAITI

7B

Mexico and Central America: From the "Grito de Dolores" to Monarchy

World events outside of Latin America dictated the terms, to some degree, of Latin America's independence struggles. First, the American Revolution against Great Britain proved that thirteen small colonies in North America could separate from one of the world's preeminent European powers. Later, in 1789, the French Revolution changed the political, social, and economic trajectory of the world's leading power (France) during the eighteenth century. The Haitian Revolution of the late eighteenth and early nineteenth century was significant in shaping the Latin American independence movements, as was the Napoleonic invasion of Iberia in 1807–1808. Charles IV abdicated in favor of his son Ferdinand VII; both father and son were abducted by Napoleon, who placed his brother Joseph on the Spanish throne. In America, the creole elite asked simple, but profoundly significant, questions: The legitimate king is gone, so does this mean we are free? What, precisely, connects us to the crown, if the king has been forced to abdicate?

The wars for independence in Latin America began in the early nineteenth century; the Mexican phase started in mid-September 1810 in the small town of Dolores, where great tension arose between the ruling Spanish/creole elite and the poor. A terrible drought in 1807–1808 had caused widespread famine, and instead of releasing grain to the people, Spanish merchants decided to hold food in storage, speculating that the drought (and shortage) would drive up prices and profits. This, and other forms of abuse against the poor, raised the indignation of the early leader of Mexican independence, a parish priest in Dolores, Guanajuato named Miguel Hidalgo y Costilla. Hidalgo was more interested in politics, reading, and lecturing than the day-to-day routine of the priesthood. He was fed up with the treatment of the poor indigenous people and could no longer tolerate the conditions of enslavement in which most of them were held by their lighter-skinned overseers. Thus, on September 16, 1810, he issued the famous "Grito de Dolores," (the "Shout of Dolores"), which concluded with "long live the Virgin of Guadalupe, death to the Spaniards!"

Hidalgo's cry of independence unleashed pent-up anger, and thousands were killed in this early rampage. Hidalgo himself was sent before a Spanish firing squad in 1811, and the movement he began was taken up by another priest, Father José María Morelos. Morelos was captured and executed in 1815. The Mexican Vicente Guerrero held out with a small group of rebels, but overseas events would dictate the contour of Mexican independence. A "liberal" revolution in Spain, which cut into the power of the Roman Catholic Church, created a situation in Mexico whereby Mexican conservatives favored "independence" from Spain rather than acceptance of the 1812 liberal Spanish constitution. The restored King Ferdinand VII reluctantly accepted this constitution after a series of military uprisings in 1820 created significant disorder in Spain. Meanwhile, in Mexico, Agustín de Iturbide managed to negotiate a truce with the rebels (led by Guerrero) and establish an agreement known as the Plan de Iguala of 1821. Under this agreement, Mexico would become a constitutional empire and the church would maintain all of its power, privilege, and property. Clearly, Mexico had gained independence from Spain, but in 1822, Iturbide was crowned Iturbide I, emperor of Mexico. One year later, he was overthrown. Mexicans had not sacrificed and struggled, with blood and property, for twelve years simply to trade one empire for another. The kingdom of Guatemala annexed itself to Mexico in 1822, but Iturbide's abdication in March 1823 resulted in Central American independence. On July 1, 1823, the United Provinces of Central America was established.

BIBLIOGRAPHY

Anna, Timothy. 1983. *Spain and the Loss of America.* Lincoln: University of Nebraska Press.

———. 1998. *Forging Mexico, 1821–1835.* Lincoln: University of Nebraska Press.

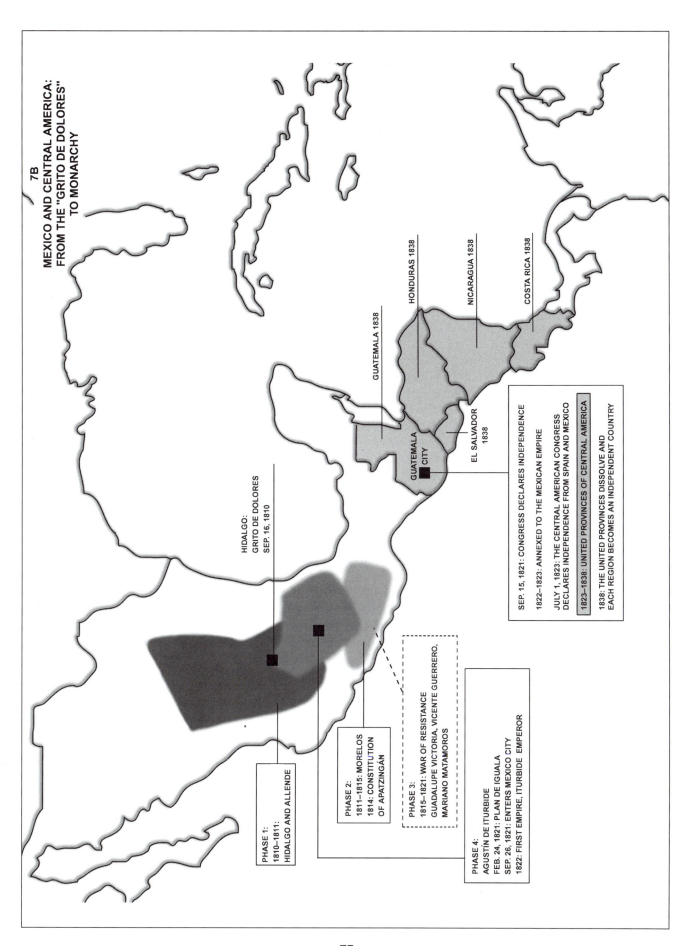

HIDALGO:
GRITO DE DOLORES
SEP. 16, 1810

GUATEMALA 1838

HONDURAS 1838

NICARAGUA 1838

COSTA RICA 1838

GUATEMALA
CITY

EL SALVADOR
1838

SEP. 15, 1821: CONGRESS DECLARES INDEPENDENCE

1822–1823: ANNEXED TO THE MEXICAN EMPIRE

JULY 1, 1823: THE CENTRAL AMERICAN CONGRESS
DECLARES INDEPENDENCE FROM SPAIN AND MEXICO

1823–1838: UNITED PROVINCES OF CENTRAL AMERICA

1838: THE UNITED PROVINCES DISSOLVE AND
EACH REGION BECOMES AN INDEPENDENT COUNTRY

PHASE 1:
1810–1811:
HIDALGO AND ALLENDE

PHASE 2:
1811–1815: MORELOS
1814: CONSTITUTION
OF APATZINGÁN

PHASE 3:
1815–1821: WAR OF RESISTANCE
GUADALUPE VICTORIA, VICENTE GUERRERO,
MARIANO MATAMOROS

PHASE 4:
AGUSTÍN DE ITURBIDE
FEB. 24, 1821: PLAN DE IGUALA
SEP. 26, 1821: ENTERS MEXICO CITY
1822: FIRST EMPIRE, ITURBIDE EMPEROR

73

War Among Creoles and Against Spaniards: The Andean Phase

At the beginning of 1810, about nine months before the "Grito de Dolores" in Mexico, tensions began mounting in northern South America, as the question of monarchical legitimacy in the "absence" of the Spanish king loomed large.

In Caracas, a group of wealthy creoles decided to depose the Spanish captain-general and form a *junta*, which would rule in the name of Ferdinand VII, the legitimate Spanish monarch. The man who emerged as leader of this group, Simón Bolívar—one of the wealthiest men in the Americas—would play a decisive role in the process of liberating northern South America from Spanish control. Bolívar had spent time in Europe during the post–French Revolution period and watched Napoleon crown himself emperor in Notre Dame Cathedral. Bolívar had decided, even before Napoleon rolled over the Iberian Peninsula, that Latin Americans should be allowed to choose their own political destiny. In 1811, when Venezuela declared itself independent, Spanish troops arrived to crush the American rebellion. Bolívar organized an army of slaves, who were promised freedom and land at the conclusion of the independence struggle, and *llaneros,* tough mestizo cowboys who lived on the Venezuelan plains, or *llanos;* Bolívar liked to refer to the *llaneros* as *los niños malvados*—the bad boys.

A brilliant military strategist, politician, philosopher, and one of the premier thinkers of his day, Bolívar achieved numerous military victories against royalist forces. When he united with José Antonio Páez, the Venezuelan leader of the *llanos,* the military campaign moved forward with great success. By 1819, Bolívar's forces controlled Venezuela, and—after the Battle of Boyacá on August 7, 1819—they controlled much of what is today Colombia. Fearing disorder, disunity, and chaos in the absence of Spanish authority, Bolívar, in late 1819, created Gran Colombia, a federation of three states: Venezuela, Colombia, and Ecuador. The constitution for this organization was declared at Cúcuta in May 1821. Next, Spanish resistance in Ecuador was finally brought under control at the Battle of Pichincha (1822), a victory for the grand field marshal of Ayacucho, the Venezuelan Antonio José de Sucre.

The final battle for independence, in 1824, occurred in Ayacucho, Peru. Peru proved to be a stronghold of royalist sentiment and, generally, Latin American independence dates from January 1826, when royalist forces surrendered the important port of Callao (Lima)—thus ending organized Spanish resistance in the Americas.

But as soon as the fighting ended with Spain, fighting began anew over how to organize and govern "America." Bolívar's dream of a "Gran Colombia" quickly collapsed when Venezuela and Ecuador pulled out of the federation in 1830. Latin Americans, particularly in the mountainous regions of Ecuador, Colombia, and Venezuela, were closely linked to regional culture, and the idea of a grand federation could not coexist with their strong attachment to local affairs. The complex geography of the region compounded this problem and made Bolívar's dream an impractical impossibility. In 1830, he was driven out of Bogotá—the capital of the federation he helped found some eleven years earlier. He marched off toward Santa Marta (Colombia) where he died, defeated and depressed, on December 17 at the age of forty-seven. His final words illustrate his mood: *¿cómo saldré yo de este laberinto?* (how will I ever get out of this labyrinth?), as does an oft-repeated phrase, uttered by Bolívar during his final days: he offered a haunting prediction for the fortunes of Latin America when he said, "America is ungovernable: those who have served the revolution have plowed the sea."

BIBLIOGRAPHY

García Márquez, Gabriel. 1990. *The General in His Labyrinth.* New York: Alfred A. Knopf.

Munro, Dana Gardner. 1942. *The Latin American Republics: A History.* New York: D. Appleton-Century.

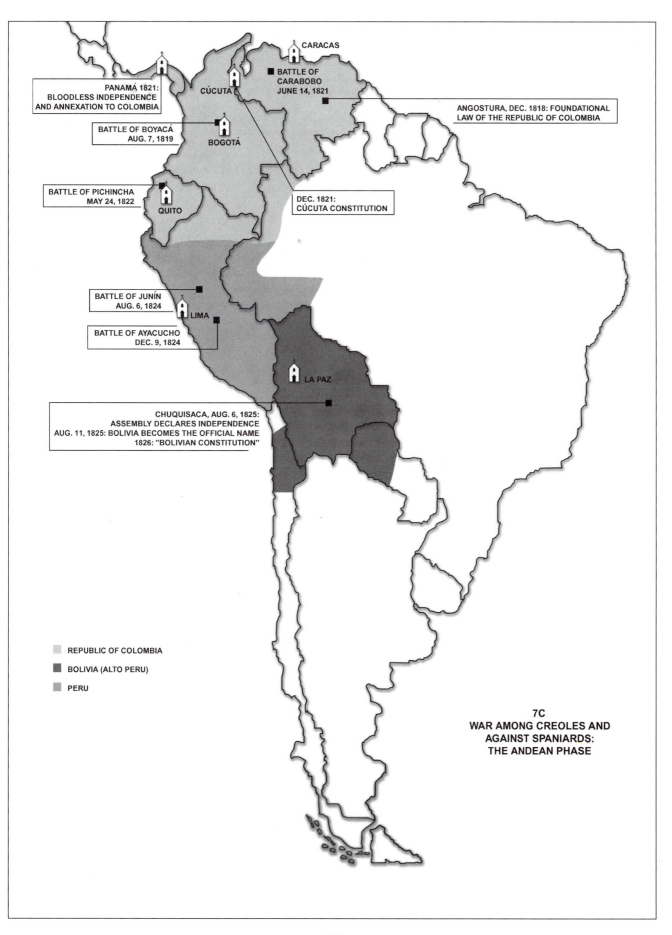

PANAMÁ 1821:
BLOODLESS INDEPENDENCE
AND ANNEXATION TO COLOMBIA

CARACAS

BATTLE OF
CARABOBO
JUNE 14, 1821

CÚCUTA

ANGOSTURA, DEC. 1818: FOUNDATIONAL
LAW OF THE REPUBLIC OF COLOMBIA

BATTLE OF BOYACÁ
AUG. 7, 1819

BOGOTÁ

BATTLE OF PICHINCHA
MAY 24, 1822

QUITO

DEC. 1821:
CÚCUTA CONSTITUTION

BATTLE OF JUNÍN
AUG. 6, 1824

LIMA

BATTLE OF AYACUCHO
DEC. 9, 1824

LA PAZ

CHUQUISACA, AUG. 6, 1825:
ASSEMBLY DECLARES INDEPENDENCE
AUG. 11, 1825: BOLIVIA BECOMES THE OFFICIAL NAME
1826: "BOLIVIAN CONSTITUTION"

REPUBLIC OF COLOMBIA

BOLIVIA (ALTO PERU)

PERU

7C
WAR AMONG CREOLES AND
AGAINST SPANIARDS:
THE ANDEAN PHASE

7D

The Southern Cone Independence Process and Brazilian Independence

The Southern Cone countries (Argentina, Chile, and Paraguay) gained their independence during a sweeping, dramatic campaign led by the Argentine General José de San Martín.[1]

In 1817, a year after the congress at Buenos Aires declared independence, San Martín organized a group of about 5,000 soldiers at the western city of Mendoza. The force crossed the Andes, swept down into Santiago, surprising the Spaniards, and won a rapid independence for Chile. This striking military victory was important for morale in the Americas, as it demonstrated that Americans could act decisively, dramatically, with skill and precision—and defeat the Spaniards. With Buenos Aires and Santiago in the hands of the rebels, the Southern Cone of Latin America was all but independent. San Martín, after liberating Chile, marched north to Lima and declared independence there in 1821, although Peru would not be completely independent until the port city of Callao was taken from the Spaniards, in 1826. Historians date the end of the independence wars as either 1826 or 1824 (the Battle of Ayacucho in Peru); both dates demonstrate the strength of Peruvian opposition to independence.

From Peru, San Martín marched north to Guayaquil, Ecuador, where he held a famous meeting with Simón Bolívar. No one really knows what happened at the meeting, except that San Martín quit the revolutionary struggle, gave up all his titles, and left for Europe. He was never to return to America.

The Brazilian story is quite different in that Brazilian "independence" occurred with minimal bloodshed. But, similar to the other independence processes in the Americas, the Brazilian phase was largely shaped by European events. In 1807, when Napoleon took over Portugal, and later Spain, the entire royal court at Lisbon boarded a fleet of ships and fled to Rio de Janeiro. The Portuguese monarch, João VI, opened up Brazilian trade (which benefited the British) and the court established a thriving culture in the American tropics at Rio de Janeiro. But, with Napoleon

defeated by 1815, João VI returned to Portugal, leaving his son Pedro I behind as crown prince regent. As Brazil grew wealthy and powerful, the Portuguese Cortes (an early version of Parliament) attempted to return Brazil to its former colonial status. Pedro responded to calls by his father for his return to Portugal with a simple declaration of independence in 1822: *Eu fico*, or I'm staying here! Essentially, Brazil was independent, though some fighting broke out in the northeast of the country in opposition to Pedro.

The contrasts between Spanish-American and Portuguese-American independence movements could not have been sharper. Spanish America was devastated during about sixteen years of warfare and dislocation. Mining centers collapsed, agriculture lagged, and trade was interrupted. Men on horseback—the *caudillos*—would come to play a critically important role throughout Spanish America in the immediate aftermath of independence; they would serve as leaders during the transition from monarchy to republic. In Brazil, the rule of Pedro I, and his son, Pedro II, assured a smooth monarchical legitimacy combined with constitutional input and procedure. The nineteenth century in Brazil is characterized by slavery, coffee, political continuity, and stability. Hispanic America's nineteenth century can be described as chaotic in many places—especially Mexico, Colombia, and Central America; there, caudillos ruled in an arbitrary fashion, civil wars broke out with great frequency, and foreigners invaded, appropriating land and resources.

NOTE

1. Uruguay was created in 1828 by a treaty between Brazil and Argentina and with the support of the British. It was designed as a sort of buffer zone between the two South American powers. Paraguay dates its independence as May 1811, when it proclaimed independence from Spain.

BIBLIOGRAPHY

Barman, Roderick J. 1988. *Brazil: The Forging of a Nation, 1798–1852.* Stanford: Stanford University Press.

Costa, Emília Viotti da. 1985. *The Brazilian Empire.* Chicago: University of Chicago Press.

Macaulay, Neill. 1986. *Dom Pedro.* Durham, NC: Duke University Press.

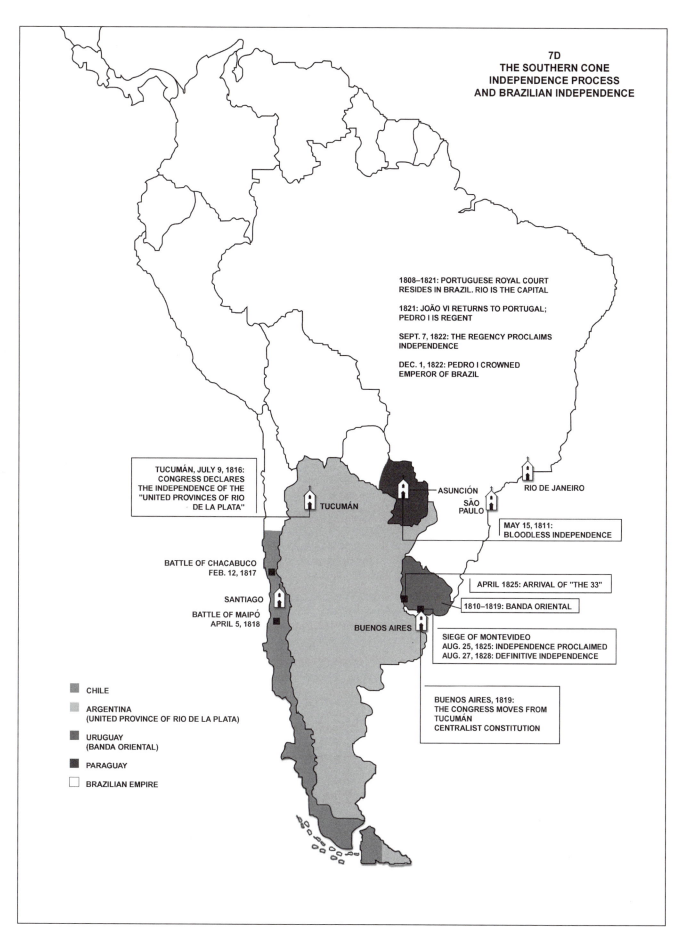

7D
THE SOUTHERN CONE
INDEPENDENCE PROCESS
AND BRAZILIAN INDEPENDENCE

1808–1821: PORTUGUESE ROYAL COURT
RESIDES IN BRAZIL. RIO IS THE CAPITAL

1821: JOÃO VI RETURNS TO PORTUGAL;
PEDRO I IS REGENT

SEPT. 7, 1822: THE REGENCY PROCLAIMS
INDEPENDENCE

DEC. 1, 1822: PEDRO I CROWNED
EMPEROR OF BRAZIL

TUCUMÁN, JULY 9, 1816:
CONGRESS DECLARES
THE INDEPENDENCE OF THE
"UNITED PROVINCES OF RIO
DE LA PLATA"

TUCUMÁN

ASUNCIÓN

RIO DE JANEIRO

SÃO
PAULO

MAY 15, 1811:
BLOODLESS INDEPENDENCE

BATTLE OF CHACABUCO
FEB. 12, 1817

APRIL 1825: ARRIVAL OF "THE 33"

SANTIAGO

1810–1819: BANDA ORIENTAL

BATTLE OF MAIPÓ
APRIL 5, 1818

BUENOS AIRES

SIEGE OF MONTEVIDEO
AUG. 25, 1825: INDEPENDENCE PROCLAIMED
AUG. 27, 1828: DEFINITIVE INDEPENDENCE

BUENOS AIRES, 1819:
THE CONGRESS MOVES FROM
TUCUMÁN
CENTRALIST CONSTITUTION

CHILE

ARGENTINA
(UNITED PROVINCE OF RIO DE LA PLATA)

URUGUAY
(BANDA ORIENTAL)

PARAGUAY

BRAZILIAN EMPIRE

8

LATIN AMERICA IN THE NINETEENTH CENTURY

8A

Mexico and Central America

The period immediately following independence in Hispanic America was a time of turmoil and disunity: it was a period defined largely by *caudillo* rule throughout the region. The rise of caudillos was a logical response to the disorder, destruction, and collapse of rule during and after independence. Much has been made of the *caudillo* in academic and nonacademic literature, for his fiery, charismatic personality has, since the early nineteenth century, captured the imaginations of social scientists and novelists alike.

Caudillos in Latin America were men on horseback. They were often products of the disbanded Latin American militaries (which, in some places, never really disbanded). They had authority and charisma and understood that independence, while offering great change in Latin America, did not fundamentally change the prevailing social structure or ingrained sense of hierarchy in the region. The *caudillo* held authority by mere virtue of the fact that he commanded large armies of men who were dislocated and unemployed in the period after independence. The *caudillo* was the patron, and the armies were his clients. Each understood his role in the system, and the *caudillo* army with the most men (i.e., the army that could distribute the most patronage) usually held the most power. In the absence of clear laws, governmental structures, or external authority, the *caudillo* filled a central—and functional—role in early nineteenth-century Latin American history.

However, *caudillismo* created problems as well. The case of Mexico is a prime example of how the arbitrary rule and mismanagement of self-aggrandized *caudillos* resulted in grave problems, including foreign intervention and the loss of about half of the country's territory by 1848. Antonio López de Santa Anna was the epoch's primary example of a *caudillo*. He was less interested in ruling Mexico and far more motivated by conquest, leading men into battle, and making, or unmaking, governments. He even, at one point, took down his own government! Santa Anna was certainly colorful: after losing a leg in the so-called "Pastry War" (1838) against French forces, he had the leg exhumed, ceremoniously paraded through the streets, and reburied with full military honors. He was not wedded to any one political party or ideology, and he switched positions when it was convenient to do so. But the "charm" of his leadership wore off by 1846, when the young, restless United States invaded for the express purpose of expanding its territorial borders. The U.S. forces occupied Mexico City and, via the Treaty of Guadalupe Hidalgo (1848), the United States officially took control of the territory known today as the states of Arizona, New Mexico, Texas, Utah, California, and Colorado.

Incredibly, Santa Anna managed to influence political affairs in Mexico through 1855, when he was finally ousted from power and forced into exile. An important era had passed in Mexico, but not without great loss to the Mexican nation and psyche.

In Guatemala, Rafael Carrera was a leader of critical importance in the period immediately after independence. He ruled from the early 1840s until his death in 1865. Carrera governed as *caudillo,* and later dictator, on behalf of the indigenous peoples of his country (he himself was indigenous). He was a conservative who enjoyed strong backing and support of the Roman Catholic Church. Carrera's tenure is one of few examples in Latin America in which an indigenous person has held power, and his policies created a period of relative peace and stability in Guatemala. Carrera's death in 1865 resulted in tension and turbulence. Liberal-conservative infighting defined Guatemalan politics until Justo Rufino Barrios rose to power and ruled until 1885. He firmly established the Liberal Party in the Guatemalan power structure, even though "rule" in Guatemala was little more than dictatorship designed to completely lock out opposing parties and ideas. The concept of "democracy" never took hold in Latin America in the nineteenth century—it eluded Guatemala for most of the twentieth century as well. The legacy of *caudillo* rule flourished in Guatemala (because it generally benefited outside economic interests) and laid the foundation for the country's political tragedies during the twentieth century.

BIBLIOGRAPHY

Handy, Jim. 1984. *Gift of the Devil: A History of Guatemala.* Boston: South End Press.
Lynch, John. 1992. *Caudillos in Spanish America, 1800–1850.* New York: Oxford University Press.
Roa Bastos, Augusto Antonio. 1987. *Yo el supremo.* Madrid: Cátedra.

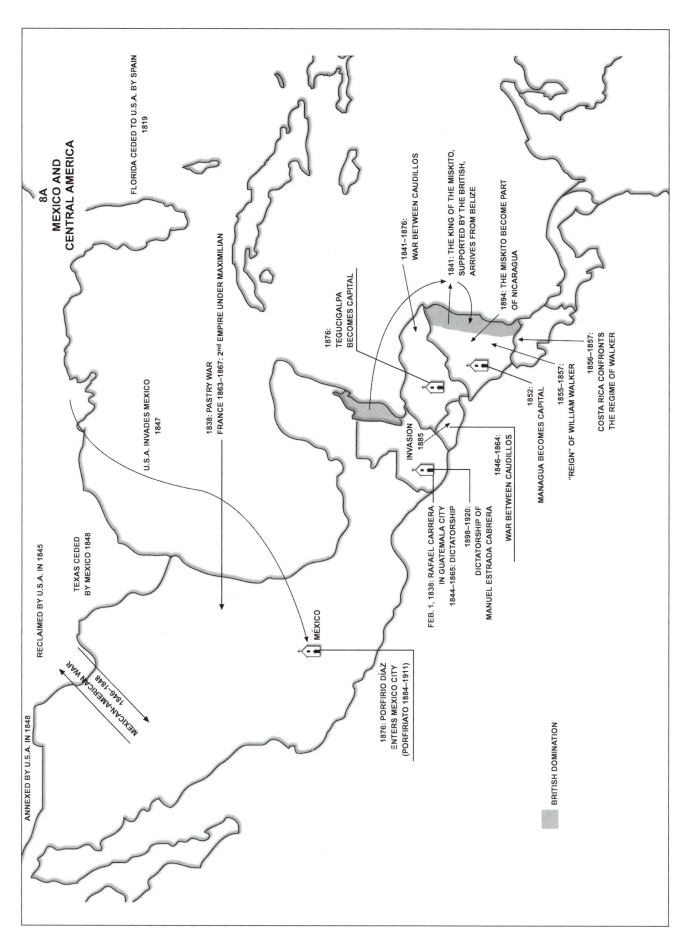

8A
MEXICO AND
CENTRAL AMERICA

FLORIDA CEDED TO U.S.A. BY SPAIN
1819

1838: PASTRY WAR
FRANCE 1863–1867: 2nd EMPIRE UNDER MAXIMILIAN

U.S.A. INVADES MEXICO
1847

1876:
TEGUCIGALPA
BECOMES CAPITAL

1841–1876:
WAR BETWEEN CAUDILLOS

1841: THE KING OF THE MISKITO,
SUPPORTED BY THE BRITISH,
ARRIVES FROM BELIZE

1894: THE MISKITO BECOME PART
OF NICARAGUA

1856–1857:
COSTA RICA CONFRONTS
THE REGIME OF WALKER

1855–1857:
"REIGN" OF WILLIAM WALKER

1852:
MANAGUA BECOMES CAPITAL

1846–1864:
WAR BETWEEN CAUDILLOS

INVASION
1885

FEB. 1, 1838: RAFAEL CARRERA
IN GUATEMALA CITY

1844–1865: DICTATORSHIP

1898–1920:
DICTATORSHIP OF
MANUEL ESTRADA CABRERA

MÉXICO

1876: PORFIRIO DÍAZ
ENTERS MEXICO CITY
(PORFIRIATO 1884–1911)

RECLAIMED BY U.S.A. IN 1845

TEXAS CEDED
BY MEXICO 1848

MEXICAN-AMERICAN WAR
1846–1848

ANNEXED BY U.S.A. IN 1848

BRITISH DOMINATION

8B

South America

Arbitrary caudillo rule was not confined to Mexico and Central America during the first half of the nineteenth century. The South American continent counted its share of *caudillos,* and they proved to be just as versatile, colorful, and dictatorial as their northern counterparts. *Caudillos* could be identified in almost every region of Latin America after independence, but the focus in this essay will be on three leaders: Gaspar Rodríguez de Francia in Paraguay, Juan Manuel de Rosas in Argentina, and Antonio Guzmán Blanco in Venezuela.

Gaspar Rodríguez de Francia ruled Paraguay from about 1814 until his death in 1840 as "El Supremo" or the Supreme One—his self-imposed title. He decided that tiny Paraguay would benefit from near-total isolation from the complex and cumbersome outside world, and he managed, surprisingly, to seal off the country from the outside world for about twenty-five years. This odd form of rule resulted in relative peace and stability in Paraguay, when compared, for example, to neighboring Argentina during the same time period. But the costs were high. No one was ever allowed to offer advice to the Supreme One, the church was completely under his authority, and the period is generally characterized as "bizarre" or "gloomy" in scholarly literature.

Juan Manuel de Rosas, governor of Buenos Aires, emerged as the undisputed leader in Argentina after about 1829. Rosas was a tyrant and ruled on behalf of the "Federalists," or Federales—those Argentines, generally from the interior, who wished to organize a loose confederation of semi-autonomous states. The opposition party, the Unitarians or "Unitarios," called for a strong central government radiating out from Buenos Aires that would be run by the aristocracy. Rosas' rule, to the complete exclusion of Unitarians, was brutal, and his authority even extended over the Roman Catholic Church. He promised to maintain order and counted on the support of the common people in the interior.

He was also able to "buy off" competing *caudillos* in the interior, and in so doing, he won their loyalty. Rosas's authoritarian and aggressive policies led him to invade tiny Uruguay, a move that upset British merchants, the French, and Rosas's detractors at home. Eventually, in 1852, the dictator's forces were defeated, and he fled into exile in England.

Venezuela's Antonio Guzmán Blanco defined politics and society in that country during the latter half of the nineteenth century. A liberal leader, he established himself as an absolute dictator and enjoyed hearing himself referred to as "The Illustrious American, Regenerator of Venezuela." Concerned with issues of trade, infrastructure development, and restricting the power of the Roman Catholic Church, Guzmán Blanco's policies were very much in line with those of other Latin American liberal leaders of the time. His rule lasted until the late 1880s, when a series of political mistakes cost him the loyalty of his supporters.

One feature common to all *caudillos* in nineteenth-century Latin America was a complete lack of democratic procedure, or even the pretense of democratic practice. The 300-year colonial model of hierarchy, power from above, and adherence to authority left a lasting legacy in Latin America. Politically, the nineteenth century in Latin America is seen, by many, as a sort of transition century: society could not switch seamlessly from monarchical colonial rule to electoral democracy. Even today, more than a century later, true democracy still eludes much of Latin America, for it is based not just on "electoralism" but on an adherence to the principles of meaningful social and economic justice.

BIBLIOGRAPHY

Burns, E. Bradford. 1980. *The Poverty of Progress: Latin America in the Nineteenth Century.* Los Angeles: University of California Press.
Lynch, John. 2001. *Argentine Caudillo: Juan Manuel de Rosas.* Wilmington, DE: SR Books.
Sarmiento, D.F. n.d. *Life in the Argentine Republic in the Days of the Tyrants; Or, Civilization and Barbarism.* New York: Hafner.

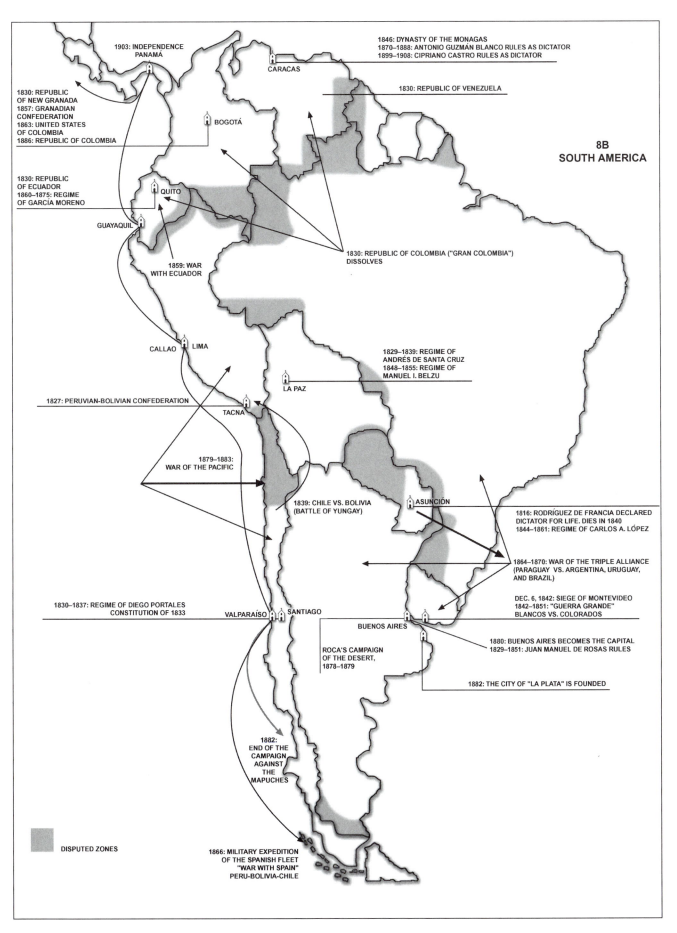

1903: INDEPENDENCE PANAMÁ

1846: DYNASTY OF THE MONAGAS
1870–1888: ANTONIO GUZMÁN BLANCO RULES AS DICTATOR
1899–1908: CIPRIANO CASTRO RULES AS DICTATOR

CARACAS

1830: REPUBLIC OF VENEZUELA

1830: REPUBLIC
OF NEW GRANADA
1857: GRANADIAN
CONFEDERATION
1863: UNITED STATES
OF COLOMBIA
1886: REPUBLIC OF COLOMBIA

BOGOTÁ

8B
SOUTH AMERICA

1830: REPUBLIC
OF ECUADOR
1860–1875: REGIME
OF GARCÍA MORENO

QUITO

GUAYAQUIL

1830: REPUBLIC OF COLOMBIA ("GRAN COLOMBIA")
DISSOLVES

1859: WAR
WITH ECUADOR

CALLAO   LIMA

1829–1839: REGIME OF
ANDRÉS DE SANTA CRUZ
1848–1855: REGIME OF
MANUEL I. BELZU

LA PAZ

1827: PERUVIAN-BOLIVIAN CONFEDERATION

TACNA

1879–1883:
WAR OF THE PACIFIC

ASUNCIÓN

1839: CHILE VS. BOLIVIA
(BATTLE OF YUNGAY)

1816: RODRÍGUEZ DE FRANCIA DECLARED
DICTATOR FOR LIFE. DIES IN 1840
1844–1861: REGIME OF CARLOS A. LÓPEZ

1864–1870: WAR OF THE TRIPLE ALLIANCE
(PARAGUAY VS. ARGENTINA, URUGUAY,
AND BRAZIL)

DEC. 6, 1842: SIEGE OF MONTEVIDEO
1842–1851: "GUERRA GRANDE"
BLANCOS VS. COLORADOS

1830–1837: REGIME OF DIEGO PORTALES
CONSTITUTION OF 1833

VALPARAÍSO   SANTIAGO

BUENOS AIRES

1880: BUENOS AIRES BECOMES THE CAPITAL
1829–1851: JUAN MANUEL DE ROSAS RULES

ROCA'S CAMPAIGN
OF THE DESERT,
1878–1879

1882: THE CITY OF "LA PLATA" IS FOUNDED

1882:
END OF THE
CAMPAIGN
AGAINST
THE
MAPUCHES

DISPUTED ZONES

1866: MILITARY EXPEDITION
OF THE SPANISH FLEET
"WAR WITH SPAIN"
PERU-BOLIVIA-CHILE

8c

Export-led Economic Growth: Mid-Century

Historian E. Bradford Burns's 1980 book, *The Poverty of Progress,* suggests that "progress" (as defined in European and North American terms) actually led to growing "poverty" in Latin America. Burns studied the entire Latin American region to formulate his thesis but focused special attention on the cases of Argentina, Brazil, and Mexico. Nineteenth-century Latin American political leaders, impressed with European political and economic ideology, embraced policies that upheld colonial patterns—that is, Latin Americans exported "raw" goods and imported "finished industrial" goods from Europe. Burns defined this as "dependency." Dependent economic growth allowed industrial nations to become wealthy, while the countries that only produced primary products were characterized by sporadic, uneven economic development.

In Argentina, during a twenty-year period that started roughly in 1853 (a year after the fall of the *caudillo*-dictator Juan Manuel de Rosas), overall exports grew by 700 percent. From 1876 to 1900, wheat exports grew from 21 tons to 2,250,000 tons. A number of interrelated factors help explain this phenomenal growth. First, there was enormous demand for Latin American agricultural products in far-off industrializing countries, especially after the repeal of the British Corn Laws in the late 1840s. Second, political change in Argentina led to a renewed focus on the export economy and the subsequent growth of the port city of Buenos Aires as the commercial, transportation, and manufacturing center of the nation. Third, the opening up of wide expanses of grasslands, known as the *pampas,* for agricultural use and cattle raising was fundamental to the expansion of export-led growth. Finally, a steep decline in freight rates during the second half of the nineteenth century enhanced profit margins for those involved in exporting primary products out of Buenos Aires. But wealth was not evenly distributed in Argentina during this time period, and the economy moved through many boom–bust cycles, which hampered long-term development and led to political and social strife.

In Brazil, the nineteenth century is associated with the production of coffee and the expansion of the coffee trade. From 1833 to 1889 (the year the Brazilian Republic was born), exports grew by over 600 percent. The dynamic sector of the Brazilian economy had moved, by the nineteenth century, to the southeastern quadrant of the country. According to one authority on Latin American economic development, "coffee exports grew from a mere 480,000 bags in 1830 to 3,827,000 in 1870/1 and 14,760,000 in 1901."[1]

The growth of the export economy in Brazil is directly related to European immigration and the concurrent growth of an urban metropolis. São Paulo became the most dynamic city in the country, replacing the eighteenth-century dominance of the city of Ouro Preto in Minas Gerais and the seventeenth- and sixteenth-century northeastern dominance of Salvador, Bahia, and Recife, Pernambuco. In 1885, only 6,000 individuals migrated to São Paulo; two years later, that number rose to 32,000, and by 1888, 90,000 arrived to São Paulo via the port of Santos. The inflow of Europeans continued, most of whom arrived from Southern and Eastern Europe, reaching a level of about 100,000 to 150,000 during the first years of the twentieth century. As was the case of the United States and Argentina, immigration from Europe declined dramatically with the onset of World War I.

Mexico achieved phenomenal growth during a period known as the Porfiriato, the thirty-five-year rule of Porfirio Díaz. Díaz's rule, from about 1876 to 1911, represented the height of export-led growth in that country. Exports from 1877 to 1900 increased by 400 percent, but the newfound expansion in export trade did not mean that all Mexicans enjoyed a higher standard of living. In fact, about 96 percent of the communal villages in Mexico (the *ejidos*) lost title to their land during this time period. Land speculators and surveyors, working in tandem with the Díaz government, cheated poor, indigenous persons out of their communally held lands. In his book, Professor Burns explains how "progress" meant poverty for the majority of Mexicans: the price of land increased dramatically, peasants were pushed off their lands, the price of basic staples increased (in the case of corn, the price quadrupled from 1899 to 1908), and wages on the large haciendas were paid in the form of "coupons" at the company store.[2]

Export-led economic growth in Latin America created tensions and contradictions in the region and exacerbated established patterns of inequality. In most cases, a small percentage of the population (generally lighter-skinned people of European descent) came to control vast fortunes, while the majority of the citizens saw relatively little personal benefit from the export-led model.

NOTES

1. Roberto Cortés Conde, "Export-led Growth in Latin America: 1870–1930," *Journal of Latin American Studies* 24 (1992): 173.

2. E. Bradford Burns, *The Poverty of Progress* (Los Angeles: University of California Press, 1980), pp. 144–145.

BIBLIOGRAPHY

Burns, E. Bradford, and Julie A. Charlip. 2002. *Latin America: A Concise Interpretive History.* 7th ed. Upper Saddle River, NJ: Prentice Hall.

Keen, Benjamin, and Keith Haynes. 2004. *A History of Latin America.* 7th ed. Boston: Houghton Mifflin.

8C
THE BIRTH OF THE EXPORT-LED ECONOMY:
PRODUCTS, PORTS, AND METROPOLIS

U.S.A.

COPPER
ZINC
SILVER
GOLD
LEAD
HENEQUEN
RUBBER
COFFEE
COCHINEAL

ENGLAND
FRANCE
GERMANY

VERACRUZ

SUGAR

ACAPULCO

BANANAS

COFFEE

COFFEE

COFFEE

COFFEE
BANANAS

CARTAGENA
BARRANQUILLA
SANTA MARTA

MARACAIBO

LA GUAIRA

EUROPE

EUROPE

COFFEE

TOBACCO
QUININE
COFFEE
COTTON

BUENAVENTURA

EUROPE

CACAO

GUAYAQUIL

U.S.A.

GUANO
SUGAR
WOOL
SILVER
COPPER
RUBBER
COTTON

SUGAR
COFFEE
WHEAT
RUBBER
CACAO
GOLD

PARAÍBA

RECIFE

EUROPE

EUROPE

CALLAO

EUROPE

TIN

MOLLENDO

CALIFORNIA

RIO

SANTOS

ASUNCIÓN

PORTO ALEGRE

SILVER
COPPER
NITRATES
WHEAT

MEAT
WHEAT
CEREALS

ENGLAND

MEAT

VALPARAÍSO

BUENOS
AIRES

MONTEVIDEO

ENGLAND

CONCEPCIÓN

■ PORT CITY

85

Liberal Reforms in Latin America

Events abroad have had an important effect on the political and economic history of Latin America. The repeal of the "Corn Laws" presented a new opportunity for Latin Americans, generated significant liberal reforms, and signaled the end of arbitrary, often tyrannical, rule by *caudillo* in many areas of Latin America.

Reformers in Latin America who attached themselves to liberal political and economic programs generally did so in the name of "progress," or the civilizing paradigms found in the cities of foreign (especially European) capitals. The reformers also believed in the export model of economic development. Mid-nineteenth-century liberals in Latin America espoused a mixture of policies that included freer trade and commerce, lowering tariffs, fighting against the power and influence of the church, and divorcing the church from education policy.

Part of the liberal reformers' plan was to "shed" the colonial past, which meant curbing the power of the institutions associated with the colonial period. The military and church were singled out for "reform." The military *fuero*, or special exemption from civil law, was eliminated via the Juárez Law in Mexico in 1855. Other laws from this period stopped the church from holding land outside of the buildings used to administer the sacraments of the Mass; additionally, the church was prevented from charging fees for sacraments. These laws, the so-called Reform Laws, represented an epic struggle between the civil president (Benito Juárez, in this case), and the Roman Catholic Church hierarchy. The ensuing civil war, the War of the Reform, claimed the lives of tens of thousands of Mexicans and pitted the modernizing liberal state against the more conservative elements of society and the Roman Catholic Church.

Argentina, particularly under the rule of Domingo F. Sarmiento (1868–1874), moved away from *caudillo* rule (personified by Juan Manuel de Rosas, who ruled from 1829 to 1852) toward rule by an educated elite based in the city of Buenos Aires. Sarmiento was deeply distrustful of rural peoples and practices, and viewed civilization and progress as residing in the city. He wrote an important work in 1845, *Civilization and Barbarism,* where he criticized his political opponents, advocated increased trade with Europe, and pushed for educational reforms—based on his elitist model. Sarmiento and others stressed European immigration as a way to "improve" the racial stock of the people living in the hinterland of the country. His views further divided society, but in Argentina, enormous tensions already existed between modernity and backwardness, between civilization and barbarism. These dichotomies were similar to the liberal-conservative divide that tore apart Mexico during the same time period.

In Colombia, liberal reform is most closely tied to the policies of General Tomás Cipriano de Mosquera, president from 1846 to 1849. He worked to improve infrastructure in the country by constructing roads and introducing steam navigation on the Magdalena River, which flows to the north and empties into the Caribbean Sea. Like many liberals of his day, Mosquera ran into trouble with the traditional elites and the church; these conflicts led inexorably toward civil war. The church fought against all reforms during this time period, and those working to build modern nations in nineteenth-century Latin America were often times cast as "heretics," or worse. The Colombian civil wars came to a halt in 1886 with the passage of a new constitution and a conservative victory under the rule of Rafael Núñez. Núñez preferred to live in his hometown, the northern coastal city of Cartagena, some 1,000 kilometers from the capital. He also chose to make peace with the church via the signing, in 1887, of a "concordat," a treaty between the Holy See and the Colombian nation. That treaty effectively tied the Colombian state to the Roman Catholic Church, and conservative rule lasted for close to forty-five years until the liberals assumed power via the electoral process in 1930.

The nineteenth century concluded, in Colombia, with a civil war between Liberals and Conservatives: the War of a Thousand Days lasted from 1899 until 1902 and claimed about 70,000 lives. The mid-nineteenth-century tensions between church and state, tradition and modernity, city and countryside, and export-led economic development and reliance on the "great estates" continued as themes well into the twentieth century throughout much of Latin America.

BIBLIOGRAPHY

Burns, E. Bradford. 1980. *The Poverty of Progress: Latin America in the Nineteenth Century.* Berkeley: University of California Press.

Bushnell, David. 1992. *The Making of Modern Colombia: A Nation in Spite of Itself.* Los Angeles: University of California Press.

Fuentes, Carlos. 1992. *The Buried Mirror: Reflections on Spain and the New World.* Boston: Houghton Mifflin.

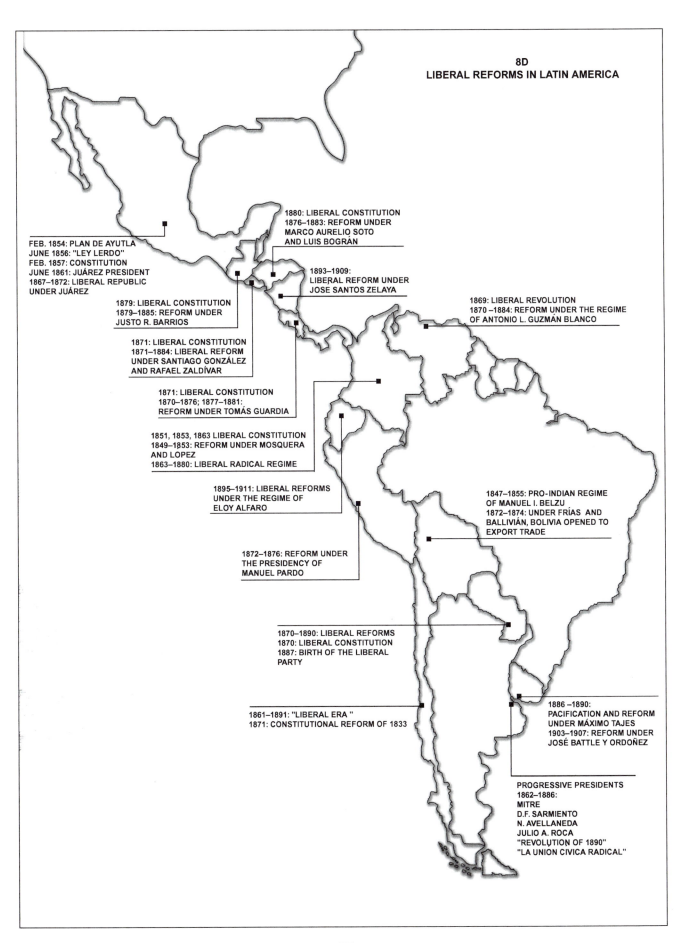

8D
LIBERAL REFORMS IN LATIN AMERICA

1880: LIBERAL CONSTITUTION
1876–1883: REFORM UNDER
MARCO AURELIO SOTO
AND LUIS BOGRÁN

FEB. 1854: PLAN DE AYUTLA
JUNE 1856: "LEY LERDO"
FEB. 1857: CONSTITUTION
JUNE 1861: JUÁREZ PRESIDENT
1867–1872: LIBERAL REPUBLIC
UNDER JUÁREZ

1893–1909:
LIBERAL REFORM UNDER
JOSE SANTOS ZELAYA

1869: LIBERAL REVOLUTION
1870–1884: REFORM UNDER THE REGIME
OF ANTONIO L. GUZMÁN BLANCO

1879: LIBERAL CONSTITUTION
1879–1885: REFORM UNDER
JUSTO R. BARRIOS

1871: LIBERAL CONSTITUTION
1871–1884: LIBERAL REFORM
UNDER SANTIAGO GONZÁLEZ
AND RAFAEL ZALDÍVAR

1871: LIBERAL CONSTITUTION
1870–1876; 1877–1881:
REFORM UNDER TOMÁS GUARDIA

1851, 1853, 1863 LIBERAL CONSTITUTION
1849–1853: REFORM UNDER MOSQUERA
AND LOPEZ
1863–1880: LIBERAL RADICAL REGIME

1895–1911: LIBERAL REFORMS
UNDER THE REGIME OF
ELOY ALFARO

1847–1855: PRO-INDIAN REGIME
OF MANUEL I. BELZU
1872–1874: UNDER FRÍAS AND
BALLIVIÁN, BOLIVIA OPENED TO
EXPORT TRADE

1872–1876: REFORM UNDER
THE PRESIDENCY OF
MANUEL PARDO

1870–1890: LIBERAL REFORMS
1870: LIBERAL CONSTITUTION
1887: BIRTH OF THE LIBERAL
PARTY

1861–1891: "LIBERAL ERA "
1871: CONSTITUTIONAL REFORM OF 1833

1886 –1890:
PACIFICATION AND REFORM
UNDER MÁXIMO TAJES
1903–1907: REFORM UNDER
JOSÉ BATTLE Y ORDOÑEZ

PROGRESSIVE PRESIDENTS
1862–1886:
MITRE
D.F. SARMIENTO
N. AVELLANEDA
JULIO A. ROCA
"REVOLUTION OF 1890"
"LA UNION CIVICA RADICAL"

8E

The United States Discovers a Continent

The U.S. government's concern with the viability of the Latin American republics dates back to about 1823, when the famous Monroe Doctrine was pronounced during the presidency of James Monroe. The doctrine stated that the United States would look with displeasure upon any attempts by European powers to reconquer, or in any way interfere with, the sovereignty and independence of the newly liberated Latin American republics. Albeit unenforceable, the doctrine was directed mainly at the British and French and demonstrated the degree to which the United States viewed Latin America as part of its special sphere of influence.

The first major event of the nineteenth century whereby the United States' "discovery" of Latin America manifested itself was the U.S. invasion of Mexico in 1846, the so-called "Mexican-American War." The war amounted to little more than a land grab and an attempt by U.S. southerners to extend slavery into the former Mexican territories. It ended with the Treaty of Guadalupe Hidalgo (1848), wherein Mexico ceded about one-half of its national territory to the United States. The Mexican-American War is frequently cited today as a prime example of Manifest Destiny (the belief that U.S. domination of Latin America is part of God's divine plan), and it damaged relations between the United States and Latin America for the remainder of the century.

Shortly after this war, two bizarre episodes gave further credence to U.S. interest in Latin America. First, in 1854, the Ostend Manifesto, through which the United States sought to "purchase" Cuba from Spain for 120 million dollars, was drafted. If Spain refused to sell, the United States would invade and take control of the island. Ultimately, this manifesto was never realized. Second, two years later, there was the William Walker affair. Walker, a Tennessean filibuster, had himself elected president of Nicaragua in 1856. He reinstituted slavery and made English the official language of that country, but his venture was to be short-lived; Walker was eventually captured and executed in Honduras.

A longer-lasting, closer focus on Latin America by the United States would occur after the conclusion of the U.S. Civil War. With the ending of slavery and the dominance of the northern industrial model, the United States began rapidly to modernize: this meant the growth of urban centers (especially in the north), the expansion of transportation networks, and a growing need for primary products—some of which were in scarce supply within the United States. Economists questioned the pace of U.S. industrialization, particularly after the economic depression of 1893–1894. The U.S. economy appeared unable to absorb the productive capacity of U.S. industry, prompting economists to advise a search for new markets abroad. This advice came while military officials, politicians, and statesmen were still debating the work of Alfred T. Mahan, the naval captain who had published, in 1890, *The Influence of Sea Power on History*. Captain Mahan, in a sweeping historical analysis of the creation of world military powers, advised the formation of a powerful "two-ocean" navy in the United States. Mahan's work implied a need for foreign bases in the Caribbean and Pacific, an interoceanic canal, and massive government expenditures on shipbuilding. All of this came to fruition within thirteen years of the publication of Mahan's book.

The character of the United States changed dramatically in 1898, when the young republic became an imperialist power, taking possessions from Spain in what came to be called the Spanish-American War. The war lasted only a few months, and Spain, through the Treaty of Paris (1898), ceded possession of its Caribbean territories as well as Guam and the Philippines in the Pacific. The war put the United States in de facto control of Cuba and Puerto Rico, as the interest, and influence, of the United States in the region expanded. The Platt Amendment of 1901 ensured a strong United States presence in Cuba, and two years later, a U.S.-supported independence movement in the Province of Panama (previously controlled by Colombia) demonstrated the country's intention to construct an interoceanic canal—on its terms and with its military protecting the canal zone. In fact, a ten-mile-wide strip of Panama became a virtual U.S. colony within a sovereign nation, an arrangement that lasted from the birth of the Panamanian republic (November 1903) until December 31, 1999.

Finally, in 1904, President Theodore Roosevelt expressed his intentions in Latin America via his "Roosevelt Corollary to the Monroe Doctrine"; he stated that the United States would intervene militarily wherever it saw fit in Latin America in order to ensure the safety of American lives and/or property. This sweeping "doctrine of intervention" would have profound effects on U.S.–Latin American relations up through the Franklin Delano Roosevelt administration of the early 1930s.

BIBLIOGRAPHY

LaRosa, Michael, and Frank O. Mora, eds. 1999. *Neighborly Adversaries: Readings in U.S.–Latin American Relations*. Lanham, MD: Rowman & Littlefield.

Black, George. 1988. *The Good Neighbor: How the United States Wrote the History of Central America and the Caribbean*. New York: Pantheon Books.

8E
THE U.S. DISCOVERS A CONTINENT

1823: MONROE DOCTRINE
1840s: MANIFEST DESTINY
1904: "ROOSEVELT COROLLARY"

STANDARD OIL CO.
R.G. GRACE
UNITED FRUIT CO.

1846–1848
1870
1876
1914

1832–1824

1898–1902
1906–1909

1905

1891

1824
1898

1855

1849: E. SQUIER

1840s: N. MICHLER

1838–1839:
CHARLES WILKES

1854 1898
1855 1899
1894 1907
1896 1912

1860
1885
1895
1901–1914
1908

1868
1873
1895

1835

1860s: THAYER

1851: W. L. HERNDON

1894

1840s: T.Y. PAGE

1859

BUSINESS BETWEEN LATIN AMERICA AND U.S.A.

FROM U.S.A.

1880s: KEROSENE
LUMBER
GRAIN
ICE
COAL
BARBED WIRE
SEWING MACHINES
RIFLES
WINDMILLS
LOCOMOTIVES

FROM LATIN AMERICA

FOODSTUFFS
INDUSTRIAL RAW MATERIALS

1840s:
J.M. GILLIS

1833
1852–1853
1868

1855
1858
1868

1891

SCIENTIFIC EXPEDITIONS

SELECT U.S. MILITARY INTERVENTIONS

MAJOR U.S. CORPORATIONS IN LATIN AMERICA

89

Brazil: Monarchy to the First Republic

Brazil's history took a different path from that of Hispanic America (Spanish-speaking Latin America), particularly in the nineteenth century. The Napoleonic invasion of Iberia in 1807–1808 forced the Portuguese monarchy, the Braganzas, to flee to Rio de Janeiro, where they established the continuation of the Portuguese monarchy. Thus, while Hispanic America was convulsed in an epic, sixteen-year independence struggle that cost the lives of hundreds of thousands, relative order, preservation of tradition, and monarchical continuity prevailed in Brazil. Though tensions existed, especially as exerted by the Portuguese crown, which felt compelled to try and pull Brazil back into the former colonial structure, the Brazilian process proceeded free from the all-consuming chaos that defined Hispanic-American independence.

The first ten years after independence were difficult, but Pedro I (having established himself as constitutional monarch) managed to maintain the territorial unity of Brazil despite many separatist rebellions. By 1831, he decided to return to Portugal, and he died in 1834. Pedro I left his son, Pedro II, to rule over Brazil. In 1840, at the age of fourteen, Pedro II took on the title Dom Pedro II and began what would be a forty-nine-year reign. The period between the abdication of Pedro I and Dom Pedro II's oath of July 23, 1840 (where he agreed to uphold the constitution as constitutional monarch) is known as the Regency. This nine-year period was characterized by relative stability. The Brazilian Regency lacked the disorder, *caudillo* armies, and civil wars that defined the turbulent histories of Mexico, Colombia, and Argentina during the same period.

Dom Pedro II was an able ruler who led Brazil as a constitutional monarch with "moderating" powers. Essentially, he could override the legislature as he saw fit. Still, Pedro II was Brazilian—he was born and raised in Brazil—and fleeing to Portugal was not a viable option for him; he had to try to achieve balance at home. Pedro II was educated in the liberal, enlightened tradition of the period and established the important precedence of working to solve problems rather than resorting to conflict. Given the enormity of the Brazilian landmass, this proved to be an important legacy, or characteristic, of the "Brazilian way."

There were some notable exceptions to this portrait of a peaceful, moderate Brazilian state. From 1865 to 1870, Brazil joined with Argentina and Uruguay in the War of the Triple Alliance against tiny Paraguay, which had developed independently and refused to trade with its more powerful neighbors. The war, which lasted six years, was a disaster for Brazil (and of course Paraguay, which lost nearly all of its adult male population). The conflict clearly challenged Dom Pedro's authority and leadership, and began a process of "introspection" that led—eventually—to the overthrow of Dom Pedro and the birth of the republic in 1889.

The second half of the nineteenth century in Brazil has been characterized using three terms: slavery, coffee, and monarchy. Brazil holds the dubious distinction of being the last country in the Western Hemisphere to eliminate slavery, in 1888. Joaquim Nabuco was Brazil's most outspoken critic of slavery and worked tirelessly to abolish the institution from Brazilian soil. Unlike other societies in the Americas that abolished slavery only after bloody conflict (the United States or Cuba), Brazil's article of abolition (the Golden Law of May 13, 1888) was promulgated without incident. The overseas slave trade ended in 1830, but slaves continued to arrive in Brazil as late as 1852; thus, the price of slaves skyrocketed as the availability declined, and their average age rose markedly. Brazilians adopted a more pragmatic approach to ending slavery. Simply put, it was no longer profitable or viable; it was interfering with Brazilian's self-perception as a modern, progressive society organized around the concept of positivism—"order and progress."[1] Many ex-slaves lived on the margins of society in escaped slave communities known in Brazil as *quilombos*.

The end of slavery meant a dramatic increase in the number of Europeans willing to migrate to Brazil; they would work in the expanding and profitable coffee economy based in the southeastern region of the country, surrounding the city of São Paulo and the port of Santos. One year after the abolition of slavery, the Brazilian Republic was born, for slavery and monarchy were connected in the minds of the people as representative of the "past"; a free society under constitutional rule represented a move toward modernity.

NOTE

1. The words *Ordem e Progresso* (Order and Progress) are emblazoned on the Brazilian flag.

BIBLIOGRAPHY
Levine, Robert M., and John J. Crocitti, eds. 1999. *The Brazil Reader.* Durham, NC: Duke University Press.
Worcester, Donald E. 1973. *Brazil: From Colony to World Power.* New York: Charles Scribner's Sons.

8F
BRAZIL: FROM MONARCHY
TO THE FIRST REPUBLIC (1889)

RUBBER

INCORPORATED
TERRITORIES
AFTER 1832

BELÉM

FORTALEZA

CATTLE

COTTON

PARAÍBA

RECIFE

PEASANT
MIGRATION

SUGAR

CACAO

SALVADOR

CATTLE

MINERALS

MINERALS

COFFEE

SÃO PAULO

NITERÓI: METAL INDUSTRY

RIO DE JANEIRO: CAPITAL OF THE EMPIRE

1822–1831: PEDRO I
1831–1840: REGENCY
1840–1889: EMPIRE, PEDRO II
1889–1929: FIRST REPUBLIC

CATTLE

PORTO ALEGRE

AREA OF EUROPEAN
IMMIGRATION

TERRITORY INCORPORATED
AFTER 1832

91

The Vestiges of Empire: Cuba, Puerto Rico, and the Guyanas

The independence movements in the early part of the nineteenth century did not provide freedom and independence for all Latin Americans. In fact, millions of people still lived under colonial rule. The Latin American independence struggles can be thought of as four essentially independent phenomena: First, the Mexican struggle involving what we today call Mexico and northern Central America. That struggle was led, at the beginning, by the Catholic priests Father Miguel Hidalgo and Father José María Morelos. Second, Simón Bolívar's campaigns helped liberate much of northern South America. Third, the so-called Southern Cone countries (Argentina, Paraguay, and Chile) were liberated by the Argentine general José de San Martín. Fourth was Brazil's distinct path to independence, which occurred via the establishment of a sustained, relatively peaceful constitutional monarchy.

While independence struggles raged in most countries within the region, political independence eluded the islands of Cuba and Puerto Rico in the Caribbean—they remained part of a greatly reduced Spanish overseas empire after 1826. (Other Spanish possessions during the nineteenth century included Guam and the Philippine Islands in the South Pacific.)

Despite efforts by the United States to purchase the island of Cuba in the mid-nineteenth century, and the United States' growing interest in the Caribbean basin as expressed through the Monroe Doctrine of 1823, Cuba and Puerto Rico remained Spanish colonial possessions until 1898. A disturbing contradiction developed after about 1865 (the conclusion of the U.S. Civil War), when U.S. business interests on the island of Cuba eclipsed Spanish commerce with the island. Cuba "belonged" to Spain, but for reasons mostly related to geography, the island was increasingly connected to and controlled by capitalists living in the United States. The Cuban patriot and intellectual José Martí frequently wrote about this contradiction until his death of the hands of Spanish military forces in 1895.

Puerto Rico and Cuba were "liberated" from Spain by the United States in 1898; Puerto Rico never gained complete independence and Cuba's path to independence was complicated. Cuba remained under U.S. tutelage until about 1934—the year the Platt Amendment was abrogated. Fidel Castro's rise to power in the late 1950s is directly related to the island's colonial tradition, dating back to the earliest days of Spanish conquest. Puerto Rico, a protectorate of the United States, exists as neither completely independent nor completely integrated with the United States of America. This complex and contradictory situation deeply affects Puerto Rican culture and identity; residents of Puerto Rico are citizens of the United States, but not "full" citizens, as they do not enjoy all of the rights and privileges that U.S. citizenship brings.

Other areas that form part of geographic South America include Guyana, Suriname, and French Guiana (or Cayenne) on the north-northwest section of the continent. The independent nation of Guyana was colonized by the British and gained independence in 1966. The official language is English, and the economy is dominated by the export of agricultural and mineral products. Neighboring Suriname, to the east of Guyana, was colonized by the Netherlands and only gained independence in 1975. Suriname exports mineral and agricultural products primarily to the Netherlands, the United States, and the United Kingdom. French Guiana is still a colonial territory of France. This territory was settled by the French in 1604 and was part of a larger French presence in the Americas that included, at one time, all of Louisiana, parts of Canada, Haiti, and other islands in the Caribbean. The French planted sugar cane and profited from colonial structures and the institution of slavery. France used French Guiana as a penal colony for 100 years from 1850 to about 1950, and after World War II, Guiana became an "overseas department of France," similar to the political status of Martinique and Guadeloupe.

When scholars define Latin America, they sometimes use a linguistic categorization; that is, they consider as "Latin America" those independent nations that were colonized by countries with Latin-derived languages. Brazil and Mexico are part of Latin America: Jamaica is not. Guyana, Suriname, and French Guiana, technically, are not defined as "Latin America"; however these societies, along with Cuba and Puerto Rico, have been shaped by long periods of colonialism, exploitative labor systems, dependence on plantation-style agriculture, and massive profit outflows to other areas of the world—generally Europe. In most of the Caribbean today, true independence (political, social, and economic) eludes the vast majority of the citizens, and the variety of political structures present in that region is a clear reflection of the long-lasting, damning consequences of centuries of colonial rule.

BIBLIOGRAPHY

Knight, Franklin W. 1990. *The Caribbean.* 2d ed. New York: Oxford University Press.
United States. Central Intelligence Agency. 2004. *The World Factbook.* Available at www.cia.gov/cia/publications/factbook/geos/fg.html.

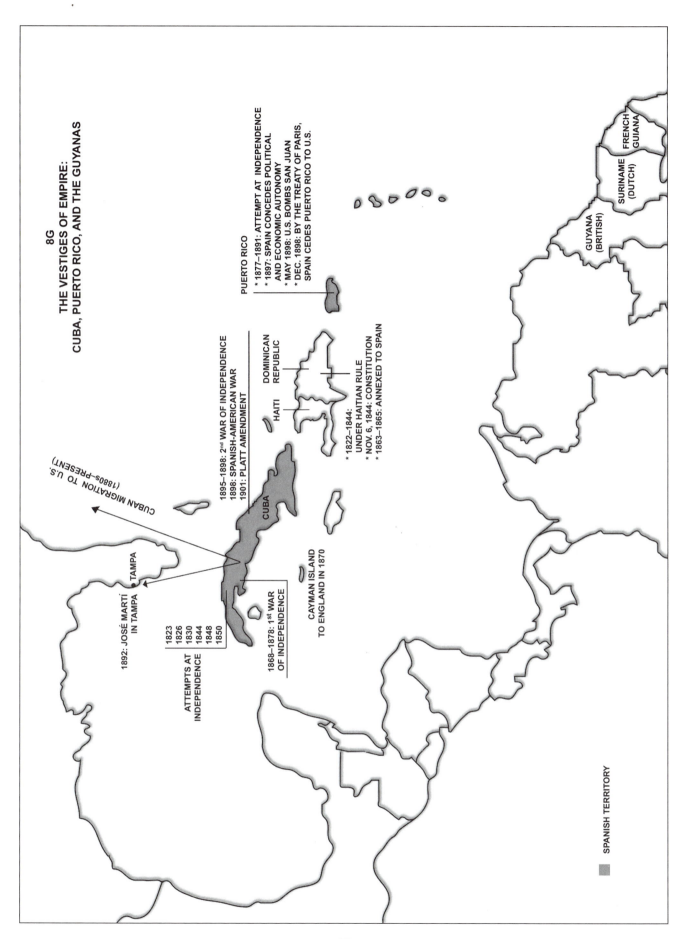

8G
THE VESTIGES OF EMPIRE:
CUBA, PUERTO RICO, AND THE GUYANAS

PUERTO RICO

* 1877–1891: ATTEMPT AT INDEPENDENCE
* 1897: SPAIN CONCEDES POLITICAL AND ECONOMIC AUTONOMY
* MAY 1898: U.S. BOMBS SAN JUAN
* DEC. 1898: BY THE TREATY OF PARIS, SPAIN CEDES PUERTO RICO TO U.S.

1895–1898: 2ⁿᵈ WAR OF INDEPENDENCE
1898: SPANISH-AMERICAN WAR
1901: PLATT AMENDMENT

DOMINICAN REPUBLIC

HAITI

* 1822–1844: UNDER HAITIAN RULE
* NOV. 6, 1844: CONSTITUTION
* 1863–1865: ANNEXED TO SPAIN

CUBAN MIGRATION TO U.S. (1880s–PRESENT)

TAMPA

1892: JOSÉ MARTÍ IN TAMPA

1823
1826
1830
1844
1848
1850

ATTEMPTS AT INDEPENDENCE

CUBA

1868–1878: 1ˢᵗ WAR OF INDEPENDENCE

CAYMAN ISLAND TO ENGLAND IN 1870

GUYANA (BRITISH)

SURINAME (DUTCH)

FRENCH GUIANA

SPANISH TERRITORY

93

9

LATIN AMERICAN ECONOMIES IN THE TWENTIETH CENTURY

9A

From England to the United States: North American Investment Through 1929

Foreign investment in Latin America became much more significant with the repeal of the British Corn Laws in 1846. British capitalists in the north wrestled concessions from the agrarian south, which collapsed protectionist tariffs on foodstuffs and allowed Latin American wheat, corn, and flour to flow to Europe. Expanding markets in Europe, fueled by the Industrial Revolution and the newfound belief in classical economics and comparative advantage, meant a growing focus on Latin American agricultural production and infrastructural development.

Thus, by about mid-century, an emphasis on political stability and support of the export sector of the economy (or the liberal triumph) dictated the economic mood in much of Latin America. Latin Americans wanted to take full advantage of the European appetite for their primary products, and new investment in mines, railroads, port facilities, and cities was part of the mid-nineteenth-century push toward modernity. Much of the investment, of course, would come from Europe (primarily Great Britain), and this pattern would remain intact until the start of World War I.

The prevailing philosophy at this time in Europe and Latin America was positivism—the idea that societies moved through different stages of development at different times and that predictable "scientific" patterns dictated this process of development and modernization. "Order and progress" were the central concepts of positivism: order, for a Latin American positivist, came to mean the absence of revolutionary struggles, while progress meant the importation of all things European—machinery, products, philosophy, educational structures, fashion, and architecture. Investment from Europe stimulated the Latin American positivists and provided a sort of self-fulfilling prophecy for Latin American elites who uncritically accepted European advice, expertise, and investment.

Thus, between 1870 and 1919 (shortly after the conclusion of World War I), foreign investment in Latin America amounted to about 10 billion dollars. The vast majority of this investment came from Great Britain, but Germany and France were also significant investors. The British invested most heavily in Argentina (railroads and port works) and Brazil during this period. In fact, in 1889, one-half of Great Britain's total foreign investment went to one country—Argentina, which at that time surpassed India in terms of overseas British investment.

U.S. investment in the region developed gradually, especially after the conclusion of World War I. Two significant events in the early 1890s focused U.S. attention on overseas markets: First, in 1890 at the Inter-American Conference, Secretary of State James Blaine called for a dramatic increase in "hemispheric" trade and helped refocus policy makers away from the conventional view of Latin America as a military or defense "problem." Next, the economic depression of 1893–94 was, in real terms, worse than the 1929 depression would be and caused economists in the United States to think critically about expanding markets and investment abroad as a way of selling off the excess production of U.S. factories. The U.S. market seemed "saturated" in the early 1890s, and the prevailing view stressed the need to open new markets abroad.

After about 1900, the dynamic of investment changed dramatically. With the United States taking on empire status following the conclusion of the Spanish-American War in 1898 (whereby the United States came to dominate Puerto Rico, Cuba, the Philippines, and Guam—the final vestiges of the once powerful Spanish Empire in America), U.S. economic commitment to the region increased dramatically. At the turn of the century, the United States invested heavily in Cuba and Mexico, and by the eve of World War I, total foreign investment in Latin America could be summed up as follows: Great Britain, 5 billion dollars; France, $1.7 billion; the United States, $1.6 billion; and Germany, a little more than one billion dollars.

World War I changed the flow of the world economy: Europe was devastated and the United States became the safest place on the planet for investment capital. U.S. banks were bursting with investment dollars and were willing to loan out the money at generous rates. From 1926 to 1928, about one billion dollars in loans flowed to Latin America, and on the eve of the Wall Street stock market crash of 1929, 40 percent of all U.S. foreign investment was going to Latin America.

President William Taft (1909–1912) spoke of "dollar diplomacy," which meant that the power of Wall Street investment firms would be used—rather than the military—to reshape "small" countries in Central America and the Caribbean. The central goal of this diplomacy, though, involved protection of U.S. investments in those countries. Some have referred to this period as a time of *neocolonialism*—using the power of investment to create colonial-like ties without actually ruling the countries in question.

BIBLIOGRAPHY

Burns, E. Bradford, and Julie A. Charlip. 2002. *Latin America: A Concise Interpretive History.* 7th ed. Upper Saddle River, NJ: Prentice Hall.

Chasteen, John Charles. 2001. *Born in Blood and Fire: A Concise History of Latin America.* New York: W.W. Norton.

Winn, Peter. 1999. *Americas: The Changing Face of Latin America and the Caribbean.* Berkeley: University of California Press.

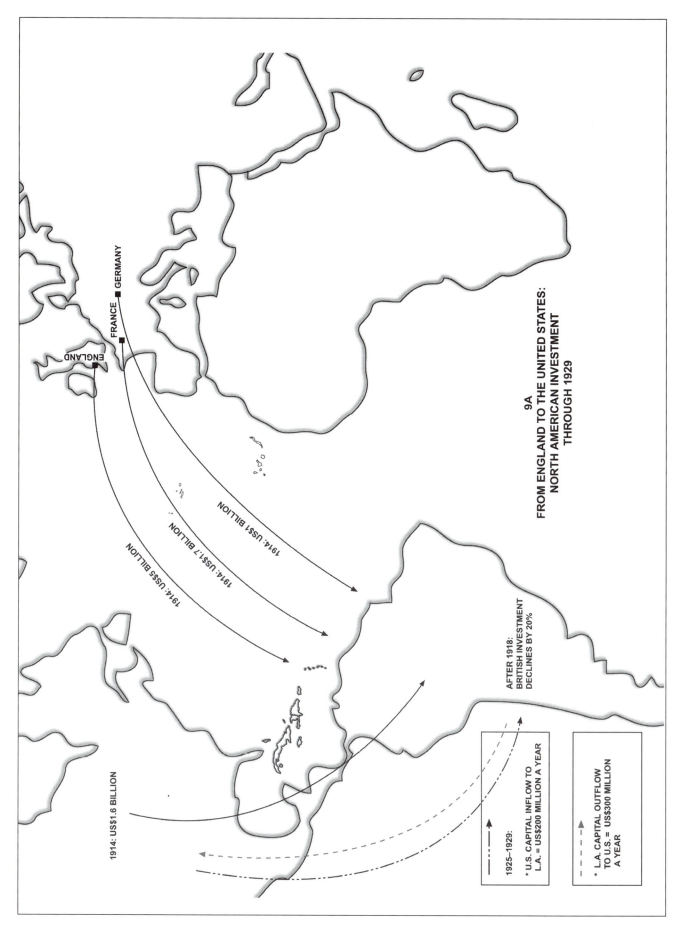

FROM ENGLAND TO THE UNITED STATES:
NORTH AMERICAN INVESTMENT
THROUGH 1929

9A

ENGLAND

FRANCE

GERMANY

1914: US$5.6 BILLION

1914: US$1.7 BILLION

1914: US$1 BILLION

1914: US$1.6 BILLION

AFTER 1918:
BRITISH INVESTMENT
DECLINES BY 20%

1925–1929:

* U.S. CAPITAL INFLOW TO
L.A. = US$200 MILLION A YEAR

* L.A. CAPITAL OUTFLOW
TO U.S. = US$300 MILLION
A YEAR

9B

Modernization in Transportation and Communications

Transportation and communication have posed major challenges throughout Latin American history. The earliest chroniclers and conquistadors commented on the difficulties of geography, of imposing mountain ranges, vast deserts, and complex rivers. The European version of the conquest of America usually alludes to European man conquering both the natural environment and the human societies that flourished in the Americas.

However, the Spaniards were never completely able to dominate the complexity of Latin America's geography. Their primary objectives centered on removing the silver at Potosí (in modern-day Bolivia) and Zacatecas (in Mexico). They developed new techniques for smelting silver and created a convoy system, the flotilla, to transport mined silver and gold bullion back to Europe. This voyage was far from easy; the logistics involved many stops, overland transfers of cargo, dangers associated with trolling pirates in the Caribbean, hurricanes, and a myriad of potential misfortunes.

But, Spain's dominance of the Caribbean and trans-Atlantic trade from the Americas was relatively short-lived. Other European powers—especially the English, Dutch, and French—would come to play a significant role in commerce and trade. The conclusion of Spain's colonial rule (by the early part of the nineteenth century) meant changes in trade patterns and an increased reliance on Northern European priorities and technology. With the recovery of mining and agriculture in the period after independence (by the early 1830s), British investment flowed to Latin America—particularly Argentina, Chile, and later Brazil. The British were concerned with moving agricultural and mineral products from the Latin American interior to the ports, and from there, to Britain. The British desperately needed wheat, corn, tallow, minerals, cotton, and wool to support their burgeoning industrialization in the primary northern industrial cities of Leeds, Manchester, Birmingham, and Liverpool.

In 1852, British-financed railroads were operational in Chile, and began operation in Brazil just two years later, in 1854. The first tracks were laid in Argentina in 1857, and by 1915 more than 22,000 miles of railroad track could be counted in that country (financed almost exclusively by Britain—a figure that compared favorably with per capita railroad construction in the United States of the same time period). In Argentina, General Julio Roca's "Campaign of the Desert" (1878–1879) pushed Native Americans off their land, opening up the vast, grassy plains (the pampas) for cattle grazing and the expansion of trade in hides, tallow, beef, and wheat. The railroads that were built constituted a "hub-and-spoke" system, radiating out from the hub (Buenos Aires) into the pampas. The railroads were not designed to facilitate national development or integration—the system was designed to move products from the pampas to the port for exportation to Europe.

With the development of the refrigerated steamship in 1876, frozen/fresh beef, rather than salted beef, could be shipped to Europe, which helped expand commerce between Buenos Aires and the northern industrial cities of Great Britain. Just a quarter of a century later, almost 300 of these ships were running routes between Argentina and Britain alone.

Steam-powered riverboats, the telegraph, and barbed wire all helped "tame" the Argentine pampas, and supported the export economy in Argentina and elsewhere in Latin America. In Mexico, railroad development proceeded much like it had in Argentina, with foreigners investing in railroads, port facilities, and telegraph lines. During the thirty-four-year period from 1876 to 1910, the Mexican railroad system grew from 400 miles of track to 15,000 miles. According to E. Bradford Burns, exports expanded eight-and-a-half times during this same time period.[1]

Electrification of cities and the development of streetcars in the primary cities of Buenos Aires, Mexico City, and Bogotá were important projects in the modernization of Latin America. Unfortunately, by the end of the nineteenth century, despite the arrival of "modernity"—defined by miles of railroad track and the construction of telegraph systems—(including a trans-Atlantic line laid in 1874, connecting Brazil to Europe), a vast chasm still separated the Latin American city from the interior. Modernization in terms of transportation and communication only affected a small number of people in the cities who were directly connected to the export economy. The projects were not designed to unite the individual countries of Latin America or develop the region. They created, borrowing a phrase from the economic historian John Coatsworth, a pattern of "growth against development" throughout Latin America.

NOTE

1. E. Bradford Burns, *The Poverty of Progress* (Los Angeles: University of California Press, 1980), p. 136.

BIBLIOGRAPHY
Chasteen, John Charles. 2001. *Born in Blood and Fire: A Concise History of Latin America.* New York: W.W. Norton.

92,000
23,345
96,000

4,891
67,000

240
2,000

1,159

1,459

604

327

217

158

665

4,000
993
22,000

24,000
2,609
28,000

665
6,000

122,000
32,478
163,000

19,000
2,880

2,253
2,000

468
2,000

36,000
8,937
44,000

212,000
37,978
291,000

2,731

ROADS IN KM.

RAILWAYS IN KM.

TELEPHONE LINES

The Impact of the Great Depression of 1929 in Latin America

The Great Depression, beginning with the U.S. stock market collapse of October 1929, had a profound influence on Latin American economies, politics, and societies. The effects differed from region to region, but all areas were affected to some degree. The economies that exported, to the United States and Europe, one or two primary products—such as El Salvador, Cuba, and Honduras—suffered the most. Simply stated, products from these countries—sugar, bananas, tropical fruits, and coffee—were not "staples" and were considered luxury goods at the time. The depression, which led to a staggering 33–40 percent unemployment rate in the United States, meant that U.S. consumers could no longer afford to buy Latin American goods.

By 1929, the extent of primary export economic growth in Latin America was astounding: Seventy-one percent of the Brazilian economy depended on coffee exportation, while Chile's economy was linked primarily to the export of copper and nitrates (84 percent). Venezuela's petroleum export sector accounted for 76 percent of its exports, and Bolivian tin constituted 73 percent of its economy.

During the first thirty years of the twentieth century, foreign investment flowed toward the export sectors of the Latin American economies, and large agro-businesses—such as the United Fruit Company—operated as virtual enclave economies in Honduras, Costa Rica, Guatemala, and Colombia. About 70 percent of all Latin American trade involved four outside trading partners: the United States, the United Kingdom, France, and Germany. The emphasis on overseas trade and discouragement of local and intraregional trade left Latin American societies largely at the mercy of powerful industrial nations. The dramatic decline of the terms of trade after 1929 spelled disaster for many economies in the region. In the four years immediately following the Great Depression, from 1929 to 1932, the volume of trade in Latin America declined by about 65 percent.

The immediate effects on individual countries within Latin America can be measured in the specific decline (in dollars) of export revenues. For example, in Argentina, exports of beef and grains (primarily) declined from 1.57 billion dollars in 1929 to 561 million dollars in 1932. In Cuba, foreign trade in 1932 represented a mere 10 percent of pre-1929 levels. Uruguay witnessed an 80 percent decline during the same period. In Brazil, exports plummeted from 446 million dollars in 1929 to 181 million in 1932. Brazil's poor economic performance was directly related to the dramatic decline in the price of coffee. Since few people in the industrial West could afford coffee after 1929, the price fell from 22.5 cents per pound in 1929 to about 8 cents per pound on the international market two years later. The situation was equally grim in Cuba, where the price of sugar declined by about 60 percent, and according to Louis A. Pérez, Jr., "The value of tobacco, the island's second largest export, declined from $43 million in 1929 to $13 million in 1933."[1]

The world economy recovered slowly, spurred on by the onset of war in Europe. But the Great Depression dramatically, and permanently, altered the terms of trade between the Latin American economies and the economies of the "developed world." The prices for primary commodities from Latin America never recovered their pre-1929 levels in real terms. Compounding this reality was a concerted effort by the United States to convince Latin American nations to hold down the prices for the scarce commodities deemed "critical" to the war effort: these products included Venezuelan and Mexican oil, Brazilian quartz, Chilean copper and nitrates, and Bolivian tin.

Some countries were able to recover relatively quickly from the Great Depression; those with the most diversified economies tended to pull out of the economic crisis during, and immediately after, the war. But countries such as Honduras, Nicaragua, El Salvador, Uruguay, Paraguay, and Panama—small countries with only one or two primary exports and no significant industrial structure at the time—had a much more difficult time recovering.

There was, however, a silver lining to the economic crisis of the 1930s in Latin America. The Latin American nations learned about the dangers of relying on one or two primary products destined for two or three nations. This realization fostered the development of import-substitution industrialization as a model for economic development. Latin American leaders began to believe that "industry" was the key to economic stability and long-term growth for the region. The challenge, then, during the period after World War II, would be to finance, develop, and sustain national industries that could compete with imports from the industrialized countries such as the United States and Western Europe. This project would shape the political and, to some degree, social agenda in Latin America for about a thirty-five-year period after 1945.

NOTE

1. Louis A. Pérez, Jr., *Cuba: Between Reform and Revolution,* 2d ed. (New York: Oxford University Press, 1995), p. 253.

BIBLIOGRAPHY

Burns, E. Bradford, and Julie A. Charlip. 2002. *Latin America: A Concise Interpretive History.* 7th ed. Upper Saddle River, NJ: Prentice Hall.
Lee, C.H. 1969. "The Effects of the Depression on Primary Producing Countries." *Journal of Contemporary History* 4, no. 4 (October).
Skidmore, Thomas E., and Peter H. Smith. 2005. *Modern Latin America.* 6th ed. New York: Oxford University Press.

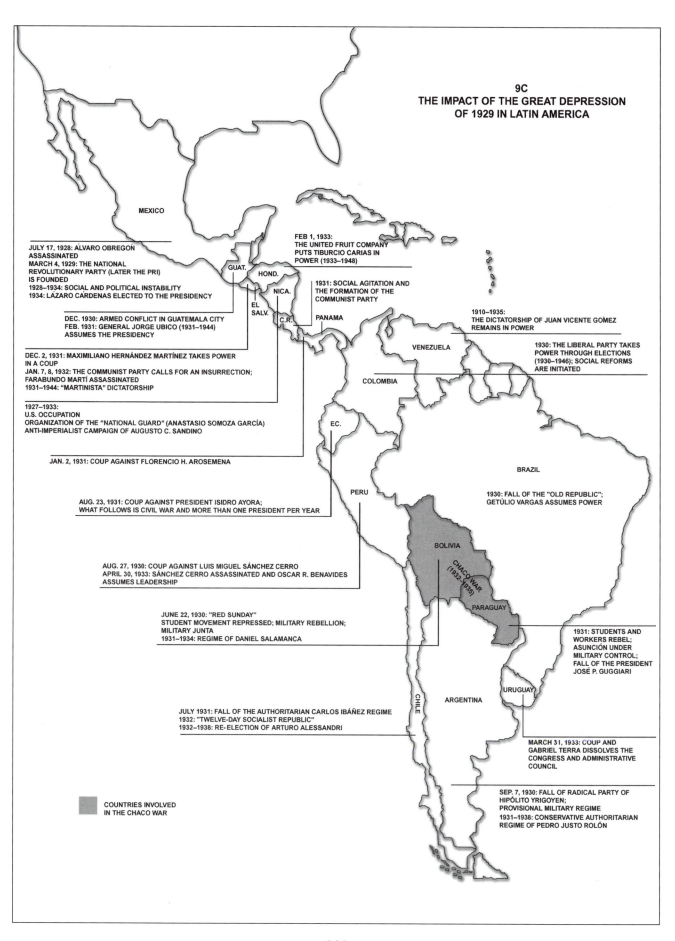

9C
THE IMPACT OF THE GREAT DEPRESSION
OF 1929 IN LATIN AMERICA

MEXICO

JULY 17, 1928: ÁLVARO OBREGÓN
ASSASSINATED
MARCH 4, 1929: THE NATIONAL
REVOLUTIONARY PARTY (LATER THE PRI)
IS FOUNDED
1928–1934: SOCIAL AND POLITICAL INSTABILITY
1934: LÁZARO CÁRDENAS ELECTED TO THE PRESIDENCY

GUAT.

HOND.

FEB 1, 1933:
THE UNITED FRUIT COMPANY
PUTS TIBURCIO CARIAS IN
POWER (1933–1948)

EL
SALV.

NICA.

1931: SOCIAL AGITATION AND
THE FORMATION OF THE
COMMUNIST PARTY

DEC. 1930: ARMED CONFLICT IN GUATEMALA CITY
FEB. 1931: GENERAL JORGE UBICO (1931–1944)
ASSUMES THE PRESIDENCY

C.R.

PANAMA

1910–1935:
THE DICTATORSHIP OF JUAN VICENTE GÓMEZ
REMAINS IN POWER

DEC. 2, 1931: MAXIMILIANO HERNÁNDEZ MARTÍNEZ TAKES POWER
IN A COUP
JAN. 7, 8, 1932: THE COMMUNIST PARTY CALLS FOR AN INSURRECTION;
FARABUNDO MARTÍ ASSASSINATED
1931–1944: "MARTINISTA" DICTATORSHIP

VENEZUELA

1930: THE LIBERAL PARTY TAKES
POWER THROUGH ELECTIONS
(1930–1946); SOCIAL REFORMS
ARE INITIATED

COLOMBIA

1927–1933:
U.S. OCCUPATION
ORGANIZATION OF THE "NATIONAL GUARD" (ANASTASIO SOMOZA GARCÍA)
ANTI-IMPERIALIST CAMPAIGN OF AUGUSTO C. SANDINO

EC.

JAN. 2, 1931: COUP AGAINST FLORENCIO H. AROSEMENA

BRAZIL

AUG. 23, 1931: COUP AGAINST PRESIDENT ISIDRO AYORA;
WHAT FOLLOWS IS CIVIL WAR AND MORE THAN ONE PRESIDENT PER YEAR

PERU

1930: FALL OF THE "OLD REPUBLIC";
GETÚLIO VARGAS ASSUMES POWER

AUG. 27, 1930: COUP AGAINST LUIS MIGUEL SÁNCHEZ CERRO
APRIL 30, 1933: SÁNCHEZ CERRO ASSASSINATED AND OSCAR R. BENAVIDES
ASSUMES LEADERSHIP

BOLIVIA

CHACO WAR
(1932–1935)

PARAGUAY

JUNE 22, 1930: "RED SUNDAY"
STUDENT MOVEMENT REPRESSED; MILITARY REBELLION;
MILITARY JUNTA
1931–1934: REGIME OF DANIEL SALAMANCA

1931: STUDENTS AND
WORKERS REBEL;
ASUNCIÓN UNDER
MILITARY CONTROL;
FALL OF THE PRESIDENT
JOSÉ P. GUGGIARI

JULY 1931: FALL OF THE AUTHORITARIAN CARLOS IBÁÑEZ REGIME
1932: "TWELVE-DAY SOCIALIST REPUBLIC"
1932–1938: RE-ELECTION OF ARTURO ALESSANDRI

CHILE

ARGENTINA

URUGUAY

MARCH 31, 1933: COUP AND
GABRIEL TERRA DISSOLVES THE
CONGRESS AND ADMINISTRATIVE
COUNCIL

COUNTRIES INVOLVED
IN THE CHACO WAR

SEP. 7, 1930: FALL OF RADICAL PARTY OF
HIPÓLITO YRIGOYEN;
PROVISIONAL MILITARY REGIME
1931–1938: CONSERVATIVE AUTHORITARIAN
REGIME OF PEDRO JUSTO ROLÓN

9D

Mining and Petroleum

Latin America is rich in mineral wealth—the European conquerors noticed this reality almost as soon as they set foot on the continent. Driven by a mercantilist mentality in the early days of the conquest, Spaniards settled in centers where minerals were easily extracted, which meant a focus on Mexico, Peru, and Bolivia.

In the seventeenth century, new areas of mining became important in Latin America. The southwestern area of what is today Colombia held significant gold deposits, and miners moved out from the city of Popayán to exploit gold in the western Chocó, and later, in and around the northwestern city of Medellín. Minas Gerais (or General Mines) became an important gold, diamond, and mineral base in Brazil: the development of mining in Minas Gerais represented an important historic shift away from an economy dominated by northeastern sugar barons.

Throughout Latin America, especially in the eighteenth century, plantations or "estates" developed near major mining regions as a way to provide goods and services to the mining centers. François Chevalier's research on the great estates of Mexico clarified this process; estates in Peru, Colombia, Brazil, and Bolivia developed in tandem with the mining sector as well. Mining centers needed human labor, food, clothing, and animal labor—all of which could be found at the large estates.

The length and savagery of the wars for independence during the nineteenth century had a deleterious effect on mining throughout Hispanic America. Mines, especially in Mexico and Peru, were abandoned, sabotaged, or flooded, and mining revenues declined sharply during, and immediately after, independence. Shortly after independence had been won from Spain, mining activity slowly recovered.

Industrialization in the latter half of the nineteenth century, and the relationship between industrial development and petroleum, meant new opportunities for Latin American economies. Areas with vast petroleum reserves, mainly Venezuela, Colombia, Mexico, and Ecuador, experienced economic booms. Scarce mineral reserves of tin, copper, zinc, nickel, and quartz in the United States gave some Latin American countries bargaining power, especially in the period between the world wars. Bolivian tin, Brazilian quartz (for radio transmission), and Chilean copper were critically important wartime products: in the early 1950s, Bolivia accounted for about 20 percent of the world's tin production while Chile produced 18 percent of the world's copper. Mexico and Peru held deposits of zinc and lead. As late as 1998, Latin America produced significant amounts of important mineral products in terms of overall global output, including silver (40 percent), copper (39 percent), bauxite (28 percent), and tin (25 percent).

Petroleum resources became a major concern for the industrial West, especially after the 1973 oil embargo. The United States and other industrial countries began looking for reliable sources of crude oil and focused, in a more determined fashion, on Latin America. In the mid-1950s, Venezuela alone accounted for about 82 percent of the entire Latin American region's petroleum and natural gas production; Mexico lagged significantly behind at about 9 percent. By the mid-1990s, Venezuela was producing about 4.5 percent of the world's crude oil, with Brazil, Argentina, Colombia, and Ecuador trailing in descending order of production. Estimated oil reserves in Venezuela are greater than any other area in the Americas; Mexico has the second largest reserves in the region. Politics have been dramatically altered by oil reserves in Latin America: President Lázaro Cárdenas's decision to nationalize Mexican oil reserves in 1938 sent a clear message to the industrial nations of "the north," and current political tensions and U.S. policies in Ecuador, Colombia, and Venezuela are shaped to some degree by oil reserves and the "politics of oil."

BIBLIOGRAPHY

Campodónica, Humberto. 2004. "Reformas e inversión en la industría de hidrocarburos de América Latina." United Nations, CEPAL (Comisión Económica para América Latina y el Caribe), SERIE #78: Recursos naturales e infraestructura, October.

Franko, Patrice M. 1999. *The Economic Puzzle of Latin American Development.* Lanham, MD: Rowman & Littlefield.

United Nations. Economic Commission for Latin America and the Caribbean (ECLAC). 1957. *Economic Survey of Latin America: 1955.* New York: United Nations.

———. 1957. *Economic Survey of Latin America: 1956.* New York: United Nations.

Winn, Peter. 1999. *Americas: The Changing Face of Latin America and the Caribbean.* Berkeley: University of California Press.

9D
MINING AND PETROLEUM

IRON
GOLD
COPPER

NICKEL
COPPER
GOLD
IRON
MANGANESE

IRON
NICKEL
GOLD
SILVER

LEAD GOLD
ZINC IRON
SILVER COPPER

GOLD
MARBLE
BAUXITE
COPPER

IRON
TUNGSTEN

GOLD
ZINC
LEAD
SILVER

IRON   COPPER
LEAD   SILVER
GOLD   BAUXITE
COAL   NATURAL GAS

GOLD
BAUXITE
SULPHUR
IRON ORE
MANGANESE

COPPER
COAL

GOLD
NICKEL
COAL
EMERALDS
NATURAL GAS

ZINC
GOLD
SILVER
COPPER
NATURAL GAS

TIN
IRON
LEAD
GOLD
COPPER
URANIUM
MANGANESE
NATURAL GAS

TIN
ZINC
IRON
GOLD
COAL
LEAD
SILVER
COPPER
TUNGSTEN

TIN
ZINC
IRON
LEAD
SILVER
COPPER
TUNGSTEN
NATURAL GAS

IRON
ZINC
COAL
LEAD
SILVER
URANIUM
NATURAL GAS

IRON

GOLD
SILVER
COPPER

PETROLEUM PRODUCING NATION

9E

Import-Substituting Economic Development

Economic policies adopted in Latin America changed significantly after the Great Depression of 1929. The rapidly declining fortunes of essentially mono-crop Latin American economies led to new ways of thinking about the economy and to the creation of new policy options designed to modernize Latin American economies and break them out of endemic, polarizing boom–bust cycles.

Latin American economic planners, increasingly skeptical of the sanctity of classical economic theory (and taking significant cues from John Maynard Keynes) came to realize that they would forever be subject to the vagaries of the international economic system as "price takers" if their economies remained essentially agricultural, mono-crop, and nonindustrial. Thus, Latin Americans began to speak of import-substitution industrialization during this time period as a way to break the traditional cycles of instability, poverty, and underdevelopment.

By the conclusion of World War II, import-substituting industrialization, or ISI, had become the "norm" for countries across the region. The basic premise of ISI centered on decreasing Latin American dependence on the world economy by encouraging rapid industrial growth through heavy state involvement in economic development. By "artificially" stimulating the growth of industry within the region via policy (including high tariffs and quotas, limiting imports, and by providing state subsidies, tax breaks, and targeted lending), ISI was designed to nurture the growth and development of domestic companies. Through import-substituting industrialization, Latin America would attempt to manufacture the industrial goods that had previously been imported from abroad.

Raúl Prebisch, an Argentine economist, played a central role in the development of post–World War II economic policy in Latin America and the developing world. His *Economic Development of Latin America and Its Principal Problem* (1949) became an influential text that helped explain why Latin American economies remained underdeveloped (at the "periphery," as he referred to them) while the developed economies of the Northern Hemisphere (Europe and the United States/Canada) were at the "center." According to Prebisch, the industrial center grew at the expense of the periphery, resulting in a dramatic imbalance and "declining terms of trade" for Latin America, as industrial goods gained value against primary products. In a dramatically unequal world of industrial versus nonindustrial nations, classic economic models based on "comparative advantage" were antiquated at best and destructive at worst. Rapid industrialization was the prescription of Mr. Prebisch; his leadership and scholarship gained him the chairmanship of the United Nations Economic Commission for Latin America and the Caribbean, which was created in 1948.

In terms of output, ISI was successful in Latin America, but only in the largest markets (Argentina, Brazil, and Mexico). Between 1950 and 1970, gross domestic product (GDP) in the region tripled. In fact, the growth rates in Latin America during this period exceeded those of other more industrialized nations. However, it is important to note that there were negative consequences associated with ISI. In most Latin American countries, ISI led to incomplete industrial growth and lowered production efficiency. While the production of finished industrial goods (textiles) grew significantly, Latin American countries (with the exception of Brazil and Mexico) never developed the ability to produce intermediate capital goods (steel) used in the manufacture of finished goods. Likewise, in the long run, the protectionist policies adopted and enacted in Latin America during this time hurt Latin American industries' ability to compete in the international arena. Growth and accumulation of wealth through ISI was concentrated in the large metropolitan areas of the most populous Latin American countries. Rural areas and primarily agrarian nations were left out of the "progress" attributed to ISI. Furthermore, ISI exacerbated unequal distribution of wealth by further concentrating wealth and power in the hands of industrial elites.

BIBLIOGRAPHY

Franko, Patrice M. 1999. *The Puzzle of Latin American Economic Development.* Lanham, MD: Rowman & Littlefield.
Skidmore, Thomas E. 1997. *Brazil: Five Centuries of Change.* New York: Oxford University Press.
Skidmore, Thomas E., and Peter H. Smith. 2005. *Modern Latin America.* 6th ed. New York: Oxford University Press.

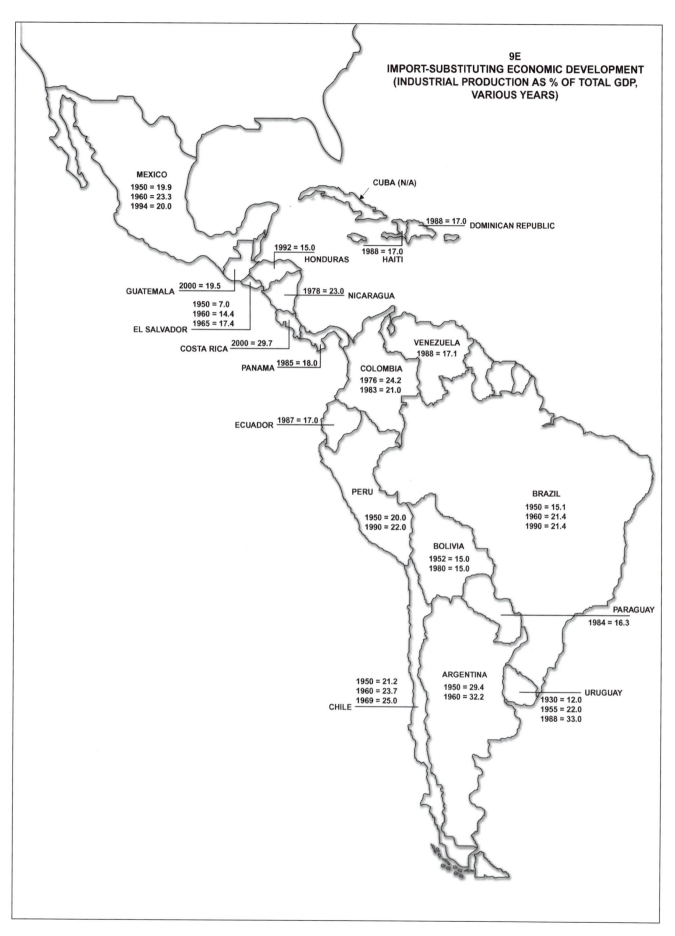

9E
IMPORT-SUBSTITUTING ECONOMIC DEVELOPMENT
(INDUSTRIAL PRODUCTION AS % OF TOTAL GDP,
VARIOUS YEARS)

MEXICO
1950 = 19.9
1960 = 23.3
1994 = 20.0

CUBA (N/A)

1988 = 17.0   DOMINICAN REPUBLIC

1992 = 15.0
HONDURAS

1988 = 17.0
HAITI

GUATEMALA   2000 = 19.5

1978 = 23.0   NICARAGUA

1950 = 7.0
1960 = 14.4
1965 = 17.4
EL SALVADOR

COSTA RICA   2000 = 29.7

VENEZUELA
1988 = 17.1

PANAMA   1985 = 18.0

COLOMBIA
1976 = 24.2
1983 = 21.0

ECUADOR   1987 = 17.0

PERU

1950 = 20.0
1990 = 22.0

BRAZIL
1950 = 15.1
1960 = 21.4
1990 = 21.4

BOLIVIA
1952 = 15.0
1980 = 15.0

PARAGUAY
1984 = 16.3

1950 = 21.2
1960 = 23.7
1969 = 25.0
CHILE

ARGENTINA
1950 = 29.4
1960 = 32.2

URUGUAY
1930 = 12.0
1955 = 22.0
1988 = 33.0

9F

Production by Nation

At the conclusion of World War II, Latin Americans, having provided much assistance to the Allies' cause, expected grants and loans to flow to the region from the United States. After all, Latin Americans had participated in the war effort (Brazilians died in Italy alongside Allied soldiers, and Mexican pilots flew missions in the South Pacific), and they had sold basic commodities to the United States at below-market prices. Yet, despite these efforts, U.S. priorities lay in "re-building the destroyed European economies via the Marshall Plan."[1] Using the theories and rhetoric of import-substituting industrialization (discussed in the previous section), and emerging nationalism, Latin Americans pursued internal industrial development, especially in those areas with large populations, abundant natural resources, and a stable labor force. This meant that Argentina, Brazil, and Mexico would lead industrial production. Those three economies made up approximately 80 percent of all Latin American industrial output by the early 1960s. Latin American countries also began to restructure commercial networks and placed a new emphasis on trade with Europe and Asia in the mid-twentieth century.

Reflecting the new nationalism of the postwar period, together with the push for industrialization (1950–1970), manufacturers' share of GDP for the entire region grew from 20 percent to 26 percent while overall GDP from agriculture shrank from 24.6 percent to 15.4 percent during the same period.

Brazil's industrial sector grew aggressively during this time and continued to grow during a period known simply as "the miracle." Under strict military rule after 1964, and with centralized planning of the economy, manufacturing became an obsession of the Brazilian military rulers, and impressive gains were realized. Industrial exports constituted 3 percent of the economy in 1960, but 30 percent by 1974. Brazilian economic growth reached levels of 10 percent per year, and Brazilian factories were producing automobiles, steel, and other "heavy" manufactured goods.[2]

Mexican industrialization benefited from close proximity to the United States. Additionally, Mexico counted on a large internal market and an educated, organized industrial work force. The Mexican automobile industry produced about 50,000 cars in 1960. Ten years later, 193,000 cars were assembled in Mexico.[3] The growth of the automobile industry positively affected other industrial sectors of the economy, including rubber and glass manufacturers and, of course, the oil industry. The Mexican oil industry (or PEMEX) was born shortly after 1938, the year when the populist President Lázaro Cárdenas na-

tionalized foreign oil properties in Mexico. Petroleum production, automobile manufacturing, and other heavy industry allowed the Mexican economy to post impressive gains: during a twenty-year period, from 1960 to 1980, the GDP grew from $US31.5 billion to 107 billion, representing a 340 percent increase.

In Argentina, GDP climbed from $US27.9 billion to 53.6 billion during a twenty-year period, 1960–1980, despite political tensions, military intervention, and cyclical economic instability. The Argentine economy relied heavily on the beef industry; however, petroleum and manufacturing of light and durable factory goods were significant components.

Copper production and exports contributed to the growth of the Chilean economy. By 1972, copper represented 10 percent of Chile's GDP and 70 percent of total exports. At present the Chilean economy is much more diversified, and thanks to changing tastes in Europe and the United States, along with significant advances in transportation, Chilean fresh fruit competes with American-grown fruit in the U.S. economy. The Chilean wine industry has grown dramatically in the past twenty years, and Chilean wines can be purchased almost anywhere in the United States and throughout Latin America. The Argentine wine industry (based at the city of Mendoza) is now making impressive inroads in a Latin American industry once dominated almost exclusively by Chileans.

In considering production by nations after 1945, a critical component of Latin Americans' drive to industrialize centered on their desire to achieve "status" in the club of industrial nations. Latin American sensibilities were offended when, after World War II, the United States prioritized rebuilding Europe rather than rewarding Latin American cooperation and solidarity during the war effort. Postwar political leaders in Latin America recognized that industrialized nations had more bargaining power in the newly competitive, postwar industrial world.

NOTES

1. E. Bradford Burns and Julie A. Charlip, *Latin America: A Concise Interpretive History*, 7th ed. (Upper Saddle River, NJ: Prentice Hall, 2002), p. 237.
2. Ibid. p. 292.
3. Patrice M. Franko, *The Puzzle of Latin American Economic Development* (Lanham, MD: Rowman & Littlefield, 1999), p. 71.

BIBLIOGRAPHY

Economic and Social Progress in Latin America: Annual Report. 1972. Washington, DC: Inter-American Development Bank.
———. 1980–1981. Washington, DC: Inter-American Development Bank.
United Nations. Economic Commission for Latin America and the Caribbean (ECLAC). ECLAC Department of Economics and Social Affairs. 1965. *Economic Survey of Latin America: 1963.* New York: United Nations.

9F
PRODUCTION BY NATION
(2006 GDP PER CAPITA IN U.S. DOLLARS)

GDP: 7,926
1, 2, 7, 8, 11, 17, 18
D, G, H, I, J, K, P, Q, Y

GDP: N/A
6, 7, 18
C, D, K, P, Q, V, Y

GDP: 3,074
2, 6, 7, 18
D, I, K, N, Q, V

GDP: 2,065
2, 3, 18
A, D, I, Q, Y, Z

GDP: 1,225
2, 3, 9
A, D, Q, R

GDP: 918
2, 6, 7, 18
D, I, K, N, Q

GDP: 2,597
1, 2, 3, 8
D, G, I, Q, S

GDP: 906
1, 2, 8, 9,11
A, D, G, I, K, Q

GDP: 4,646
1, 2, 14
A, D, I, Q, R

GDP: 5,804
1, 2, 12, 13, 17
B, D, I, M, Q

GDP: 4,955
7, 19
A, D, I, K, Q

GDP: 3,019
1, 2, 7, 8, 9, 17
A, C, D, I, K, L, Q, S, V, X

GDP: 2,652
1, 2, 3, 4, 5
A, B, C, D, E, F

GDP: 5,507
2, 5, 7, 9, 11, 13, 16, 17
B, D, E, G, H, I, J, M, P, Q, S

GDP: 3,000
1, 2, 4, 7, 9, 10
A, C, D, F, G, K, L, M, N

GDP: 1,103
1, 8, 9
C, D, G, H, K, L, R

GDP: 7,214
1, 2, 3, 4, 7, 12, 13, 15
F, I, J, M, R, T, U

GDP: 1,255
2, 3, 5, 6, 7, 8
D, G, H, I, J

GDP: 5,055
1, 2, 8, 11
I, J, K, O, P

GDP: 5,496
1, 2, 8, 9, 11, 15, 17, 18
E, J, M, N, S, P, T

INDUSTRY:

1: FOOD PROCESSING
2: TEXTILES
3: WOOD PRODUCTS
4: FISHING
5: LUMBER
6: SUGAR PROCESSING
7: CEMENT
8: BEVERAGES
9: CLOTHING
10 : SHIPBUILDING
11: CHEMICALS
12: COPPER
13: STEEL
14: FERTILIZER
15: WINE
16: AIRCRAFT
17: MOTOR VEHICLE
18: TOURISM
19: BREWING

FARM AND ANIMAL PRODUCTS:

A: BANANAS OR PLANTAINS
B: COCOA
C: POTATOES
D: SUGAR CANE
E: CATTLE
F: FISH
G: COTTON
H: SOY BEANS
I: CORN
J: WHEAT
K: RICE
L: COCAINE
M: BEEF
N: WOOL
O: BARLEY
P: LIVESTOCK
Q: COFFEE
R: TIMBER
S: VEGETABLE OIL
T: GRAPES
U: FRUITS
V: TOBACCO
X: CUT FLOWERS
Y: BEANS
Z: RUBBER

SOURCE: IMF WORLD ECONOMIC OUTLOOK, APRIL 2006.
LÁTIN BUSINESS CHRONICLE

9G

Public Expenditures in Latin America

The rapid reemergence of traditional trade patterns between the United States and Latin America after the conclusion of World War II—whereby the United States sought to continue supplying Latin America with manufactured goods in exchange for primary mineral and agricultural products—fueled a backlash of nationalism in the region.

Latin American countries received very little (from the United States) in return for their support during the war; they got advice on eliminating communists from their societies, limited military aid, and outdated military technology/hardware. But the new nationalism in Latin America—sparked in good measure by changing social realities, including the rapid growth of cities—necessitated a focus on public programs to support health, education, and basic sanitation infrastructure in the cities. Public spending on the military consumed a large part of Latin American budgets during this time, reflecting the historic importance of the military in the overall power balance in most nations of the region.

Between 1945 and 1954, public expenditures grew across Latin America in tandem with economic growth after the war, as manufacturers tried to keep pace with pent-up postwar demand. Nine percent of the Mexican GDP was dedicated to public expenditures in 1954; the figure was 19 percent in Argentina. Venezuela, Chile, and Brazil ranked behind Argentina with 18, 17, and 10 percent, respectively. Guatemala was the only country in which public expenditures decreased as a percentage of GDP during this period. To break down the numbers further, in Argentina, spending on health represented 5 percent of GDP for 1946, 1950, and 1954, while the education budget remained virtually unchanged as well, at 17, 18, and 16 percent of GDP, respectively. The military budget declined from 37 to 23 percent during the nine-year period. This decrease in military spending reflects the populist program of Juan Perón, who insisted on social spending as a way to connect "Peronisimo" to the common people. In Brazil, military spending declined from 37 percent in 1946 to 33 percent in 1954, the year that the populist leader Getúlio Vargas committed suicide in the presidential palace. The case of Costa Rica stands in sharp contrast to those of Brazil and Argentina: the Costa Rican numbers are reversed, reflecting much more emphasis on education (37, 35, and 34 percent of GDP respectively) and less on defense (14, 10, and 12 percent of GDP during this period). Costa Rica outlawed its military and has depended on a national police force to maintain order.

The Cuban Revolution of 1959—which placed a new emphasis on public expenditures, health, and education for the people of Cuba—represented a new stage in the region's commitment to public spending. Fueled with credit from the United States under the Alliance for Progress, Latin American governments continued to increase their spending on social programs during the 1960s. Yet, by 1965, Cuba was spending more than nine times as much as Mexico on healthcare coverage per person. More students were enrolled in school than ever before, and a house was provided to every family with an affordable rent. In Venezuela, between 1958 and 1971, per capita spending on education grew more than 400 percent: while this figure might be related to increased revenues from the petroleum industry, public spending on social programs was primarily seen as an effective countermeasure to revolutionary programs—especially those unfolding in nearby Cuba.

Public expenditures for health and education faltered in the late 1960s and early 1970s, as Latin American economies began to experience balance-of-payment difficulties. But in these Cold War years, Latin American leaders were strongly encouraged to increase spending on already-bloated military budgets. Brazil, in 1968, spent about 7 percent of GDP on education—the lowest percentage in Latin America. The 1980s, known as the "lost decade," witnessed further declines in social spending, as public debt and economic stagnation gripped the region. By the mid-1990s, it is estimated that Latin American governments spent about 25 billion dollars on their militaries, representing 1.3 percent of GDP for the entire region and a little less than 10 percent of total government spending.

Latin American societies today are still seeking a more balanced equation between social and military spending; frequent protests, marches, and work stoppages by teachers and health professionals demonstrate the ongoing, daily struggle to balance investment in health and human capital versus investment in defense.

BIBLIOGRAPHY

Burns, E. Bradford, and Julie A. Charlip. 2002. *Latin America: A Concise Interpretive History.* 7th ed. Upper Saddle River, NJ: Prentice Hall.

Economic and Social Progress in Latin America: Annual Report, 1972. 1972. Washington, DC: Inter-American Development Bank.

Farley, Rawle. 1972. *The Economics of Latin America: Development Problems in Perspective.* New York: Harper and Rowe.

Lahera, Eugenio, and Marcelo Ortúzar. 1998. "Military Expenditure and Development in Latin America." ECLAC Division of Statistics and Economic Projections, *CEPAL Review,* no. 65 (August).

Pérez, Louis A., Jr. 1995. *Cuba: Between Reform and Revolution.* New York: Oxford University Press.

United Nations. Economic Commission for Latin America and the Caribbean (ECLAC). 1957. *Economic Survey of Latin America.* New York: United Nations.

9G
PUBLIC SOCIAL SPENDING
IN LATIN AMERICA, 1998–1999
(AS % OF TOTAL PUBLIC SPENDING)

MEXICO
58.5

CUBA
N/A

DOMINICAN REPUBLIC
39.7

HAITI
N/A

HONDURAS
34.3

GUATEMALA
46.2

EL SALVADOR
27

NICARAGUA
37

COSTA RICA 43.1

PANAMA
38.6

VENEZUELA
37.3

COLOMBIA
35.5

ECUADOR
N/A

PERU
38.3

BRAZIL
60.4

BOLIVIA
56.5

PARAGUAY
46.2

CHILE
66.8

ARGENTINA
63.6

URUGUAY
72.5

9H

Latin American Trade Blocs

Trading partnerships designed to link comparative advantages among and between smaller economies in Latin America have met with varying degrees of success over the years.

The Central American nations, with relatively similar export patterns and products, developed a political structure in 1951 known as the Organization of Central American States. This structure formed the basis for the General Treaty on Central American Economic Integration, better known as the CACM, or Central American Common Market. During the early 1960s, the CACM was extremely effective as a means of stimulating trade and growth in the region. For example, intraregional exports as a percentage of total exports grew from 7 to 26 percent from 1960 to 1970, but declined to 14.7 percent by 1985. Growth rates were uneven, with El Salvador deriving the greatest benefits and Honduras registering a negative balance of payments, particularly in the mid-1960s. Dramatic differences in population density–to–landmass ratios between El Salvador (with 400 people per square mile in the 1960s) and neighboring Honduras (55 per square mile) resulted in strained relations between the two countries. Political instability after the Soccer War[1] hindered the growth of the CACM; this, combined with mistrust generated by the conflict, political turbulence in Guatemala, El Salvador, and Nicaragua, the 1979 Sandinista Revolution in Nicaragua, and U.S. intervention during the Reagan years, contributed to the stagnation and decline of the CACM from 1969 through the late 1980s. The real challenge for CACM, and Central American economies in general, involved the passage of NAFTA in 1993, which shifted trade patterns along an axis between the three giant North American economies. After intense debate and lobbying in both Central America and the United States—and with strong support from U.S. manufacturing sectors and fierce opposition from U.S. sugar producers—the Central American Free Trade Agreement, or CAFTA-DR, passed the U.S. House of Representatives by a vote of 217 to 215 in July 2005, having already passed the U.S. Senate.

The Andean countries—defined as Bolivia, Colombia, Peru, Venezuela, and Ecuador—set the stage for the gradual emergence of a common market among the five nations; the goal was to create greater employment levels and enhanced standards of living for the nations' citizens. The 1969 Cartagena Agreement, signed in May 1969, set up the Andean Group. During the 1990s, integration pressures increased within the region largely in response to NAFTA and to the Washington Consensus, which pushed Latin American economies to promote free trade, open markets, and appropriate integration strategies while at the same time reducing tariffs and ending protectionist policies. By 1996, the Andean Community

had been established as a sort of successor to the Andean Group. It functioned primarily as a customs union whereby common external tariffs were established among the member nations. An official common market, defined as the unimpeded circulation of goods, services, peoples, and capital, was the next goal. The total Andean Community includes more than 120 million people and has a combined GDP of 260 billion dollars. True economic integration has proven difficult due to geographic constraints and political crises in all of the Andean countries during the 1990s. The 1991 war between Ecuador and Peru, and current border tensions between Venezuela and Colombia, have hardly facilitated trade negotiations. To hasten efforts at integration, Washington has signed Free Trade Agreements (FTAs) with Peru (December 2005) and Colombia (February 2006).

MERCOSUR is a trading bloc established on January 1, 1995, between Argentina, Brazil, Paraguay, and Uruguay. The push for economic integration in the Southern Cone began in 1986, when Presidents José Sarney of Brazil and Raúl Alfonsín of Argentina recognized that benefits would accrue to their societies through regional trade agreements and reduced tariffs. From 1990 to 1996, intraregional trade grew from 4 billion dollars to 16.7 billion. MERCOSUR has operated as an actual common market. Economic crises in Brazil (1999) and Argentina (late 2000) negatively affected growth rates among MERCOSUR nations. Chile, reflecting historic isolation from its Latin American neighbors, chose not to participate in MERCOSUR and instead decided to negotiate, in 2003, an FTA directly with the United States.

Other Latin American trading blocs include the CARICOM, or the Caribbean Common Market, consisting of many of the small states in and around the Caribbean basin.

NOTE

1. Following the June 1969 World Cup playoffs between El Salvador and Honduras, the so-called Soccer War erupted. The conflict lasted four days and resulted in 3,000 deaths.

BIBLIOGRAPHY

"Central American Common Market." 1995. Library of Congress, Federal Research Division, Area Handbook Series. Honduras, Appendix B. Available at http://lcweb2.10c.gov/frd/cs/honduras/hn_appnb.html. Accessed on November 14, 2004.

Krueger, Anne O. 1999. "Are Preferential Trading Agreements Trade-Liberalizing or Protectionist?" *Journal of Economic Perspectives* 13, no. 4 (Autumn): 105–124.

Woodward, Ralph Lee, Jr. 1999. *Central America: A Nation Divided.* 3d ed. New York: Oxford University Press.

The World Bank, Data and Statistics. 2000. "Regional Trade Blocs." *World Development Indicators 2000,* Table 6.5. Available at www.worldbank.org/data/wdi2000/pdfs/tab6_5.pdf. Accessed on November 16, 2004.

BAHAMAS

MEXICO

CUBA

DOMINICAN REPUBLIC

HONDURAS

GUATEMALA

EL SALVADOR

NICARAGUA

JAMAICA HAITI

COSTA RICA

PANAMA

VENEZUELA

COLOMBIA

ECUADOR

PERU

BRAZIL

BOLIVIA

PARAGUAY

ARGENTINA

URUGUAY

CHILE

CAFTA-DR

CACM

MERCOSUR

ANDEAN COMMUNITY

CARICOM (CARIBBEAN COMMON MARKET)

ALADI (ASOCIACIÓN LATINOAMERICANA DE INTEGRACIÓN)

North American Trade Blocs

Over the past two decades, economists and politicians have debated "globalization," which can essentially be defined as the increasing ease of movement of people, goods, and services throughout the world. Technological advances in air freight shipping and increased disparities in labor costs between the northern "industrial" powers and the underdeveloped "third world" have prompted countries to look outside of their political borders for a comparative advantage. The United States, Canada, and Mexico viewed their comparative advantage in terms of previously established trading patterns, highly developed infrastructure networks (which facilitated trade and transportation), and the enormous quantity of goods and services moving across the North American continent each year; in 2004, it is estimated that one-third of all foreign trade out of the United States was negotiated with just two countries—Canada and Mexico.

The North American Free Trade Agreement, or NAFTA, traces its origins to the U.S.–Canada Free Trade Agreement, which was signed into law by Ronald Reagan in 1987 and implemented on January 1, 1989. The premise of this agreement was that lowering, or eliminating, external tariffs between Canada and the United States would help increase trade flows and employment in both countries. Given similarities in wage structures, levels of education, and political/cultural traditions, the move to free trade between the two nations did not dramatically alter existing trade patterns.

Adding Mexico to a North American free trade scenario had obvious implications for all three countries. Three groups in particular, two of them from the United States, were opposed to NAFTA from its inception. Labor unions saw the agreement as a potential drag on wages paid to U.S. workers, given the close proximity of lower-wage Mexican labor on the other side of the U.S.-Mexican border. Environmentalists were concerned about limited environmental protections in Mexico, lax enforcement of those standards, and the "migration" of air and water toxins across borders. Mexican farmers complained about heavy U.S. government subsidies paid to farmers in the form of reduced prices for water and tax breaks. The average farmer in the United States, in 2004, received a 16,000 dollar subsidy.

The Clinton administration lobbied in support of NAFTA in the U.S. Senate, and the agreement was passed in the fall of 1993. The 1992 independent presidential candidate Ross Perot had opposed the treaty, arguing in televised presidential debates that a "giant sucking sound" would signal the transfer of millions of high-paying U.S. jobs to Mexico. Other critics included conservative commentator and candidate Pat Buchanan, who worried that undocumented Mexican laborers would migrate north without bothering to regularize their immigration status once in the United States.

NAFTA was supposed to help keep low-wage laborers in Mexico by increasing opportunities for them in their home country, especially along the 2,000-mile border separating the United States from Mexico. Maquiladoras, assembly plants primarily employing women, have grown up along the U.S.-Mexican border in record numbers over the past twenty years. The plant owners benefit from low labor costs (about 9 dollars a day) and minimal import tariffs to the United States. Women who migrate from the Central Valley of Mexico or southern regions can double their earning capacity by working in these assembly plants. However, most face hidden costs such as increased crime rates, housing shortages, pollution, and a lack of clean drinking water.

As a response to the implementation of NAFTA on January 1, 1994, a rebel group, the EZLN (Zapatista National Liberation Army), formed in San Cristóbal de las Casas, Chiapas, to declare itself in open conflict with the Mexican government of Ernesto Zedillo. This group vowed to take its struggle to all regions of the country. The EZLN, or "Zapatistas," took their name from Emiliano Zapata, the revolutionary hero who fought to help the poor gain access to land. The Zapatistas have questioned the degree to which NAFTA will help poor, landless tenant farmers in the south of Mexico—people without formal education or access to land, credit, and health care.

While the need for radical structural reforms brought to light by the Zapatistas has not been fully addressed, NAFTA has helped increase trade volume dramatically between the United States, Canada, and Mexico. From 1994 to 2000, trade grew from 109 billion dollars to 622 billion. Total trade between the United States and Mexico during that same time period grew from 100 billion dollars to 230 billion, and the average annual growth of Mexican exports to the United States increased from 10 percent (1989–1994) to 16 percent in the post-NAFTA years (1994–2001). NAFTA has increased U.S. interest in Mexico, as seen through direct foreign investment in that country, which shifted upward from 18 billion to 52 billion dollars between 1994 and 2001. In January 2004, Chile was added to the North American trade structure as the push for regional trade alliances continued. However, a hemisphere-wide free trade agreement (Free Trade Agreement of the Americas, or FTAA) seems unlikely to pass given the opposition of the MERCOSUR countries (led by Brazil) to such an arrangement.

BIBLIOGRAPHY

Fuentes, Carlos. 1997. *A New Time for Mexico.* Los Angeles: University of California Press.

The World Bank, Data and Statistics. 2000. "Regional Trade Blocs." *World Development Indicators 2000,* Table 6.5. Available at www.worldbank .org. Accessed November 13, 2004.

U.S. TRADE AGREEMENTS WITH
LATIN AMERICAN COUNTRIES

MEXICO

CUBA

DOMINICAN REPUBLIC

HAITI

HONDURAS

GUATEMALA

EL SALVADOR

NICARAGUA

COSTA RICA

PANAMA

VENEZUELA

FREE TRADE AGREEMENT (FTA) SIGNED FEB. 2006

COLOMBIA

ECUADOR

BRAZIL

FTA SIGNED DEC. 2005

PERU

BOLIVIA

PARAGUAY

FTA RATIFIED 2004

ARGENTINA

URUGUAY

CHILE

NAFTA: JAN. 1, 1994 (MEXICO, U.S.A., CANADA)

CAFTA–DR (2005)

INDIVIDUAL FTA AGREEMENTS

FTAs UNDER NEGOTIATION

9ᴊ

A Deforestation Estimate

Latin America is covered with significant tropical forests, which are some of the most biodiverse and productive ecosystems on Earth. Subtropical and temperate forests are found in the northern and southernmost latitudes. South America alone contains more tropical forest area (620,514 hectares, most of which lies in the Amazon basin) than any other continent. Depending on factors such as precipitation and altitude, tropical forests may be dry, humid, wet, rain, or cloud forests. Forest cover in Latin America is unequally distributed among regions and even more so among nations: 50 percent of the land area in South America is forested versus 30 percent in Central America and Mexico; 64 percent of Brazil is forested versus only 3 percent of Haiti. Current forest coverage is a result of the natural distribution of forests, and net cumulative deforestation and reforestation.

Deforestation is the human-driven process of replacing forest ecosystems with nonforested land covers. Trees are the essential unit of forests, but forests are habitats for diverse flora and fauna—from soil micro-organisms to insects and large predators. In Latin America and the Caribbean, forests are also home to over 70 million people. Forests provide both direct and indirect benefits to the human population in the form of goods like lumber and fuelwood, and ecosystem services including soil-water cycle maintenance and climate regulation. Deforestation results in the loss of most, to nearly all, of the biodiversity and associated ecosystem goods and services. The impacts of deforestation are not limited to the cut or burned area, as indirect effects are caused by the fragmentation of forest, which may have deleterious consequences for remaining patches, expediting species extinction by isolating subpopulations.

Forests help dampen the effects of natural disasters. The loss of forest contributed to the severity and frequency of mudslides and floods that devastated Honduras and Nicaragua during Hurricane Mitch in 1998 and wreaked havoc on Haiti when Hurricane Jeanne struck in 2004.

Net loss of tropical forest in Latin America was approximately 4.5 percent from 1980 to 1990. The rate of deforestation is perhaps the most important statistic for policy concerns. Nearly 12 percent of forests were lost in Central America and Mexico between 1990 and 2000, with notable rates of 37 percent and 26 percent loss of forest during the same period in El Salvador and Nicaragua. Though Brazil's 1990–2000 deforestation rate (4.1 percent) was below the regional average,

that figure represents deforestation of an area roughly the size of Mississippi and Louisiana combined.

The factors contributing to deforestation are complex and have varied across Latin America and over time. Conversion of forest land to large-scale agriculture is currently the predominant cause of deforestation in Latin America. Cutting forests for timber and fuelwood, slash-and-burn small-scale agriculture, mining, and industrial development are other leading contributors to forest loss. Pressures on forests are related both to practical factors such as proximity to developed land, and intangibles like international market demand for forest products.

Deforestation is not an irreversible process, as forests may return through human aid or as a result of natural succession. However, land is often reforested in the form of monotypic plantations, which require maintenance and do not harbor the diversity present in older forests.

Placing forest land in preserves and national parks is one measure being taken to protect forests. Some countries have protected a significant portion of their remaining forest area: Venezuela (66 percent), Costa Rica (36 percent), Panama (35 percent), and Guatemala (35 percent). Yet cordoning off forests often displaces those human communities living within or on the edges of forests and depend on forest goods. Additionally, forest fragmentation occurs when protected areas are isolated. Promoting commensurate relationships between human communities and forests through the selective harvest of timber, fruits, nuts, and fibers is an emerging conservation initiative in Latin America.

Valuation of forests using traditional economics—whether based on the potential income of wood products or the profits that can be derived from the land after it is cleared—does not reflect all the ecosystem services forests currently provide or the goods they could provide should markets evolve for them. High rates of deforestation will likely continue until the accepted value of a forest in a sustainable condition is greater than the value of alternative land uses or its products.

BIBLIOGRAPHY

Food and Agricultural Organization of the United Nations (FAO). 2002. *Global Forest Resources Assessment 2000.* Main Report. FAO Forestry Paper 140. Rome.

Harrison, Paul, and Fred Pearce. 2000. *AAAS Atlas of Population and the Environment.* Berkeley: University of California Press/American Association for the Advancement of Science.

Millennium Ecosystem Assessment. 2005. "Ecosystems and Human Well-Being: Synthesis Report." Washington, DC: Island Press.

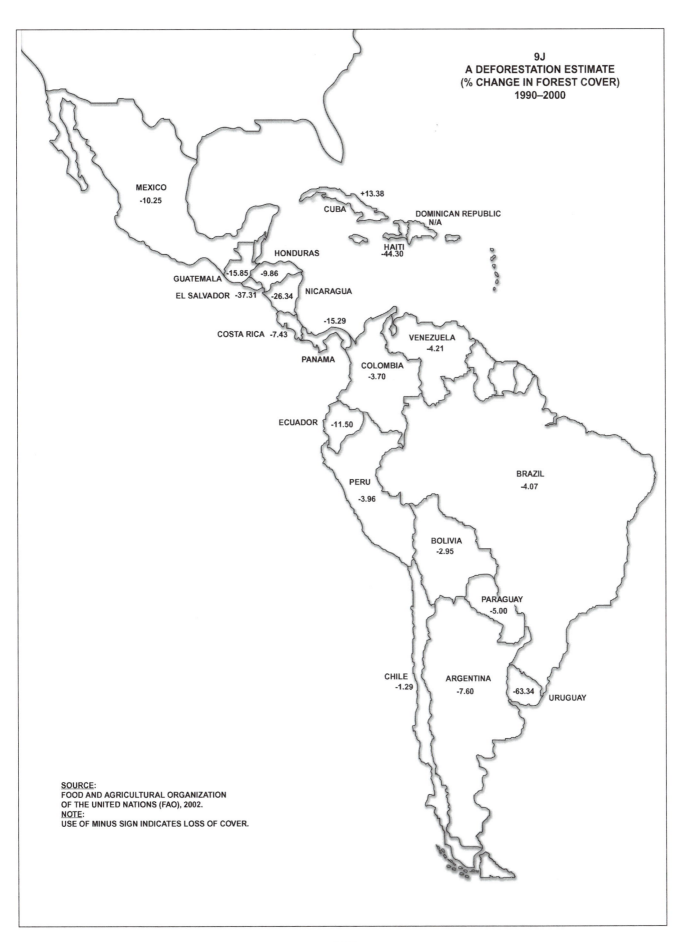

9J
A DEFORESTATION ESTIMATE
(% CHANGE IN FOREST COVER)
1990–2000

MEXICO
-10.25

+13.38

CUBA

DOMINICAN REPUBLIC
N/A

HONDURAS

GUATEMALA
-15.85 -9.86

HAITI
-44.30

EL SALVADOR -37.31 -26.34 NICARAGUA

-15.29

COSTA RICA -7.43

VENEZUELA
-4.21

PANAMA

COLOMBIA
-3.70

ECUADOR -11.50

BRAZIL
-4.07

PERU
-3.96

BOLIVIA
-2.95

PARAGUAY
-5.00

CHILE
-1.29

ARGENTINA
-7.60

-63.34 URUGUAY

SOURCE:
FOOD AND AGRICULTURAL ORGANIZATION
OF THE UNITED NATIONS (FAO), 2002.
NOTE:
USE OF MINUS SIGN INDICATES LOSS OF COVER.

10

DEMOGRAPHICS AND POPULATION IN THE TWENTIETH CENTURY

10A

The Birth of the Major Metropolitan Areas

Latin America contains a number of *mega cities* with populations of well over 8 million: Buenos Aires, Rio de Janeiro, São Paulo, Bogotá, Mexico City, and Lima are among the largest cities in the Americas today, but their initial growth began in the late nineteenth century.

The growth of cities in Latin America corresponded to fundamental trends of modernization, immigration from abroad, and liberal elite preference for cities over the rural sector. One of the fastest growing cities in Latin America at the end of the nineteenth century was Buenos Aires, the capital of Argentina. It is no surprise that this city grew quickly, given its close proximity to the ocean and its attraction as a port of entrance for European laborers. Additionally, Argentina, during the mid-nineteenth century, developed under the vision of intellectuals/political leaders such as Domingo F. Sarmiento, who viewed the "interior" as hopelessly backward and uncivilized. He extolled the virtues of the city in terms of its modernizing, civilizing influence on society. His book, *Civilization and Barbarism* (1852), offered a clear plan of development for Argentina, which stressed the city over the countryside, and white Europeans over Native Americans and Afro-Argentines. The population growth figures for Buenos Aires were dramatic: approximately 250,000 people lived in the city in 1860. Just thirty years later the population had doubled. Argentina's urban growth proceeded at an astounding rate, and by 1914, 53 percent of the country's population resided in urban areas.

Rio de Janeiro, the capital of Brazil when the republic was born in 1889, grew exponentially in November 1807 when "the entire [Portuguese] court and more than ten thousand courtiers and hangers-on set sail" for Rio, fleeing Napoleon's invasion of the Iberian Peninsula.[1] They arrived in Rio, making it the first city in America to receive European royalty. With the abolition of slavery in 1888, Brazil became a preferred destination in the Americas for Southern and Eastern European immigrants. The city of São Paulo, currently the second largest city in Latin America, traces its growth to coffee production in and around the Paraíba River valley, which increased steadily during the mid-nineteenth century. Italians in particular came to the area around São Paulo to harvest coffee, and many owned small plots of land. By the middle of the twentieth century, São Paulo had become the industrial engine of Brazil, and the area between Rio de Janeiro and São Paulo is now one of the most dynamic industrial regions of the world. São Paulo's population grew to about a quarter of a million by 1900, which put it roughly on par with the populations of Montevideo, Santiago, and Havana at the same time period.[2] Ten years later, São Paulo's population had increased to half a million.

Lima, the capital of Peru and a city with about 8.6 million residents today, grew dramatically during the early part of the twentieth century. In 1920, Lima's population was about a quarter of a million. By 1931, the population had grown 68 percent, to 376,000. Growing demand for products from Peruvian mines stimulated the growth of the capital city, with its nearby port of Callao. However, it was migration from the highlands to Lima that accounted for the majority of the population growth. Today, about 40 percent of Peru's population resides in Lima; it is the dominant city in terms of culture, education, transportation, and political-economic power.

Bogotá, home to some 7.6 million people, is the largest city in Colombia, although other important cities—Medellín, Cali, and Barranquilla—each have more than a million residents. Political and economic power radiates from the capital, which is one of the few Latin American capital cities located far away from the ocean. Bogotá sits 1,000 kilometers from the Caribbean Sea at an elevation of 2,600 meters, making it an unlikely capital city. But, Bogotá's agricultural and industrial development created a vast network of trade and production through the interior of Colombia, linking the country with Ecuador and Venezuela. Trade was facilitated by way of the mighty Magdalena River, which connected the northern coastal cities with the interior. The birth of aviation in the early twentieth century also contributed significantly to Bogotá's growth.

Mexico City, the largest city in the Americas and perhaps the second largest in the world, holds a population of about 22 million. Other important cities in Mexico include Monterrey in the north, Guadalajara to the west, and Tijuana in the northwest. About one-fifth of Mexico's population resides in the capital city, one of the world's most important cultural and intellectual centers. The most significant growth of the city occurred in the latter half of the twentieth century; in 1900, the population of Mexico City was about 500,000. The rapid expansion of Mexico City is related to the country's economic development in the period after World War II, the widening of the manufacturing sector, the success of the oil industry, and the country's proximity to U.S. markets.

NOTES

1. Thomas E. Skidmore, *Brazil: Five Centuries of Change* (New York: Oxford University Press, 1999), p. 35.

2. John Charles Chasteen, *Born in Blood and Fire* (New York: W.W. Norton, 2001), p. 187.

BIBLIOGRAPHY

Chasteen, John Charles. 2001. *Born in Blood and Fire: A Concise History of Latin America.* New York: W.W. Norton.

Keen, Benjamin, and Keith Haynes. 2004. *A History of Latin America.* 7th ed. Boston: Houghton Mifflin.

10A
THE BIRTH OF THE MAJOR
METROPOLITAN AREAS

LA HABANA
2004 = 2,600,000

SANTO DOMINGO
2004 = 3,000,000

MEXICO CITY
1890 = 450,000
2004 = 22,100,000

TEGUCIGALPA
1887 = 7,032
2004 = 1,600,000

PORT-AU-PRINCE
2004 = 2,100,000

GUATEMALA CITY
1880 = 50,522
2004 = 2,700,000

MANAGUA
1898 = 25,000
2004 = 1,500,000

CARACAS
1920 = 92,000
2004 = 3,800,000

SAN SALVADOR
1905 = 50,000
2004 = 1,800,000

BOGOTÁ
1900 = 100,000
2004 = 7,600,000

PANAMA CITY
2004 = 1,100,000

SAN JOSÉ
1927 = 100,000
2004 = 1,600,000

QUITO
1950 = 209,000
2004 = 1,900,000

LIMA
1908 = 173,000
2004 = 8,600,000

BRASÍLIA
2004 = 2,200,000

LA PAZ
1900 = 53,000
2004 = 1,800,000

RIO DE JANEIRO
2004 = 11,500,000

SÃO PAULO
2004 = 19,100,000

ASUNCIÓN
1900 = 80,000
2004 = 1,400,000

CAPITAL CITY

COUNTRIES WITH MORE THAN ONE
METROPOLITAN AREA OF OVER
ONE MILLION INHABITANTS

COUNTRIES WITH ONLY ONE CITY
WITH MORE THAN ONE MILLION
INHABITANTS

SANTIAGO
1907 = 333,000
2004 = 4,900,000

MONTEVIDEO
1908 = 312,000
2004 = 1,800,000

BUENOS AIRES
1895 = 774,000
2004 = 13,300,000

119

10B

Population Growth

In 2005, the Latin American population reached 551 million. Within the region, Brazil, Mexico, Colombia, and Argentina are the most populous countries. Social scientists and politicians have long been concerned with rapid population expansion in the Latin American region. Moreover, the uneven nature of development has led many others to worry about social tensions and unrest resulting from population growth. Natural resources such as water and fuels do not reach all citizens in Latin American countries: In Brazil, some 20 percent live in abject poverty. In Venezuela, 75 percent of the population lives at or below the poverty level. Both of these countries are rich in natural resources and industry (Brazil is the tenth largest industrial nation in the world), yet the people are poor.

During the twentieth century, the population of Latin America grew at a rapid rate. In general terms, population growth has been a function of "modernization." Improved quality of and access to health care has led to declines in the death rate and infant mortality; this, along with scientific breakthroughs in treating yellow fever, malaria, and other tropical diseases, as well as relatively steady birthrates, has positively affected population growth rates in Latin America. More efficient agricultural techniques mean that less land is needed to feed more people. Cultural factors, such as the influence of a strong Roman Catholic Church (which officially discouraged any form of artificial birth control or scientific contraception when it became available in the 1960s), also contributed to population increase. In 1968, in the papal encyclical entitled *Humane Vitae,* or *On Human Life*—which staunchly defended the church's traditional opposition to artificial birth control in the age of "the pill"—the church's position was reaffirmed.

Despite the general trend of population growth in the region, the rate of that growth is slowing due to various factors. The easy availability of artificial birth control in urban areas of Latin America, combined with more intensified use of land for farming, the mechanization of farming, and constant migratory streams from the countryside to the city—especially in the period after World War II—have all led to lower birthrates in the region. Families no longer depend on having a large number of children to sustain an agriculturally based existence. Latin American governments—in conjunction with traditional allies in Europe, the United States, and

the United Nations—have worked to promote awareness of "family planning." Culturally, more opportunities for women outside the home, greater access to education for both men and women, and diminishing taboos concerning the use of contraception have translated into rapidly declining birthrates over the past fifty years. Thus, since the mid-twentieth century, population growth rates have declined markedly in the region. Between the years 2000 and 2005, the total growth rate for Latin America was 15 percent, or just under 3 percent per year, as compared to the period 1950–1955, when growth rates averaged over 5 percent per year (27 percent during the entire period).

There have been significant instances of severe population declines in Latin American history during the twentieth century: War, famine and disease, and forced migration have all had deleterious effects on populations. The Mexican Revolution (1910–c. 1920) claimed the lives of approximately 1.5 million citizens out of a total population of 14 million. In El Salvador, "La Matanza" (The Massacre) of 1932 resulted in some 30,000 deaths, representing about 2 percent of the Salvadoran population. American anthropologist Nancy Scheper-Hughes estimates that approximately one million children under the age of five die each year in Brazil due to hunger, poverty, and disease. The conflicts of the 1980s in Central America (especially El Salvador, Guatemala, and Nicaragua) and, more recently, in Colombia, have negatively affected overall population growth rates in those countries.

Yet even with declining birthrates and the slowing of population growth rates, the estimated total population of Latin America in 2050 will be close to 800 million citizens, making it one of the most populous regions of the world. How the major cities, fragile democracies, and overtaxed environment will support these people looms as the major challenge for Latin American society in the not-too-distant future.

BIBLIOGRAPHY

Brea, Jorge A. 2003. "Population Dynamics in Latin America." *Population Reference Bureau, Population Bulletin* 58, no. 1 (March). Available at www.prb.org. Accessed on December 6, 2004.

Scheper-Hughes, Nancy. 1992. *Death Without Weeping: The Violence of Everyday Life in Brazil.* Los Angeles: University of California.

United Nations. Economic Commission for Latin America and the Caribbean (ECLAC). 2002. Demographic Bulletin no. 69, Centro Latinoamericano de Demografía (CELADE). Available at www.eclac.cl/celade.

10B
POPULATION GROWTH BY COUNTRY

MEXICO
1900 = 13,600,000
1960 = 36,000,000
2000 = 98,800,000

CUBA
1900 = 1,600,000
1960 = 7,000,000
2000 = 11,200,000

DOMINICAN REPUBLIC
1900 = 600,000
1960 = 3,000,000
2000 = 8,500,000

HONDURAS
1900 = 400,000
1960 = 1,800,000
2000 = 6,500,000

HAITI
1900 = 1,300,000
1960 = 3,600,000
2000 = 8,200,000

NICARAGUA
1900 = 400,000
1960 = 1,400,000
2000 = 5,000,000

GUATEMALA
1900 = 900,000
1960 = 3,800,000
2000 = 11,400,000

VENEZUELA
1900 = 2,400,000
1960 = 7,300,000
2000 = 24,200,000

EL SALVADOR
1900 = 800,000
1960 = 2,400,000
2000 = 6,300,000

PANAMA
1900 = 300,000
1960 = 1,100,000
2000 = 2,900,000

COLOMBIA
1900 = 3,900,000
1960 = 15,400,000
2000 = 42,300,000

COSTA RICA
1900 = 300,000
1960 = 1,200,000
2000 = 4,000,000

ECUADOR
1900 = 1,300,000
1960 = 4,400,000
2000 = 12,600,000

BRAZIL
1900 = 18,000,000
1960 = 69,700,000
2000 = 170,100,000

PERU
1900 = 3,000,000
1960 = 10,000,000
2000 = 25,700,000

BOLIVIA
1900 = 1,800,000
1960 = 3,800,000
2000 = 8,300,000

PARAGUAY
1900 = 500,000
1960 = 1,700,000
2000 = 5,500,000

CHILE
1900 = 3,000,000
1960 = 7,600,000
2000 = 15,200,000

ARGENTINA
1900 = 4,600,000
1960 = 19,900,000
2000 = 37,000,000

URUGUAY
1900 = 1,000,000
1960 = 2,600,000
2000 = 3,300,000

10c
Growth of Urban Population

Latin America is predominantly urban, but this has not always been the case. In fact, up until the period after World War II, the vast majority of Latin Americans lived in rural settings.

Many factors contributed to urbanization in Latin America, but the general trend toward industrialization and the movement of jobs away from rural areas during the early/mid-twentieth century certainly stands out as one of the most important explanatory factors. Increasing foreign investment in mining, agriculture, and industry fostered a need for infrastructural development, which led to the rapid growth of the construction industry in urban centers. Latin Americans began moving to the city out of necessity, to find employment. Simultaneously (as part of the process of industrialization), the introduction of technology (e.g., farm equipment) reduced the need for rural labor and pushed people off the land at unprecedented rates; it also helped drive up the price of land and contributed to the intensification of rural conflict: In some places, like Colombia, contemporary social conflict dates to this period. El Salvador, Guatemala, and Peru all moved through phases of significant conflict as "modernization" encroached and forced people toward the cities.

Rural residents of Latin America migrated to cities in three waves during the twentieth century: first, in the period before the economic crash of 1929, then in the period after World War II, and again, in the 1970s and 1980s. From 1919 to 1931, approximately 65,000 people moved from the countryside to the Peruvian capital city, Lima. Forty percent of Lima's population was rural in origin in 1931.

After World War II, political processes had become shaped by rural-urban migration trends in Latin America. "Populist" political candidates emerged throughout the region to ease the transition, provide rhetorical support for the "urban masses," and negotiate a safe middle way between the fears of wealthy urban elites (who viewed people from the countryside with fear and suspicion) and the aspirations of recently arrived residents who had to struggle to find work and decent shelter in the city. Political leaders such as Getúlio Vargas of Brazil, Víctor Raúl Haya de la Torre of Peru, Lázaro Cárdenas of Mexico, Jorge Eliécer Gaitán of Colombia, and Juan and Evita Perón of Argentina all responded to the new urban environment and incorporated the recently arrived, lower-class Latin Americans into an urban political platform that promised better jobs, educational opportunities, and housing.

From the mid-1970s to the present, a combination of political, social, and economic factors has once again driven people to cities: In Central America, brutal civil wars in Guatemala and El Salvador, and the violence leading to a Nicaraguan revolution in 1979 (and subsequent U.S.-backed counterrevolution), contributed to urbanization in those countries. The Colombian insurgency, in effect since the early 1960s, has forced people to move from the countryside to safer locations in cities. Likewise, rapid, unplanned industrialization in Brazil, Colombia, Mexico, and other countries has pulled people toward urban centers in search of work and better living conditions.

Latin America is the world's most urban region with more than 75 percent of the total population living in cities or towns, according to statistics from 2000. Massive urbanization during the latter half of the twentieth century has been called "hyperurbanization," and six of the world's most populous cities are in Latin America, with populations ranging from 7 to over 20 million.

Yet urbanization has not necessarily translated into jobs for everyone seeking work and a better way of life in the city. In fact, rural-urban migration has culminated in an all too familiar pattern in Latin America, where wealthy elites occupy certain sections of the city surrounded by the urban poor who live in *favelas, tubúrgios,* or *pueblos jovenes*—all euphemisms for urban slums defined by inadequate housing/infrastructure and limited opportunities for decent work or advancement through education. Millions of residents of Mexico City, São Paulo, Rio de Janeiro, Bogotá, and Lima live in conditions that could be described as inhuman. Rural-urban migratory patterns, conditioned by social, political, and economic realities, combined with technological change and outside investment, have shaped the modern Latin American city. The mega cities of Latin America—dynamic centers of culture and opportunity for some—have not afforded economic, cultural, or educational advancement for the majority. The greatest challenge for the next generation of Latin American leaders will be to address this growing disparity with meaningful, creative, and transformative policies.

BIBLIOGRAPHY

Arguedas, José María. 1988. *Yawar Fiesta.* 9th ed. Lima: Editorial Horizonte.

Keen, Benjamin, and Keith Haynes. 2004. *A History of Latin America.* 7th ed. New York: Houghton Mifflin.

Levine, Robert M. 1997. *Brazilian Legacies.* Armonk, NY: M.E. Sharpe.

Stein, Steve. 1980. *Populism in Peru: The Emergence of the Masses and the Politics of Social Control.* Madison: University of Wisconsin Press.

United Nations. Secretariat, Department of Economic and Social Affairs. 2004. *World Urbanization Prospects: The 2003 Revision, Data Tables and Highlights. UN Population Division.* March. Available at www.un.org/esa/population/publications.

10C
GROWTH RATE OF URBAN POPULATIONS
(%)

MEXICO
1960 = 52
2000 = 74

CUBA
1960 = 55
2000 = 75

DOMINICAN REPUBLIC
1960 = 30
2000 = 65

HONDURAS
1960 = 23
2000 = 47

HAITI
1960 = 16
2000 = 36

GUATEMALA
1960 = 32
2000 = 40

NICARAGUA
1960 = 39
2000 = 65

VENEZUELA
1960 = 61
2000 = 87

EL SALVADOR
1960 = 38
2000 = 47

PANAMA
1960 = 41
2000 = 58

COLOMBIA
1960 = 48
2000 = 75

COSTA RICA
1960 = 37
2000 = 52

ECUADOR
1960 = 34
2000 = 62

BRAZIL
1960 = 45
2000 = 81

PERU
1960 = 46
2000 = 73

BOLIVIA
1960 = 39
2000 = 65

PARAGUAY
1960 = 36
2000 = 56

CHILE
1960 = 65
2000 = 85

ARGENTINA
1960 = 74
2000 = 89

URUGUAY
1960 = 80
2000 = 91

10D

Migration Patterns from Latin America to the United States

The United States has long benefited from Latin American migratory patterns, historically a function of politics, economics, and geographic considerations. However, it was not until the 1960s that the number of immigrants from Latin America began to rise sharply and steadily. Latin Americans now make up the dominant immigrant group entering the United States.

It is estimated, according to the 2000 U.S. Census, that 35 million residents of the United States originated from Latin America. A decade before, in 1990, data showed 22 million Latin Americans residing in the United States. This means that from 1990 to 2000 alone, the Latin American presence in the United States increased 57.9 percent. Additionally, the 2000 Census estimated that there were between 8 and 9 million undocumented Latin Americans living without citizenship in the United States.

By 2003, people of Latin American origin comprised over half (53.3 percent) of the total foreign-born population living in the United States. Of this total, 30 percent originated from Mexico, 10 percent from the Caribbean, 7 percent from Central America, and 6 percent from South America.

People of Mexican origin, whose patterns of migration have resulted from an inextricable historical link with the United States, represent the largest group of immigrants from Latin America. In 1848, Mexican migratory patterns to the United States underwent a dramatic change when the Treaty of Guadalupe Hidalgo shifted the Mexican border southward. Some Mexicans stayed in towns and cities that had formerly belonged to Mexico, most notably San Antonio, Texas. Others migrated back to their homes in what used to be northern Mexico (currently known as the southwest United States). Between 1900 and 1930, surrounding the Mexican Revolution (1910–1920), the United States witnessed another large influx of Mexicans to the Southwest region when an estimated one million Mexicans headed north, fleeing poverty and political turmoil. Since the 1990s, the lure of economic opportunity has enticed millions of Mexicans to migrate northward once more, this time beyond the traditional gateways of Texas, California, and the Southwest. While the largest populations of Mexican immigrants remain in California and Texas, the fastest growing populations are now to be found in the southeastern United States in Alabama, Arkansas, Georgia, Kentucky, North Carolina, South Carolina, and Tennessee.

Two Caribbean islands (Puerto Rico and Cuba) have sent significant numbers of people to the U.S. mainland. In 1898 the United States defeated Spain in the Spanish-American War, and, via the Treaty of Paris of 1898, Spain ceded its Caribbean holdings, including Puerto Rico and Cuba. Puerto Ricans, who hold U.S. citizenship, established a strong presence in New York City and their contribu-

tions have been integral in shaping New York's rich cultural matrix. Cubans helped develop Ybor City (Tampa, Florida), and worked primarily in that city's thriving cigar-manufacturing economy during the early part of the twentieth century. Cuban migration to Miami increased sharply after the 1959 Cuban Revolution, and Cubans' presence has been intricately connected to the economic, cultural, and political development of Miami ever since. Many Cubans also migrated to the New York area, settling —most notably—in Union City, New Jersey.

More recently, Colombians have comprised an important migratory group, settling in New York City (Queens) and South Florida, with growing populations in Los Angeles and Atlanta. Many Colombians have fled the social and political violence of their homeland, and many commute regularly between Miami and Bogotá.

It is estimated that some 500,000 Salvadorans presently live in the United States. El Salvador was devastated by societal unrest and a subsequent civil war during the 1970s and 1980s; that war ended in a peace treaty in 1992. During and after the war, many Salvadorans migrated to the Washington, DC area, and to Los Angeles, New York, and San Francisco.

Guatemalans migrated to the United States in the latter half of the twentieth century, a direct result of their country's thirty-five-year civil war (1961–1996). Hondurans have established a large and thriving metropolitan community in New Orleans, Louisiana.

Brazilians have moved to Los Angeles, South Florida, Boston, and New York. According to the 2000 U.S. Census, there were 200,000 persons of Brazilian origin in the country. That figure has certainly grown (possibly to 600,000), with established communities in South Florida and New York City. The 2000 U.S. Census reported 420,000 foreign-born Haitians living in the United States. Political and economic crises in Haiti have led to wide-scale emigration from Haiti, and most of the Haitians in the United States live in four states: Florida, New York, Massachusetts, and New Jersey.

BIBLIOGRAPHY

González, Juan. 2000. *Harvest of Empire: A History of Latinos in America*. New York: Viking Penguin.

Grieco, Elizabeth. 2003. *A New Century: Immigration and the US* (online). Retrieved from the Migration Policy Institute, Migration Information Source Web site: www.migrationinformation.org.

Guzmán, Betsy. 2001 U.S. Census Bureau, "The Hispanic Population: Census 2000 Brief" (May). Available at www.census.gov/population/www/cen2000/briefs.html.

Lowell, Lindsay, and Roberto Suro. 2002. *How Many Undocumented: The Numbers Behind the U.S.–Mexico Migration Talks* (online). Retrieved October 5, 2004, from the Pew Hispanic Center Web site: www.pewhispanic.org.

Martin, Philip, and Elizabeth Midgley. 2003. *Immigration: Shaping and Reshaping America* (online). Retrieved from the Population Reference Bureau Web site: www.prb.org.

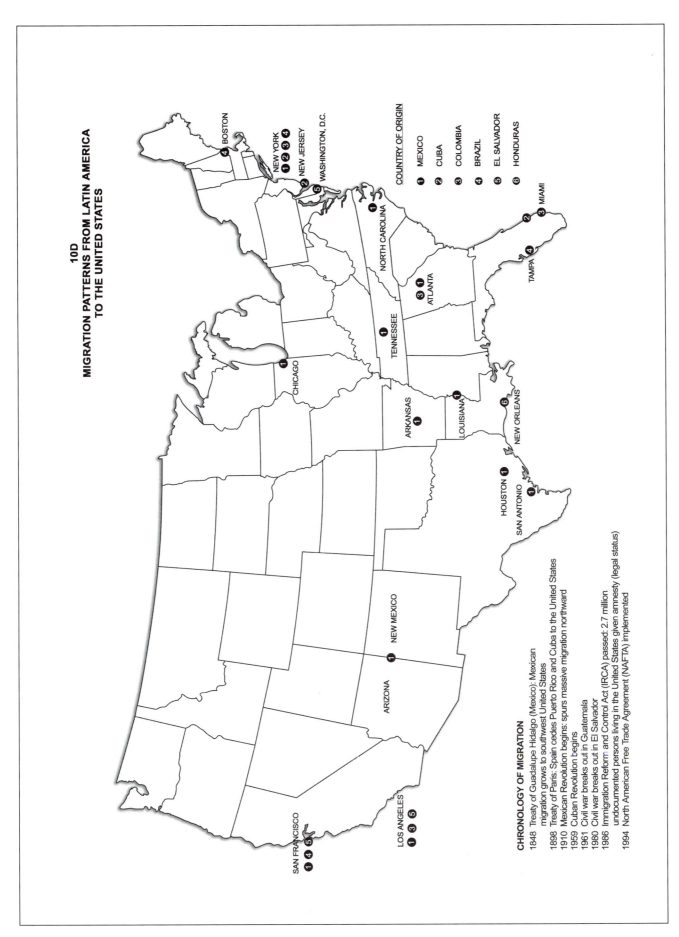

10D
MIGRATION PATTERNS FROM LATIN AMERICA
TO THE UNITED STATES

COUNTRY OF ORIGIN

❶ MEXICO
❷ CUBA
❸ COLOMBIA
❹ BRAZIL
❺ EL SALVADOR
❻ HONDURAS

BOSTON ❹

NEW YORK ❶❷❸❹
NEW JERSEY ❷
WASHINGTON, D.C. ❺

NORTH CAROLINA ❶

MIAMI ❷❸

TAMPA ❹

ATLANTA ❸❶

TENNESSEE ❶

CHICAGO ❶

ARKANSAS ❶

LOUISIANA ❶

NEW ORLEANS ❻

HOUSTON ❶

SAN ANTONIO ❶

NEW MEXICO ❶

ARIZONA ❶

LOS ANGELES ❶❸❺

SAN FRANCISCO ❶❹❺

CHRONOLOGY OF MIGRATION

1848 Treaty of Guadalupe Hidalgo (Mexico): Mexican
      migration grows to southwest United States
1898 Treaty of Paris: Spain cedes Puerto Rico and Cuba to the United States
1910 Mexican Revolution begins: spurs massive migration northward
1959 Cuban Revolution begins
1961 Civil war breaks out in Guatemala
1980 Civil war breaks out in El Salvador
1986 Immigration Reform and Control Act (IRCA) passed: 2.7 million
      undocumented persons living in the United States given amnesty (legal status)
1994 North American Free Trade Agreement (NAFTA) implemented

Migration Patterns from Latin America to Other Countries

Latin America has the highest emigration rate in the world. People leave Latin America destined to all parts of the world in search of greater employment opportunities and higher wages. They tend to migrate to industrialized, wealthy, first world countries and regions. As such, the vast majority of Latin American migrants gravitate toward the United States, Western Europe, and in Asia, Japan.

From 2000 to 2004, there was a dramatic increase in the number of Latin Americans migrating to Europe due to economic and political crises back home (particularly in Ecuador, Colombia, and Argentina). Amnesty and regularization programs, especially in Spain, further encouraged migration from Latin America. According to the Spanish Ministry of the Interior, in 2003 approximately 174,000 Ecuadorians lived within the borders of Spain; in the same year, sources that attempt to count the number of undocumented Ecuadorians estimated the population to be just under 400,000. Colombians are the second most populous Latin American national group in Spain, with an estimated population of about 160,000 in 2001. By 2003, that number might have grown to a quarter of a million, according to the Spanish National Institute of Statistics. Italy counted approximately 76,000 Latin Americans within its borders (2000), with Peruvians making up the majority (29,600). Brazilians comprised the second largest Latin American group in Italy, with a population of 19,200. In Switzerland, 21,000 Latin Americans were officially counted in 2000, most of them coming from Brazil (7,582), Chile (3,890), Peru (2,621), and Colombia (2,481). Latin American migration to Switzerland increased by 350 percent in the final decade of the twentieth century.

Unfortunately, many Latin American women who migrate to Europe end up working in the sex industry. It is estimated that as many as 60,000 Dominican women and 75,000 Brazilian women are sex workers. Of the 13,000 known foreign sex workers in Spain (in 2000) more than half were from Latin America.

Economic crises in the Southern Cone countries, together with the post-9/11 atmosphere in the United States, have had profound effects on the migratory patterns from Latin America. By the end of 2000, it is estimated that approximately 250,000 Brazilians lived in Japan; in 2001 alone, about 30,000 Brazilians moved there. This migration mirrors an important Japanese presence in Brazil, which began in the early part of the twentieth century and increased dramatically during the interwar years, when a quarter of a million Japanese moved to Brazil, creating there the largest concentration of Japanese outside of Japan. Peruvians make up the second largest Latin American group in Japan, numbering 46,000 in 2000. Argentina,

which faced a severe economic downturn beginning in 2000, has also witnessed dramatic emigration. More than 255,000 Argentineans have left the country in the past five years.

Emigrants from Latin America have often preferred migration to Southern European countries for obvious reasons involving language, culture, and heritage. As the population of Europe ages and as population growth rates in Europe remain flat, there will be a growing need for workers to help Spaniards and Italians care for their elderly, staff hospitals, and work in the service sector of the economy. Because of this, and as the United States adopts more stringent immigration policies, increasing numbers of Latin Americans will seek the former colonizing nations—and other European nations that have sent immigrants to Latin America—as points of entry into European society.

Recent research on migration trends and patterns focuses on the effects of immigration in both the host and sending country; Latin Americans remain connected to their place of origin and support relatives and friends back home, as evidenced through remittance payments. Remittances constitute an integral part of the migratory process. Approximately 35 billion dollars were remitted to Latin American countries in 2003 from outside the region (30 billion dollars alone originated from the United States). For example, in 2003, Mexicans living outside of Mexico remitted 13.2 billion dollars, which represented the third largest component of GDP in that country, after petroleum and tourism. Approximately 2 billion dollars were sent to Latin America from Europe in the form of remittances in 2003: one billion dollars originated from Spain and the other one billion dollars from the rest of Europe. Colombians, Ecuadorians, and Dominicans are the three largest groups of remittance payers from Spain to their home countries.

BIBLIOGRAPHY

Capdevila, Gustavo. 2000. "Population: Latin American Migration to Europe Expected to Grow." Inter-Press Service (June 15). Global Information Network, Lexis Nexis.

Clark, Ximena, Timothy J. Hatton, and Jeffrey G. Williamson. 2004. "What Explains Emigration Out of Latin America?" Australian National University (May). Available at http://ecocomm.anu.edu.au/people/info/hatton/wdmay2004.pdf.

Eakin, Marshall. 1998. *Brazil: The Once and Future Country.* New York: St. Martin's Griffin.

Kashiwazaki, Chikako. 2002. "Japan: From Immigration Control to Immigration Policy?" Migration Information Source (August). Available at http://migrationinformation.com.

Pellegrino, Adela. 2004. "Migration from Latin America to Europe: Trends and Policy Challenges." International Organization for Migration Policy Research Series, no. 16 (May). New York: UN Publications.

Pérez, Nieves Ortega. 2003. "Spain: Forging an Immigration Policy." Migration Information Source (February). Available at http://migration information.com.

10E
LATIN AMERICAN MIGRATION PATTERNS
(NET IMMIGRATION RATE PER 1,000)
2003

MEXICO
-2.65

-1.05
CUBA

DOMINICAN REPUBLIC

HAITI
-4.03   -3.43

HONDURAS
-1.71   -2.04

GUATEMALA
EL SALVADOR   -3.81

NICARAGUA
-1.27

PANAMA

COSTA RICA   0.51

-0.97

VENEZUELA
-0.07

COLOMBIA
-0.32

ECUADOR   -0.52

PERU
-1.03

BRAZIL
-0.03

BOLIVIA
-1.37

PARAGUAY
-0.08

CHILE
0

ARGENTINA
0.62

-0.35

URUGUAY

COUNTRY WITH MORE
EMIGRATION THAN IMMIGRATION

COUNTRY WITH LESS
EMIGRATION THAN IMMIGRATION

10F

Migration Patterns Within Latin America

Latin American migration within the continent has received relatively little attention from scholars in the United States. Researchers tend to focus on migratory patterns between specific Latin American nations and the United States or Canada. However, inter-American immigration is an important segment of the overall immigration world matrix, and migration patterns across Latin America reflect the changing dynamic and interplay of economic and political factors within the region.

Migration within Latin America reached its peak during the 1970s and 1980s and has primarily been, during the past thirty years, a function of economic conditions and political change. Venezuela's "oil boom" during the 1970s prompted migrations from middle- and lower-middle-sector Colombians; they joined Chileans who fled to Venezuela from Chile with the onset of the Pinochet regime (1973–1990). Thirty years later, the Colombian presence can still be felt in Venezuela. This group comprised more than 60 percent of the Latin American immigrant population of Venezuela as of 2001.

During much of the twentieth century, Argentina was an important point of attraction for Latin Americans. By 2001, Paraguayans made up 32 percent of Argentina's 1 million immigrants from within the region. During the same year it is estimated that there were 233,000 Bolivians living in Argentina. A significant difference in wealth and earning power between Argentina, Paraguay, and Bolivia and the geographic proximity of the countries helps explain these migratory patterns. With the economic crisis of 2000, Argentina became less attractive as a point of immigration for residents of the region; however, the relative strength of Argentine industrial capacity means that it will continue to attract immigrants from surrounding countries.

Other factors "pushing" Latin Americans out of their own countries include the growth of urban centers. During the past fifty years, rural options in many countries have dissipated due to falling prices for agricultural goods and the growing concentration of landholding. Those Latin Americans whose options are limited in the rural and urban sectors will often make the decision to migrate to neighboring countries in search of work and a higher standard of living. Migrants within the region often consider migration as a "temporary" necessity; they can travel overland, and they can return to their country of origin with relative ease. These temporary migrations are not without drawbacks however, as constant and continual movement into, and out of, regions negatively affects the ability of migrants to fully integrate into the new society.

Approximately 5 million Central Americans (or 14 percent of the Central American population) live outside of the country in which they were born; however, large numbers of these immigrants still reside within the region. Immigrants from Latin America comprise at least 15 percent of the total immigrant population in every Central American country. Eighty percent of all immigrants in Costa Rica are from Latin America, and with a total population of about 3.8 million citizens in 2000, Costa Rica counted 8 percent of its total population as foreign-born. Of those, about 300,000 came from one country, neighboring Nicaragua. Most of the Nicaraguans in Costa Rica are lower-middle-class or lower-class agriculture workers who have fled their country's political and economic instability; during the 1980s, Nicaraguans faced a left-leaning revolution, aggressively challenged by the United States, especially during the presidency of Ronald Reagan (1981–1988). The 1990s witnessed economic and political instability, as Nicaraguans attempted to reconcile the revolutionary period with more neoliberal market approaches under the leadership of President Violeta Chamorro, elected in 1990.

While migration within the region has declined significantly over the past half-century (especially during the 1990s) as Latin Americans have preferred the higher-wage regions of the United States, Canada, and Europe, intraregional migration remains important in Latin America. Many factors—geographic proximity, familiarity with language and culture, and familiarity with legal codes and traditions—influence and encourage migration within the region. People often move to places where relatives and friends live to help ease the burden of transitioning from one society to another. Economic factors also help explain migration within the region. Remittance payments demonstrate the significant inequalities between Latin American countries and suggest that people do in fact seek, in a logical manner, better economic opportunities on the Latin American continent—particularly when such opportunities are to be found on the other side of a political border. According to the Inter-American Bank, in 2002 there were approximately 1.5 billion dollars in total remittances sent by Latin Americans to other Latin Americans within the region.

BIBLIOGRAPHY

Clark, Ximena, Timothy J. Hatton, and Jeffrey G. Williamson. 2004. "What Explains Emigration Out of Latin America?" Australian National University (May). Available at http://ecocomm.anu.edu.au/people/info/hatton/wdmay2004.pdf.

Martínez Pizarro, Jorge. 2002. "Uso de los datos censales para un análisis comparativo de la migración internacional en Centroamérica." Comisión Económica para América Latina y El Caribe (CEPAL [ECLAC]), with El Centro Latinoamericano y Caribeño de Demografía (CELADE), División de Población. Organización Internacional para Las Migraciones (OIM), Serie Población y Desarrollo. Publication of the United Nations (December). Available at www.eclac.cl/celade.

The State of the Nation Project. 2001. "A Binational Study: The State of Migration Flows Between Costa Rica and Nicaragua. An Analysis of the Economic and Social Implications for Both Countries." International Organization for Migration (IOM), Studies and Reports (December). Available at www.iom.int.

González Alvarado, Ivan, and Hilda Sánchez. 2002. "Migration in Latin America and the Caribbean: A View from the ICFTU/ORIT." International Labour Organization. Available at www.ilo.org/public/english/dialogue/actrav/publ/129/19.pdf.

10F
SOME MIGRATION PATTERNS
WITHIN LATIN AMERICA

MEXICO

CUBA

DOMINICAN REPUBLIC

HONDURAS

HAITI

GUATEMALA

EL SALVADOR

NICARAGUA

COSTA RICA

VENEZUELA

PANAMA

COLOMBIA

ECUADOR

PERU

BRAZIL

BOLIVIA

PARAGUAY

URUGUAY

CHILE

ARGENTINA

129

11
POLITICAL, SOCIAL, AND CULTURAL ISSUES

11A

Indigenismo

*I*ndigenismo (or "Indian-ness") emerged as a cultural movement during the twentieth century in Latin America. The movement parallels "nationalism" and represented a repudiation of past attempts to identify the Latin American nation with all that was European. Nineteenth-century intellectuals stressed their "European-ness" and downplayed the histories of native peoples, enslaved Africans, and other "lesser" peoples, as they described them. In contrast to the well-known Argentine intellectual Domingo F. Sarmiento, late-nineteenth-century modernist writers, such as the Cuban patriot and intellectual José Martí and the Nicaraguan poet Rubén Darío, began to think of Latin America as a separate territorial entity, and envisioned it free of European (or North American) designs. Their work represented an important point of transition between nineteenth-century writers and the nationalist writers and thinkers who comprised the *indigenista* movement after World War I.

World War I dramatically altered Latin America's relationship, and love affair, with Europe. The savagery of the war was not lost on anyone, and Latin Americans, due to trade restrictions and other causes directly associated with the war, turned inward and looked more closely at their own history, culture, and citizenry. Out of this spirit of introspection emerged a renewed respect for the contributions of indigenous persons, persons of color, and other marginalized, non-European peoples of Latin America. The Mexican intellectual and education minister in the early 1920s, José Vasconcelos, laid out the contours of Latin American *indigenismo* in his book *La raza cósmica* (The Cosmic Race). That book defined Mexicans (and Latin Americans) as special people who inherited the best characteristics of European settlers, Native Americans, and Africans. Latin Americans should, he argued, show pride in their rich, complex racial and cultural make-up.

Postrevolutionary Mexico became the place where *indigenismo* flourished. Radical reinterpretations of Mexican history and culture put native societies on an elevated plane and assigned to the Europeans the unflattering role of conqueror and invader. The muralists Diego Rivera, David Alfaro Siqueiros, and José Clemente Orozco depicted this new interpretation on public walls, public buildings, and other places in an attempt to "re-educate" the people.

Brazilians, too, were deeply affected by the changes sweeping the world in the wake of World War I. In São Paulo in 1922, a "Modern Art Week" celebrated the traditions, culture, and history of the Brazilian nation. The Brazilian composer Heitor Villa-Lobos was present together with the intellectual Oswaldo de Andrade; they both emerged as towering figures in Brazilian twentieth-century intellectual life. Shortly thereafter (1933), the Brazilian sociologist Gilberto Freyre published his work *Casa grande e senzala* (translated to English as *The Masters and the Slaves*); Freyre's work shocked many, as he emphatically stated that Brazilians should be proud of their racial make-up, acknowledge the multifaceted contributions of Brazilians of African descent, and stop pretending that they were exclusively of European origin.

In Peru, important writers like Ciro Alegría and José María Arguedas focused on the "Indian question." Alegría's most important work, *El mundo es ancho y ajeno* (Broad and Alien Is the World), describes the historic and endemic exploitation of native Peruvians by cruel landlords; Arguedas was critical of *indigenista* writers and suggested that many of them were actually mere middle-class outsiders who could never truly understand Indian exploitation because they had never lived it. He published *Los ríos profundos* (Deep Rivers) in 1958, and he wrote in both Quechua, a Peruvian native language, and Spanish.

The *indigenismo* movement in Latin America is more than one universally accepted cultural or intellectual movement. It was a series of developments, in various nations of Latin America, helping to shape Latin America's history, culture, and "place" in the world.

BIBLIOGRAPHY

Deeds, Susan M., Michael C. Meyer, and William L. Sherman. 2003. *The Course of Mexican History.* 7th ed. New York: Oxford University Press.

Delpar, Helen. 1995. *The Enormous Vogue of Things Mexican: Cultural Relations Between the United States and Mexico, 1920–1935.* Tuscaloosa: University of Alabama Press.

Vasconcelos, José. 1979. *The Cosmic Race: A Bilingual Edition.* Los Angeles: California State University Press.

11A
**SOME INDIGENOUS CULTURAL FIGURES:
SELECT COUNTRIES**

1891
JOSÉ MARTÍ PUBLISHES
"NUESTRA AMÉRICA"

1915
MARIANO AZUELA
PUBLISHES *LOS DE ABAJO*
1925
JOSÉ VASCONCELOS
PUBLISHES *LA RAZA CÓSMICA*
1935
CARLOS CHÁVEZ COMPOSES
SINFONÍA INDIA

1904
RUBÉN DARÍO WRITES
"A ROOSEVELT"

1891–1984
CARLOS MÉRIDA, PAINTER
1930
MIGUEL ÁNGEL ASTURIAS
PUBLISHES *LEYENDAS
DE GUATEMALA*

1924
MANUEL QUINTIN LAME
WRITES *LOS PENSAMIENTOS
DEL INDIO QUE SE EDUCÓ DENTRO
DE LAS SELVAS COLOMBIANAS*

1922
MODERN ART WEEK IN SÃO PAULO
1924
OSWALDO DE ANDRADE
PUBLISHES *POESIAS PAU BRASIL*
1932
HEITOR VILLA-LOBOS COMPOSES
"O PAPAGAIO DO MOLEQUE"

1934
JORGE ICAZA PUBLISHES
HUASIPUNGO

1929
JOSÉ C. MARIÁTEGUI
FOUNDS THE PERUVIAN
SOCIALIST PARTY
1941
JOSÉ MARÍA ARGUEDAS
PUBLISHES *YAWAR FIESTA*

1930s
ALEJANDRO MARIO YLLÁNEZ
BEGINS HIS MURALS WITH
INDIGENOUS MOTIFS

1924
PABLO NERUDA PUBLISHES
CANTO GENERAL

1872
JOSÉ HERNÁNDEZ PUBLISHES
MARTÍN FIERRO
1926
RICARDO GÜIRALDES PUBLISHES
DON SEGUNDO SOMBRA

11B

Populism in Latin America

The growth and appeal of populism in Latin America resulted directly from the harsh social and economic realities of the 1930s, rural-urban migratory patterns, and the expansion of cities in the region. Populism marked a new way to conduct politics in Latin America.

In general, populist leaders held four common characteristics: they were extraordinarily charismatic individuals with excellent oratory skills; they maintained authority via a clear understanding of the patron–client networks that governed society; they used historic norms of social hierarchy to their advantage; and they acted as social interlocutors, preventing armed revolution while insisting on social reforms from the traditional elites. Populism in Latin America was a creative, organic solution to pressing and mounting economic, social, and political troubles on the continent: In four places—Argentina, Brazil, Mexico, and Peru—populist leaders had immense influence in charting national politics and transitioning societies through difficult times. In Colombia, populism was less successful for the charismatic populist leader Jorge Eliécer Gaitán was assassinated on April 9, 1948—a date that changed the course of Colombian history.

Populism in Argentina is associated with two figures, Juan Domingo Perón and his wife, Eva "Evita" Duarte Perón. Perón's first presidential period lasted from 1946 to 1955 amid the rapid growth of unions and an expanding, increasingly radical working class. Perón presented himself publicly as "protector" of workers and the underclass, and he was clearly connected with the urban working class in Buenos Aires, the capital city. Evita, an elegant actress with working-class roots, spent a good deal of time doling out charity to the underprivileged—the *descamisados,* or (literally) the "shirtless ones." She was able to cement a strong alliance between the poor, the urban working class, and the middle class, all of whom identified with the movement known as Peronism. The Peróns were intensely nationalistic, and they sought to steer a "third way" in terms of economic policy, which took the country on a course somewhere between socialism and unfettered, unregulated capitalism. Eva died in 1952 of ovarian cancer, and by 1955 the military moved in to remove Juan Perón after his economic plan faltered significantly.

Latin American populism was a form of social control whereby a charismatic leader would control the state and distribute patronage to the people yet avoid a major reordering of society via the revolutionary process. Populists rejected the idea of class conflict and preferred to refer to the nation as a sort of national family—the populist leaders were, of course, the father figure, or in the case of Eva Perón, the nation's mother. In fact, Brazil's populist leader, Getúlio Vargas, who ruled that country from 1930 to 1945 and again from 1950 to 1954, was referred to as *pai do povo,* or "father of the people." Vargas exerted strict control over the economic and political structure of Brazilian society. He was a masterful politician, and even though his regime became much more dictatorial from 1937 to 1945 (during what is known as the "Estado Novo"), Vargas remained popular in the eyes of the Brazilian people because of his unassuming charm, his self-deprecating sense of humor, and his comfort and ease in the presence of ordinary Brazilian citizens.

Mexico's Lázaro Cárdenas ruled from 1934 to 1940. Unlike Mexican politicians who governed before him, Cárdenas listened more than he spoke, and he distributed about 49 million acres of land for communal use, called *ejidos,* to the Indian communities. Like Perón, Cárdenas worked to strengthen organized labor movements, which won him favor with the working class and strengthened his authority in Mexico. When the working class became militant and the petroleum workers organized a strike in 1936, Cárdenas nationalized all foreign-owned oil interests and created the state-run oil company, PEMEX. By 1938, the petroleum industry was nationalized—to the sum of 24 million dollars paid to British and American oil producers—thus demonstrating the degree to which populism could create national cohesion.

In Peru, Víctor Raúl Haya de la Torre is associated with that country's populist movement. Haya founded the political party known as APRA (or the Populist Alliance for the American Revolution) in the late 1920s. An electrifying speaker, Haya de la Torre challenged the elites to distribute resources to the popular classes. He called for nationalization of key sectors of the economy and criticized the damaging effects of unchecked foreign investment in Peru. Though Haya de la Torre never arrived to the office of the presidency in Peru, he significantly impacted Peruvian politics for generations; the first APRA candidate to win the presidency was Alan García, in the mid-1980s.

Populists helped change Latin American politics and society in the twentieth century; they challenged traditional elites to distribute resources more justly, while defending the popular classes against the more extreme effects of unregulated capitalist expansion. Populists had to walk a narrow path. They had to build on nationalist sentiments by committing to reforms, while at the same time steering clear from those in society who called for more dramatic change via the revolutionary option.

BIBLIOGRAPHY

Chasteen, John Charles. 2001. *Born in Blood and Fire: A Concise History of Latin America.* New York: W.W. Norton.

Skidmore, Thomas E. 1999. *Brazil: Five Centuries of Change.* New York: Oxford University Press.

Stein, Steve. 1980. *Populism in Peru: The Emergence of the Masses and the Politics of Social Control.* Madison: University of Wisconsin Press.

11B
POPULISM IN LATIN AMERICA

LÁZARO CÁRDENAS
1934–1940

HUGO CHÁVEZ
1999–

GUSTAVO ROJAS PINILLA
1953–1957

JORGE E. GAITÁN
(DOES NOT GOVERN, BUT
INFLUENCES THE PERIOD:
1930–1948)

GETÚLIO VARGAS
1937–1945
1950–1954

VÍCTOR RAÚL HAYA DE LA TORRE
(APRA'S FOUNDER 1924)

JUAN VELASCO ALVARADO
1968–1975

ALBERTO FUJIMORI
1990–2000

JOSÉ BATTLE Y ORDÓÑEZ
1903–1907 / 1911–1915

JUAN DOMINGO PERÓN
1945–1955

CARLOS S. MENEM
1989–1999

1st WAVE

2nd WAVE

MILITARY POPULISM

NEOPOPULISM

135

11c

Armed Forces and Dictatorships

The military in Latin America has played a pivotal role in societal structure and became especially significant in the early nineteenth century, with the onset of the independence movements. Military leaders directed long campaigns during the sixteen-year struggle. Venezuelan-born Simón Bolívar and the Argentine José de San Martín are remembered as brilliant military tacticians; they demonstrated that Latin Americans could in fact organize and effectively fight against Europe to achieve political, social, and economic independence. Later, in the immediate aftermath of independence, leadership in Latin America centered around the priorities of *caudillo* rulers; these "men on horseback" gained popularity and support by exploiting patron–client relationships, traditional patterns of authority, and the general collapse of order in the early nineteenth century.

The modern Latin American military structure was also born in the nineteenth century, and any discussion of contemporary military institutions in Latin America must consider their historic origins throughout the region. One of the most intriguing stories of military misstep, change, and development over time involves the Brazilian military, which suffered two serious setbacks in the nineteenth century. First, there was the disastrous War of the Triple Alliance (Brazil, Uruguay, and Argentina versus Paraguay), which lasted from 1865 until 1870. This war provided a wake-up call to the Brazilian military, as tiny Paraguay valiantly fought off two bordering giants for almost five years. Paraguay was eventually defeated, and lost nearly all of its adult male population in the process. Second, after four arduous campaigns, the Brazilian military finally defeated the northeastern rebel community of Canudos. Some 10,000 residents died in the final assault in 1897. The Canudos debacle clearly demonstrated the military's inability to effectively "dominate" the entire Brazilian landmass.

Change and modernization began to take shape during the early twentieth century in the Brazilian military structure, especially after 1922, when the *tenentes* movement showed the discontent of younger officers who were fed up with corruption, the ruling oligarchy, and extreme hierarchy in the military structure. These younger "lieutenants" demanded more respect, better and more modern equipment, and believed that they were best equipped to defend Brazil from external or internal enemies. Luiz Carlos Prestes, a junior officer and member of the Communist Party, led a military column of more than 1,000 through the Brazilian interior from 1924 to 1927, evading the military and highlighting (once again) the weakness of the Brazilian military structure.

The Latin American military has historically played the role of power broker: militaries move into power, ostensibly to protect and save the fatherland from inept civilian rulers. This was the case in 1929 with the onset of the worldwide economic depression, which had devastating consequences for Latin American societies. Military rulers stepped in to restore order in both Argentina and Peru, and throughout the region. Getúlio Vargas took power in Brazil with strong backing from the military. A group of petty tyrants (most rising up through their respective military ranks) emerged in Central America and the Caribbean, including the Somoza family in Nicaragua, Jorge Ubico in Guatemala, Rafael Trujillo in the Dominican Republic, and Maximiliano Hernández Martínez in El Salvador.

The military interventions of the latter half of the twentieth century were a continuation of a trend established in the early days of the nineteenth century. The Brazilian military took power away from civilians in 1964 and ruled until 1985. The Argentine military ruled from 1966 to 1973, and again from 1976 until 1983. Some of the worst human rights abuses in modern Latin American history were recorded during this second intervention. After 1976, the Argentine army spoke reverently of the *patria;* to defend "the fatherland," they attacked students, members of leftist political organizations, persons of Jewish decent, intellectuals, and journalists. They called their campaign of terror *el proceso* ("the process") but others referred to it simply as *la guerra sucia* or "the dirty war." Some 20,000 Argentines were "disappeared" during an eight-year period.

In Chile, General Augusto Pinochet took power in a military coup on September 11, 1973, overthrowing the democratically elected government of Salvador Allende. His military intervention broke significantly with Chilean history, which had recorded relative stability and democratic procedure dating back to the late-nineteenth century. The brutality of the Pinochet regime shocked the world: between 10,000 and 12,000 Chileans were murdered during his military intervention and another one million Chileans fled the country, moving to exile in other countries in Latin America and Europe. Pinochet remained in office through 1990, when he lost a plebiscite. After a long legal battle, he was indicted at home in a protracted international legal struggle that has served as a sort of referendum on his seventeen-year rule.

BIBLIOGRAPHY

Feitlowitz, Marguerite. 1998. *A Lexicon of Terror: Argentina and the Legacies of Torture.* New York: Oxford University Press.

Kornbluh, Peter, ed. 2003. *The Pinochet File: A Declassified Dossier on Atrocity and Accountability.* New York: The New Press.

Levine, Robert M. 1992. *Vale of Tears.* Berkeley: University of California Press.

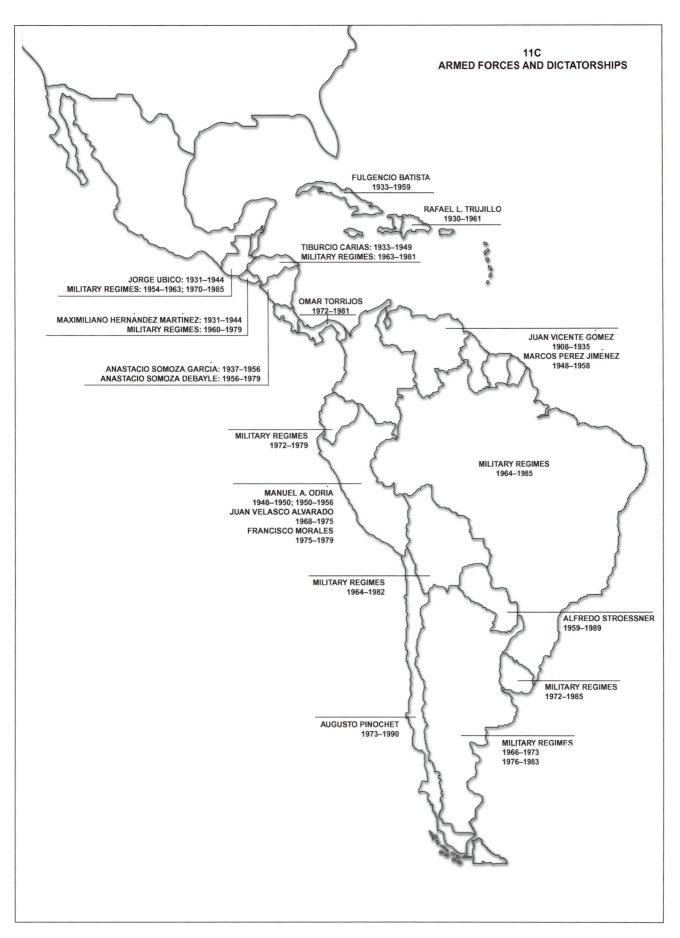

11C
ARMED FORCES AND DICTATORSHIPS

FULGENCIO BATISTA
1933–1959

RAFAEL L. TRUJILLO
1930–1961

TIBURCIO CARIAS: 1933–1949
MILITARY REGIMES: 1963–1981

JORGE UBICO: 1931–1944
MILITARY REGIMES: 1954–1963; 1970–1985

MAXIMILIANO HERNÁNDEZ MARTÍNEZ: 1931–1944
MILITARY REGIMES: 1960–1979

OMAR TORRIJOS
1972–1981

JUAN VICENTE GÓMEZ
1908–1935
MARCOS PEREZ JIMENEZ
1948–1958

ANASTACIO SOMOZA GARCÍA: 1937–1956
ANASTACIO SOMOZA DEBAYLE: 1956–1979

MILITARY REGIMES
1972–1979

MILITARY REGIMES
1964–1985

MANUEL A. ODRÍA
1948–1950; 1950–1956
JUAN VELASCO ALVARADO
1968–1975
FRANCISCO MORALES
1975–1979

MILITARY REGIMES
1964–1982

ALFREDO STROESSNER
1959–1989

MILITARY REGIMES
1972–1985

AUGUSTO PINOCHET
1973–1990

MILITARY REGIMES
1966–1973
1976–1983

137

11D

Collapse of Democracy, Birth of Debt

The 1980s is generally referred to as "the lost decade" in Latin American history and political discourse due to the large-scale accumulation of debt and financial chaos of the 1970s and 1980s. The lost 1980s can only be understood by considering the collapse of democracy in key regions of Latin America during the 1960s, the oil shock of the early 1970s, a downturn in world prices paid for Latin American commodities, and expanding debt to creditors during the 1980s.

During the 1960s and 1970s, democratically elected governments were swept away, first in Brazil (1964), then two years later in Argentina. In 1968, a left-leaning military government took power in Peru and implemented sweeping reforms. The dramatic military coup in Chile in 1973 captured the attention of the world and ushered in seventeen years of rule by the ruthless and autocratic General Augusto Pinochet. Social scientists concocted the term "bureaucratic authoritarianism" to describe the new wave of anti-democratic regimes taking power in Latin America during this period. Military elites believed that they were best equipped, technically and morally, to organize and restructure societies in light of the political and economic complexities of the day. They sidelined civilians and stated that their political ambitions were short-term, and based primarily on patriotism, or service to the *patria*.

The Brazilian military moved into power on March 31, 1964, ousting the democratically elected João Goulart from the presidency. The military generals, supported by the United States, sought to restore economic stability and remained in power until 1985. While Brazil's overall economic growth during the late 1960s and 1970s was remarkable, this was overshadowed by high levels of inflation, growing social and economic disparities, the abuse of human rights, and the curtailment of civil liberties. The civilian government that took control in 1985 inherited serious and growing social and economic problems, including a foreign debt in excess of 100 billion dollars.

The Argentine military regime was by far the most repressive, particularly when the military returned to power in 1976 and ushered in a "dirty war," which disappeared about 20,000 Argentines. They finally left power in 1983, but only after the generals provoked a conflict in 1982 with Great Britain. The so-called Malvinas War (or Falklands War) represented a humiliating defeat for Argentina and led to the collapse of the military dictatorship.

On September 11, 1973, the Chilean military, with the assistance of the Nixon administration and the CIA, overthrew the democratically elected government of Salvador Allende Gossens. After his election in 1970, President Allende had implemented labor reform, wage and price controls, and nationalized key sectors of the Chilean economy. Middle-class urbanites, wealthy landowners, and industrialists cried foul. Together with key sectors of the military, these groups began planning for what they viewed as a necessary and inevitable coup. Allende, a legitimately elected leader, was killed in the presidential palace on September 11, thus foreshadowing the violence that would grip Chile over the next seventeen years.

With democracy in recess throughout the region, a new crisis loomed when the price of oil reached thirty dollars a barrel in 1973; this price hike precipitated a deep financial crisis in Latin America. Loans that had been made to Latin American nations for capital infrastructure development projects and industry were primarily "floating" rather than fixed interest rate loans. The world economic crisis of the early 1970s drove interest rates up, which meant that Latin American nations would spend increasing amounts of money to service the debt, resulting in deep cuts in social programs. The concurrent rise in social tension was met by stiff state-sponsored repression.

The debt crisis had devastating effects, particularly on the poor, the working, and middle classes. Inflation rates in Bolivia ran over 11,000 percent in 1985, making local currency essentially worthless. Throughout the region, domestic demand could not keep up with production, given that real wages were falling due to inflationary pressures. The Mexican government was forced to borrow heavily to support food subsidies, and by the middle of the 1980s, about 45 percent of the Mexican working-age population was unemployed or significantly underemployed. In Brazil, between 1970 and 2000, the national debt rose from 4 billion to 228 billion dollars. Total debt for the Latin American region reached 400 billion dollars by the middle of the 1980s. With GDP falling, on average, 8.3 percent per capita throughout Latin America during the 1980s, this decade truly represents a period of time that many Latin Americans would like to forget.

BIBLIOGRAPHY

Burns, E. Bradford, and Julie A. Charlip. 2002. *Latin America: A Concise Interpretive History.* 7th ed. Upper Saddle River, NJ: Prentice Hall.

Chasteen, John Charles. 2001. *Born in Blood and Fire: A Concise History of Latin America.* New York: W.W. Norton.

Eakin, Marshall. 1997. *Brazil: The Once and Future Country.* New York: St. Martin's Griffin.

Franko, Patrice M. 1999. *The Puzzle of Latin American Economic Development.* Lanham, MD: Rowman & Littlefield.

Skidmore, Thomas E., and Peter H. Smith. 2005. *Modern Latin America.* 6th ed. New York: Oxford University Press.

11D
COLLAPSE OF DEMOCRACY,
BIRTH OF DEBT
(EXTERNAL DEBT IN MILLIONS
OF U.S. DOLLARS)

MEXICO
1970 = 6,969
2000 = 157,038

CUBA
2000 = 10,961

DOMINICAN REPUBLIC
1970 = 360
2000 = 4,341

HONDURAS
1970 = 91
2000 = 3,110

HAITI
1970 = 43
2000 = 691

GUATEMALA
1970 = 159
2000 = 4,326

NICARAGUA
1970 = 203
2000 = 5,545

EL SALVADOR
1970 = 183
2000 = 3,761

VENEZUELA
1970 = 1,422
2000 = 38,744

PANAMA
1970 = 229
2000 = 7,285

COLOMBIA
1970 = 2,236
2000 = 33,485

COSTA RICA
1970 = 287
2000 = 4,483

ECUADOR
1970 = 364
2000 = 13,143

BRAZIL
1970 = 4,000
2000 = 228,000

PERU
1970 = 3,211
2000 = 28,411

BOLIVIA
1970 = 588
2000 = 2,747

PARAGUAY
1970 = 112
2000 = 2,950

CHILE
1970 = 2,977
2000 = 34,859

ARGENTINA
1970 = 5,810
2000 = 154,961

URUGUAY
1970 = 363
2000 = 8,204

11E

Drug Trafficking and Informal Markets

The illegal production and exportation of narcotics inflicted significant damage on Latin American economies, especially during the difficult decade of the 1980s. As economies floundered and both public debt and unemployment mounted in the region, Latin American "entrepreneurs" discovered that massive, quick profits could be achieved through the smuggling of drugs. The leading export market in the 1980s was the United States.

Growing crime and epidemic-level use of crack cocaine in U.S. cities led to increased debate on the "drug question" in the media and political establishment. President Ronald Reagan, bowing to political pressures, declared a "war" on drugs in early 1982. Subsequent U.S. administration policies stressing "supply-side" eradication programs tended to place the responsibility of America's drug problem on the shoulders of Latin Americans. However, Latin Americans saw the problem differently: they believed that the United States should spend its resources on curtailing the demand for drugs at home. This inability to agree on methodology and tactics has led to the squandering of billions of dollars, a war on drugs that has been lost, and fluctuating periods of tension between Washington policymakers and the citizens of Latin America.

Debt and economic downturn in Latin America pushed peasants to harvest coca leaves, especially in poverty-stricken areas of Peru and Bolivia, where the plant grows easily in cool, moist climates at higher elevations. In Bolivia, for example, two-thirds of all tin miners were laid off during the 1980s as the world price for tin collapsed. Unemployment levels rose about 14 percent in the formal sector between 1980 and 1986, while the number of families involved in the cultivation of coca (the informal sector) increased some 300 percent. Facing extreme poverty and starvation, out-of-work miners chose to plant and harvest coca, and in some areas of Bolivia the plants yielded four crops annually. During the 1980s, coca leaves harvested in Peru and Bolivia were transformed into a sort of paste that would be shipped to Colombia for final processing (i.e., the addition of chemicals, and other rudimentary chemical processes). In Medellín, Colombia—the central city of the Colombian drug trade—the operation generated about 28,000 jobs for unemployed and impoverished laborers, both skilled and unskilled. Of course, drug trafficking in Latin America had a negative effect overall for workers and the poor in the region: the wealth generated from the drug trade flowed into overseas banks and real estate, having only a marginal effect on structural and capital improvements in Bolivia, Peru, or Colombia. But revenues from the drug trade were enormous. Between 1980 and 1995, it is estimated that Colombia earned 36 billion dollars in drug money, representing 5 percent of GDP during that period. Most of the profits from the drug trade remained in the United States or Europe.

Drug trafficking drew attention to the power and importance of "informal markets," or the informal sector, in Latin America and other places in the developing world. In November 1986, the Peruvian economist Hernando De Soto published *El otro sendero* (The Other Path), in which he outlined the importance and impact of the informal sector in his native Peru. De Soto described the economic activity of individuals who were itinerant street vendors, day laborers, domestic servants, and migrant agricultural workers; the author noted their primacy in making the Peruvian economy function, but, since these workers operated "off the books," their work was not recorded, taxed, or recognized by "official" society. So much of the work in Peru (and by extension in Latin America) was tied to the informal sector, according to De Soto, that official government statistics on GDP, income, and government spending were impossible to calculate. This made government planning all but impossible. De Soto claimed in his work that 60 percent of all "work" in Peru belonged to the informal sector, and stressed the need to acknowledge this force in future state planning.

Across Latin America during the 1980s, the informal sector grew rapidly—by more than 30 percent—due to the economic crisis and growing poverty throughout the region that forced workers to seek employment outside of the more traditional, diminishing formal sector. Presently, in some places in Latin America, the informal sector employs more than 50 percent of the entire working-age population. This sector also tends to be dominated by impoverished urban, unskilled laborers. In Guatemala, more than 90 percent of the working poor are employed in the informal sector.

The increase in drug trafficking from Latin America and the rapid growth of the informal economic sector are related phenomena and suggest structural problems in the region. Weak central governments and outdated, indifferent taxation policies and procedures significantly facilitated the production and shipment of illegal narcotics and the massive expansion of an informal economic sector. The push for neoliberal reforms in the region, beginning in the 1980s and continuing to the present, was designed to bring more order (and less "informality") to Latin American economies, largely through privatization of key, government-controlled sectors of the economy. However, illegal narcotics continue to flow from Latin America, and neoliberal policies, which have eliminated hundreds of thousands of jobs in Latin America, have actually pushed more people into the informal sector.

BIBLIOGRAPHY

De Soto, Hernando. 1987. *El otro sendero: La revolución informal.* 7th ed. Bogotá: Instituto Libertad y Democracia.

Franko, Patrice M. 1999. *The Puzzle of Latin American Economic Development.* Lanham, MD: Rowman & Littlefield.

Skidmore, Thomas E., and Peter H. Smith. 2005. *Modern Latin America.* 6th ed. New York, Oxford University Press.

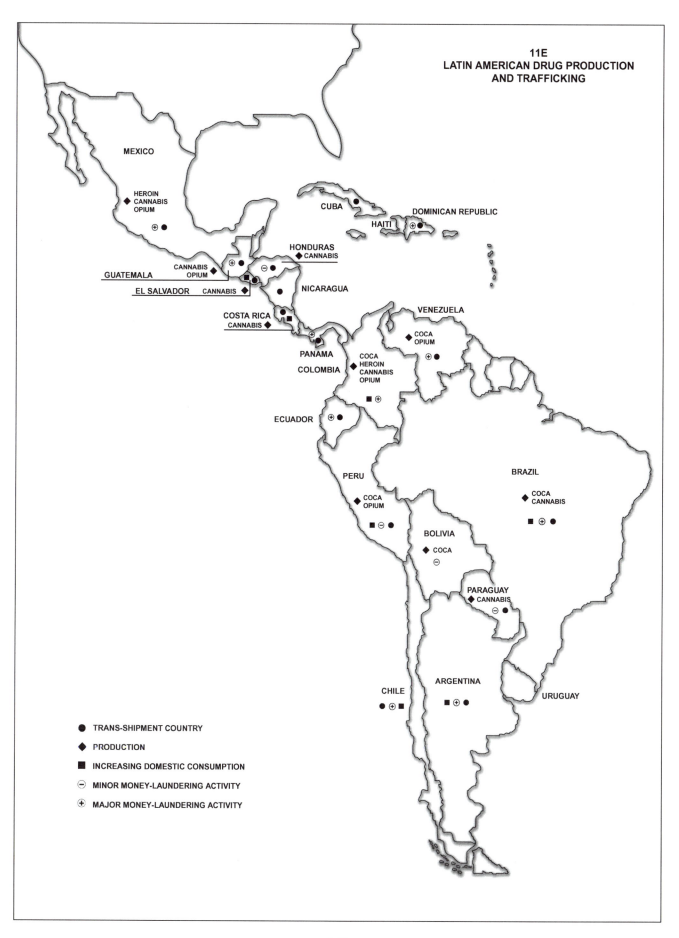

11E
LATIN AMERICAN DRUG PRODUCTION
AND TRAFFICKING

MEXICO

HEROIN
CANNABIS
OPIUM

CUBA

DOMINICAN REPUBLIC

HAITI

HONDURAS
CANNABIS

CANNABIS
OPIUM

GUATEMALA

EL SALVADOR   CANNABIS

NICARAGUA

COSTA RICA
CANNABIS

VENEZUELA

COCA
OPIUM

PANAMA

COLOMBIA

COCA
HEROIN
CANNABIS
OPIUM

ECUADOR

PERU

BRAZIL

COCA
OPIUM

COCA
CANNABIS

BOLIVIA

COCA

PARAGUAY
CANNABIS

ARGENTINA

CHILE

URUGUAY

● TRANS-SHIPMENT COUNTRY

◆ PRODUCTION

■ INCREASING DOMESTIC CONSUMPTION

⊖ MINOR MONEY-LAUNDERING ACTIVITY

⊕ MAJOR MONEY-LAUNDERING ACTIVITY

11F

Education Compared by Country

Limited access to education in Latin America has contributed to highly skewed patterns of economic and social development, as educational opportunities in the region have never adequately met societal needs or demand. Even when education was available, controversy over management and implementation of the system rendered it incapable of reaching the majority of the population.

During the colonial period, private education was sponsored primarily by the Roman Catholic Church, which fought tenaciously for the exclusive right of overseeing education on the continent. Jesuit priests constructed some of the most important institutions of higher learning, but those schools were designated for the children of the elite. As such, they excluded the poor, the indigenous, and of course, the enslaved. In Mexico, church and state (literally) went to war over the issue of the church's role in society, including those issues dealing with education. In Brazil, children of the elite were sent to Coimbra in Portugal for training in the arts, letters, law, and medicine; the first university in Brazil was not established until the twentieth century. In Colombia, via a Concordat with Rome in 1887, Catholicism was established as the official state religion and education was handed over to the Roman Catholic Church. Public education, therefore, would contain strong elements of Catholic doctrine and teachings, and would come to deeply influence the historic and social trajectory of that country.

The twentieth century witnessed a greater emphasis on making education more accessible, due in large part to the Kennedy administration's focus on education in Latin America and the Alliance for Progress. In terms of education, the Alliance proposed increasing the school enrollment rate from 6 percent to 9 percent, so that all of the projected 85 million school-age children would be enrolled in primary school by 1977. However, the Alliance never solved the problems of education in Latin America. It set clear but unattainable goals. While new schools were built in the region, bureaucratic and administrative entanglements in Washington, together with miscalculations of birthrates and a misunderstanding of the power of hierarchy and tradition in Latin America, doomed the ambitious goals of the Alliance from the program's earliest days.

While it is difficult, if not impossible, to prove causation between a lack of education and vast inequalities in the distribution of wealth and resources in Latin America, it is clear that the two phenomena are related. Taking into account the huge disparities in wealth within and among Latin American nations, especially notable in Brazil, Colombia, Guatemala, and Paraguay, it is not surprising that education continues to elude most citizens in Latin America.

Rural and indigenous persons have always been at a disadvantage in terms of access to formal education. Two out of every five children in rural areas in Latin America fail to finish primary school, compared to one in six of their urban counterparts. During the 1990s, this disparity only shrank in three countries: Chile, Honduras, and Mexico. Since education is still considered an important determinant of quality of life, limited access to education for the majority means that children still inherit the poverty of their parents.

At a recent meeting in Cochabamba, Bolivia, education ministers adopted a set of standards designed to improve education and educational access in the region. They declared that teacher training must improve and called for more participation of civil society in public education. These leaders advocated that education be seen as a fundamental human right. Yet money looms as the primary obstacle in effecting lasting educational change in the region, and the Cochabamba Declaration could neither enforce its goals nor provide the needed funds.

Figures from select countries in 1998 suggest both bright spots and inadequacies in Latin American educational systems and structures. Argentina identified 97 percent of its population as literate and spent 4.1 percent of GDP on education. Bolivia, with a wide disparity of literacy according to gender (91 percent for men, 78 percent for women) spent 5.6 percent of GDP on education. Cuba, with nearly equal rates of literacy for men and women (97 and 96 respectively) spent 6.7 percent of GDP on education. In the Cuban case, the revolution of 1959 dramatically focused attention on affording every citizen education; illiteracy was virtually eliminated within the first three years of the revolution. By contrast, Guatemala was spending only 1.8 percent of its GDP on education in 1998, and literacy rates there are among the lowest on the continent, with 75 percent of males and 60 percent of females counted as literate.

Larger allocations to train teachers might also contribute to educational improvement in the region. Argentina and Cuba, with two of the highest literacy rates in Latin America, have committed more resources to teacher training (as a percentage of GDP) than other countries in the region: each country counts about one teacher per fifty-nine citizens.

BIBLIOGRAPHY

Levinson, Jerome, and Juan de Onís. 1970. *The Alliance That Lost Its Way.* Chicago: Quadrangle Books.
United Nations. Annual Education Survey. United Nations Educational, Scientific and Cultural Organization (UNESCO). 1998. UNESCO Institute for Statistics and the Organization for Economic Cooperation and Development (OECD). Available at ww.unesdoc.unesco.org.
———. 2001. "Education Statistics 2001: Latin American and Caribbean Regions Report." *UNESCO Institute for Statistics.* Available at www.uis.unesco.org.

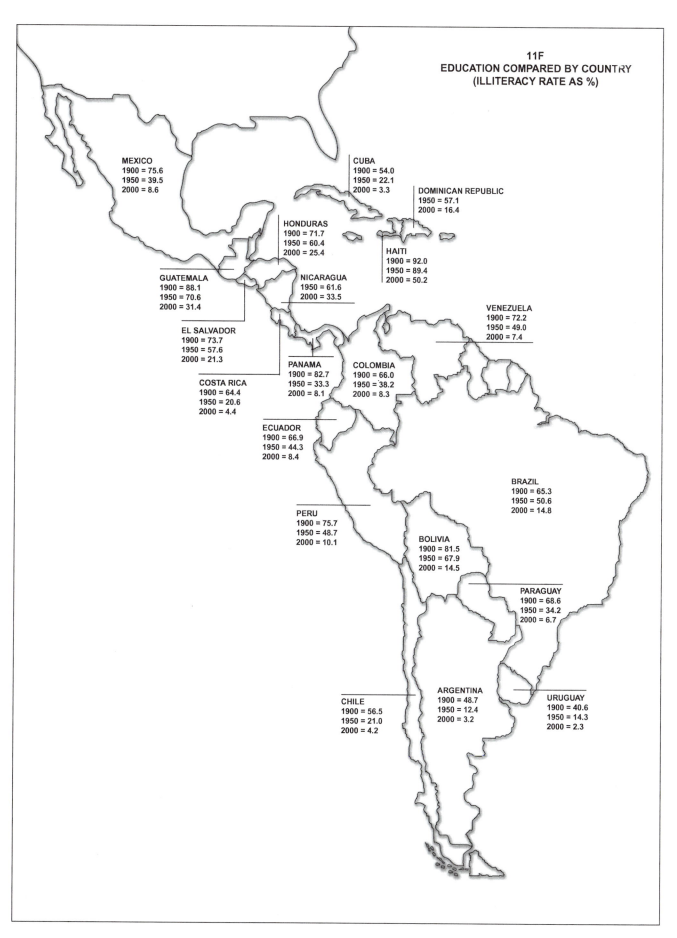

11F
EDUCATION COMPARED BY COUNTRY
(ILLITERACY RATE AS %)

MEXICO
1900 = 75.6
1950 = 39.5
2000 = 8.6

CUBA
1900 = 54.0
1950 = 22.1
2000 = 3.3

DOMINICAN REPUBLIC
1950 = 57.1
2000 = 16.4

HONDURAS
1900 = 71.7
1950 = 60.4
2000 = 25.4

HAITI
1900 = 92.0
1950 = 89.4
2000 = 50.2

GUATEMALA
1900 = 88.1
1950 = 70.6
2000 = 31.4

NICARAGUA
1950 = 61.6
2000 = 33.5

VENEZUELA
1900 = 72.2
1950 = 49.0
2000 = 7.4

EL SALVADOR
1900 = 73.7
1950 = 57.6
2000 = 21.3

PANAMA
1900 = 82.7
1950 = 33.3
2000 = 8.1

COLOMBIA
1900 = 66.0
1950 = 38.2
2000 = 8.3

COSTA RICA
1900 = 64.4
1950 = 20.6
2000 = 4.4

ECUADOR
1900 = 66.9
1950 = 44.3
2000 = 8.4

BRAZIL
1900 = 65.3
1950 = 50.6
2000 = 14.8

PERU
1900 = 75.7
1950 = 48.7
2000 = 10.1

BOLIVIA
1900 = 81.5
1950 = 67.9
2000 = 14.5

PARAGUAY
1900 = 68.6
1950 = 34.2
2000 = 6.7

CHILE
1900 = 56.5
1950 = 21.0
2000 = 4.2

ARGENTINA
1900 = 48.7
1950 = 12.4
2000 = 3.2

URUGUAY
1900 = 40.6
1950 = 14.3
2000 = 2.3

11G

Nobel Laureates and Other Significant Persons in Culture and Science

Latin America has produced some of the most prominent painters, writers, philosophers, intellectuals, and theologians in the world. Fifteen Nobel Prize laureates have called Latin America home; that prize has been awarded to Latin Americans for the promotion of peace, literary accomplishments, medicine, and chemistry. A cultural mapping of Latin America reveals a legacy of achievement despite a history marked by censorship, limited education, social and racial hierarchy, and an elite-sponsored perception that culture only develops in Europe or other "advanced" societies.

In the sixteenth century, the Peruvian Garcilaso de la Vega chronicled Inca society before the arrival of the Spaniards, and his work is still widely quoted today. One of the most creative and innovative poets of the seventeenth century was Sister Juana Inés de la Cruz, a Mexican woman considered by many the greatest baroque poet ever to have lived. Father Francisco Clavijero, during the eighteenth century, wrote a book entitled *History of Ancient Mexico,* published in 1781, which was designed to teach the history, geography, and culture of Mexico. This book helped support the slowly emerging post-Enlightenment idea that Mexico could in fact survive on its own without the tutelage of Spain.

The Latin American independence leader Simón Bolívar stands out as a military strategist and political philosopher without equal during the late eighteenth and early nineteenth centuries. Other significant figures during the nineteenth century in Latin America include the Argentine Domingo F. Sarmiento, who wrote the influential political piece *Civilization and Barbarism* (1845) and José Mármol, who authored *Amalia,* the great romantic novel of the nineteenth century in Argentina. Three significant modernist writers emerged in Latin America during the nineteenth century, each credited with redefining his country's literary traditions: Joaquim María Machado de Assis was a realist writer who rarely traveled outside his native city of Rio de Janeiro. José Martí was the great Cuban essayist, revolutionary, and political activist martyred by the Spaniards in 1895. Rubén Darío's powerful poetry expressed the anger and humiliation of United States military interventions in his native Nicaragua.

World War I changed Latin Americans' uncritical reliance on Europe for cultural and educational standards. In Mexico and Peru, *indigenista* literature challenged Latin Americans to look toward their own traditions and history for inspiration and meaning: Mexican intellectual (and minister of education in the early 1920s) José Vasconcelos's *La raza cósmica* offered such an inward glance. Later, in Peru, José María Arguedas, Ciro Alegría, and César Vallejo would define a national literature that acknowledged and celebrated Peru's Indian culture rather than ignoring it.

The twentieth century saw a remarkable flourishing of Latin American art, literature, and music. The muralist movement in Mexico inspired a generation of visual artists all over the Americas: Diego Rivera, David Alfaro Siqueiros, and José Clemente Orozco are just a few of the important Mexican painters from the early twentieth century; moved by the Mexican revolution, Rivera and others sought to "paint" the history of Mexico on public buildings as an innovative, didactic tool.

In the literary boom of the 1960s in Latin America, associated with the medium of stream-of-conscious technique and the exploration of dreams and fantasy, writers such as Mexico's Carlos Fuentes, Argentina's Julio Cortázar, Cuba's Alejo Carpentier, Chile's Pablo Neruda, Guatemala's Miguel Ángel Asturias, Brazil's Nélida Piñon, Peru's Mario Vargas Llosa, and Colombia's Gabriel García Márquez made major contributions to world literature. Neruda, Asturias, García Márquez, and the Chilean poet Gabriela Mistral have all been recognized by the Nobel Academy.

Music and dance comprise a vital part of Latin American culture. The Cuban Ernesto Lecuona was an important composer of *boleros,* romantic and slow-paced piano pieces that most likely originated in Cuba. Classical composers who have received critical acclaim include the Argentine Alberto Ginastera and Brazil's Heitor Villa-Lobos; they are regarded throughout the world for their original work that interprets, lyrically, their country's traditions and history.

The Latin American continent, throughout its history, but especially during the nineteenth and twentieth centuries, has been devastated by civil conflicts, revolutions, outside intervention, and repressive military rule. Five Latin Americans have been awarded the Nobel Peace Prize; the most recent recipient was the Guatemalan Rigoberta Menchú Tum (1992), who won for her relentless efforts to expose—to the world—the brutal conflict in her native land during the 1970s and 1980s. Other Peace Prize recipients include Argentina's Carlos Saavedra Lamas and Adolfo Pérez Esquivel, Mexico's Alfonso García Robles, and Costa Rica's Oscar Arias Sánchez.

BIBLIOGRAPHY

Bethel, Leslie, ed. 1998. *A Cultural History of Latin America: Literature, Music, and the Visual Arts in the 19th and 20th Centuries.* Cambridge: Cambridge University Press.

Fuentes, Carlos. 1999. *The Buried Mirror: Reflections on Spain and the New World.* New York: Houghton Mifflin.

Schlessinger, Bernard S., and June H. Schlessinger, eds. 1996. *The Who's Who of Nobel Prize Winners, 1901–1995.* 3d ed. Phoenix: Oryx.

11G
SOME OF LATIN AMERICA'S
CULTURAL AND SCIENTIFIC
FIGURES, TWENTIETH CENTURY

ALEJO CARPENTIER (L)
ERNESTO LECUONA (M)
JOSÉ MARTÍ (L)
JOSÉ LEZAMA LIMA (L)
NICOLÁS GUILLÉN (L)
CARLOS FINLAY (S)

OCTAVIO PAZ (NL)
DIEGO RIVERA (P)
FRIDA KAHLO (P)
CARLOS FUENTES (L)
JUAN RULFO (L)
JUAN O'GORMAN (P)
DAVID ALFARO SIQUEIROS (P)
AGUSTÍN LARA (M)
MANUEL M. PONCE (M)
CARLOS CHÁVEZ (M)
ALFONSO GARCÍA ROBLES (NP)

FERNANDO BOTERO (P)
GABRIEL GARCÍA MÁRQUEZ (NL)
GERMÁN ESPINOZA (L)
JULIO GARAVITO (S)

OSCAR ARIAS (NP)

MIGUEL A. ASTURIAS (NL)
RIGOBERTA MENCHÚ (NP)
AUGUSTO MONTERROSO (L)

ARMANDO REVERON (P)
RÓMULO GALLEGOS (L)
ARTURO MICHELENA (P)
ARTURO USLAR PIETRI (L)
BARUJ BERNACERRAF (NS)

RUBÉN DARÍO (L)
ERNESTO CARDENAL (L)

ROBERTO LEWIS (P)
RICARDO MIRÓ (L)

OSWALDO WAYASAMIN (P)
EDUARDO KINGMAN (P)
ENRIQUE TABARA (P)

CARLOS D. DE ANDRADE (L)
JORGE AMADO (L)
NÉLIDA PIÑON (L)
HEITOR VILLA-LOBOS (M)
OSCAR NIEMEYER (A)
LÚCIO COSTA (A)
ALBERTO SANTOS DUMONT (S)
CARLOS CHAGAS (S)

CÉSAR VALLEJO (L)
MARIO VARGAS LLOSA (L)
CIRO ALEGRÍA (L)
JOSÉ MARÍA ARGUEDAS (L)
ALFREDO BRYCE ECHENIQUE (L)
CARLOS MONJE (S)

JESÚS NIZAGASTI
(L)

AUGUSTO ROA
BASTOS (L)

GABRIELA MISTRAL (NL)
PABLO NERUDA (NL)
CLAUDIO ARRAU (M)
VICENTE HUIDOBRO (L)
ISABEL ALLENDE (L)
JOSÉ DONOSO (L)

MARIO BENEDETTI (L)

JORGE LUIS BORGES (L)
JULIO CORTÁZAR (L)
ADOLFO PÉREZ ESQUIVEL (NP)
ERNESTO SABATO (L)
ALBERTO GINASTERA (M)
MARIO BUNGE (S)
BERNARDO HOUSSAY (NS)
CESAR MILSTEIN (NS)
LUIS F. LELOIR (NS)
CARLOS SAAVEDRA LAMAS (NP)

NL: NOBEL LITERATURE
P: PAINTING
L: LITERATURE
NP: NOBEL PEACE
A: ARCHITECTURE
M: MUSIC
NS: NOBEL SCIENCE
S: SCIENCE

11H

Music of Latin America

The interaction of numerous cultures throughout Latin America's history produced a plethora of musical styles. Among the cultural strains, the traditional musics of indigenous, Iberian, and African cultures have been the most important in the development of folk music, which is best understood in terms of the relative degrees of influence from each cultural contribution.

Little is known about the music of pre-Columbian indigenous cultures, but most musical events seem to have been linked to religion or politics, featuring singing, dancing, and playing of instruments. Much music in traditional indigenous cultures still takes place in religious contexts, particularly shamanism.

Interaction between indigenous and Iberian music began with the earliest encounters between Native Americans and Europeans. Catholic missionaries set up schools for Native Americans in which European church music was taught; Indians soon made up the majority of musicians in some churches. Jesuit mission towns in South America were especially prominent in terms of musical acculturation. Secular Iberian music has also influenced current folk music, both in terms of instruments and genres. For instance, the Renaissance guitar developed into many characteristic variants throughout the area. The Spanish *romance,* a long epic ballad, provided the origins of the Mexican *corrido,* used originally to celebrate the exploits of revolutionary leaders and now to recount the adventures of narco-traffickers. Lyrical genres such as the Paraguayan *guarania* and the Mexican *son* are Iberian in style, as is the Paraguayan *polca,* despite the central European origin indicated by the name.

Some of the most African musical styles can be found in syncretic Afro-Brazilian and Afro-Cuban religions as well as in the Brazilian martial art/dance known as *capoeira,* all of which utilize African-derived instruments. Much secular music of African derivation is dance music, such as the Colombian *cumbia,* the Brazilian *samba,* the Cuban *huahuancó,* and the Puerto Rican *bomba.* Especially important in South America is the *zamba/cueca* complex, made up of various musical/dance styles known as *zamba* in Argentina, and *cueca, zambacueca,* or *zamacueca* in Chile, Argentina, and Bolivia. In Peru, it is now called the *marinera,* in honor of the Peruvian sailors who died in the War of the Pacific (1879–1883).

Folk music has been put to political use in a number of ways. The *nueva trova* movement, for example, made use of the traditional Cuban *trova* genre in support of the revolution of 1959. The *nueva trova* served as inspiration for the *nueva canción* movement that began in Chile in the mid-1960s, which incorporated Andean genres and musical instruments to invoke pan-Andean social and cultural unity in support of socialist ideology. Many musicians of the *música popular brasileira* movement incorporated themes of social and political protest as well. Music has also been used by the state for political purposes, with laws in some countries calling for certain percentages of radio music broadcasts to consist of folk music in order to promote a sense of musical nationalism.

Much of the Latin American commercially driven popular music, such as *salsa,* the popular Afro-Caribbean genre that draws on Cuban, Puerto Rican, and Dominican idioms, has its roots in folk music. Similarly, the *balada* can be seen as a continuation of the long-established pan-Hispanic, guitar-based romantic song embodied in the *bolero* and *canción.* Mexican *música ranchera* is the musical result of the mass migration of a rural population to urban areas, allowing former *campesinos* to cultivate a link to their roots through use of traditional folk musical styles and genres. Brazilian *bossa nova,* heavily influenced by American jazz, represents an adaptation of *samba* to a nightclub context. While Latin American rock has made inroads as a popular music, it has generally been more successful in Mexico and the Southern Cone of South America than elsewhere.

Several Latin American countries have been home to important art music composers, some of whom, especially up until about 1950, have drawn inspiration from the folk musics of their homelands. Mexico's Manuel Ponce incorporated Mexican folk idioms into romantic, impressionist, and neoclassical styles, and Carlos Chávez frequently made use of a primitivist and "Indianist" aesthetic. Many of Heitor Villa-Lobos's works draw in an eclectic fashion on his deep knowledge of rural Brazilian folk music and urban styles as well. Alberto Ginastera, while not always drawing directly from the folk music of his native Argentina, frequently wrote compositions that he maintained were characterized by a "pronounced Argentine accent," though he also made use of twelve-tone and expressionistic idioms. A number of composers turned to avant-garde experimental and electronic genres beginning in the 1960s. Though composers at the end of the twentieth and the beginning of the twenty-first centuries have made use of international models, they have transformed and incorporated them into the ongoing cultural synthesis that has operated for centuries in the music of Latin America.

BIBLIOGRAPHY

Béhague, Gerard. 1979. *Music in Latin America: An Introduction.* Englewood Cliffs, NJ: Prentice Hall.

Olsen, Dale, and Daniel Sheehy, eds. 1998. *The Garland Encyclopedia of World Music,* vol. 2, *South America, Mexico, Central America, and the Caribbean.* New York: Garland.

Stevenson, Robert. 1968. *Music in Aztec and Inca Territory.* Berkeley: University of California Press.

RANCHERA
SON JAROCHO
ARRIBEÑO
SON HUASTECO
CORRIDO
HUAPANGO
NORTEÑO
BANDA
JARABE

HUAHUANCO
TIMBA
GUAJIRA
DANZON
BOLERO
MAMBO
CHA-CHA-CHA
SON
BATA
RUMBA
HABANERA
CONGA
NUEVA TROVA
SALSA
MAMBO

SALSA
REGGAETON
BOMBA
DANZA
SEIS
PLENA

PUNTA
CHUMBA

RARA
COMPAS

MERENGUE
BACHATA
GAGA

CALIPSO

CALIPSO
SOCA

CONGO
TAMBORITO
MENTO
CALIPSO
PUNTO
DANZA

SALSA
PORRO
CUMBIA
VALLENATO
BAMBUCO
JOROPO
TORBELLINO
BUNDE
CHAMPETA

MÚSICA LLANERA
JOROPO
CALIPSO
GAITA
SANGEO

PASILLO
YARAVI
PASACALLE
BUNDE
TORBELLINO
BOMBA
CACHALLAPI
YUMBO

AXÉ MUSIC
SAMBA
AFOXE
BOSSA NOVA
CAPOEIRA MUSIC
MARACATU
CARIMBO
MPB (MÚSICA POPULAR BRASILEIRA)
XOTE
COCO
SAMBA-REGGAE
FREVO

HUAYNO
CHICHA
YARAVÍ
LANDO
MARINERA
VALS CRIOLLO
TONDERO
VIDALA

HUAYNO
SAYA
CUECA
TONADA
KALUYO
SICURI

GUARANIA
POLCA PARAGUAYA

CUECA
TONADA
VALS CHILENO
CACHIMBO
MAPUCHINA
NUEVA CANCION
TROTE

TANGO
CHACARERA
CHAMAME
MILONGA
ZAMBA
VIDALA

CANDOMBE
MURGA
MILONGA
TANGO

12
REVOLUTIONARY MOVEMENTS

12A

The Mexican Revolution

Porfirio Díaz ascended to the Mexican presidency in 1877, and his thirty-three-year rule—known as *el porfiriato*—was marked by rapid economic growth at the expense of democratic principles. He opened up the country to foreign investors and land speculators, thus replacing traditional community-based landholding patterns with private ownership. By 1910, some 90 percent of rural Mexicans had lost their land to speculators and private contractors. Wages, if paid at all to rural Mexicans, remained steady throughout the nineteenth century, but the price of food staples (corn, beans, chili peppers) doubled. Many poor Mexicans, forced off their lands, began working for the large *hacendados,* or landowners, in conditions that resembled those of medieval Europe. Public dislike and distrust of Díaz began to bubble over during the first decade of the new century, and some began calling for a revolution.

The Mexican Revolution would change the course of Mexican history. From 1910 to about 1920, about 1.5 million Mexicans died as a result of the revolution and a million more fled north to the United States. The Mexican Revolution created legendary figures such as Emiliano Zapata and Doroteo Arango (nom de guerre Pancho Villa).

One of the chief architects of the revolution was the mild-mannered jurist Francisco Madero, who called for authentic elections in 1910. Educated in Paris and Berkeley, the young Madero viewed Mexico's political structure as woefully out of step with the Western world. Díaz, however, was unwilling to relinquish power. On June 21, 1910, farcical elections returned the eighty-year-old dictator to the presidency.

Carlos Fuentes has characterized the Mexican Revolution as a series of smaller revolutions—one in the north, another in the south, and one at the center of the country, each with its own objective, personality, and leadership structure. The northern armies, organized under the leadership of Pancho Villa, were comprised of lower-middle-class cowboys, workers, small land holders, and those who wanted a greater share in the wealth of Mexico—wealth which flowed disproportionately to the few, to foreign business, and mining interests. Villa's army, closely connected in geography to the United States, saw firsthand how political and social forces in the United States condemned Mexicans to poverty and powerlessness. They were willing to fight for a greater share of Mexico's immense wealth. In the southern state of Morelos, a vastly different leader emerged—Emiliano Zapata. A horse trainer and a man with a clear sense of the injustices of landholding patterns and legal structures (which favored the wealthy and their foreign allies), Zapata organized peasants in the south to fight for *tierra y libertad,* land and liberty.

Porfirio Díaz did resign, on May 25, 1911, after an organized and determined insurgency squeezed the capital city from the north and south. But the revolution, in 1911, had barely begun. Three years after the fall of the old guard, in 1914, the revolution turned on itself, reflecting—to some degree—the conflicting ideas and ambitions of the various leaders.

After 1914, Zapata returned to the south to govern, and Morelos operated independently from the central government, reflecting local traditions, customs, and priorities. Yet provincial independence from central Mexico ran counter to the plan for a strong, centralized government. Villa's northern army was defeated by the central forces in 1915, and Morelos's independence soon came to an abrupt end.

The Constitution of 1917 had a salutary effect and its implementation suggested that the revolution had turned an important corner. Venustiano Carranza, who worked to consolidate the revolution at the center, presided over the drafting of a constitution that limited the power of the church, returned lands seized illegally to the *ejidos,* or local communities (Article 27), and guaranteed rights to urban laborers (Article 123).

Zapata was killed in April 1919 in an ambush, but his legacy lived on in southern Mexico. He was an innovative idealist who believed in the power of ordinary people to rule themselves. He preferred local government to national concerns, and the Morelos experiment in self-rule was, in the words of Carlos Fuentes, "sacrificed to greater Mexico, the dynamic, responsible, unscrupulous, centralized force that was taking shape around Carranza and his ambitious chieftains, Obregón and Calles."[1]

During the decade from 1910 to 1920, the U.S. government saw the violence to the south as destabilizing. There were two U.S. interventions in Mexico during the course of the revolution. The first occurred on April 21, 1914, when troops landed at Veracruz and occupied the city for several months. The second happened in 1916, when General John J. Pershing crossed into Mexico with 6,000 U.S. soldiers in pursuit of Pancho Villa; that expedition lasted about nine months, cost 130 million dollars, and was completely unsuccessful. Villa disappeared into the small towns of northern Mexico, and his tracks were covered by the local populace.

In 1920, the death of Carranza and the election of Álvaro Obregón to a four-year presidential term signified an end to the decade-long struggle that claimed the lives of so many Mexicans.

NOTE

1. Carlos Fuentes, *The Buried Mirror: Reflections on Spain and the New World* (Boston: Houghton Mifflin, 1999), pp. 305–306.

BIBLIOGRAPHY

Meyer, Michael C., William L. Sherman, and Susan M. Deeds. 2003. *The Course of Mexican History.* 7th ed. New York: Oxford University Press.
Womack, John, Jr. 1968. *Zapata and the Mexican Revolution.* New York: Vintage Books.

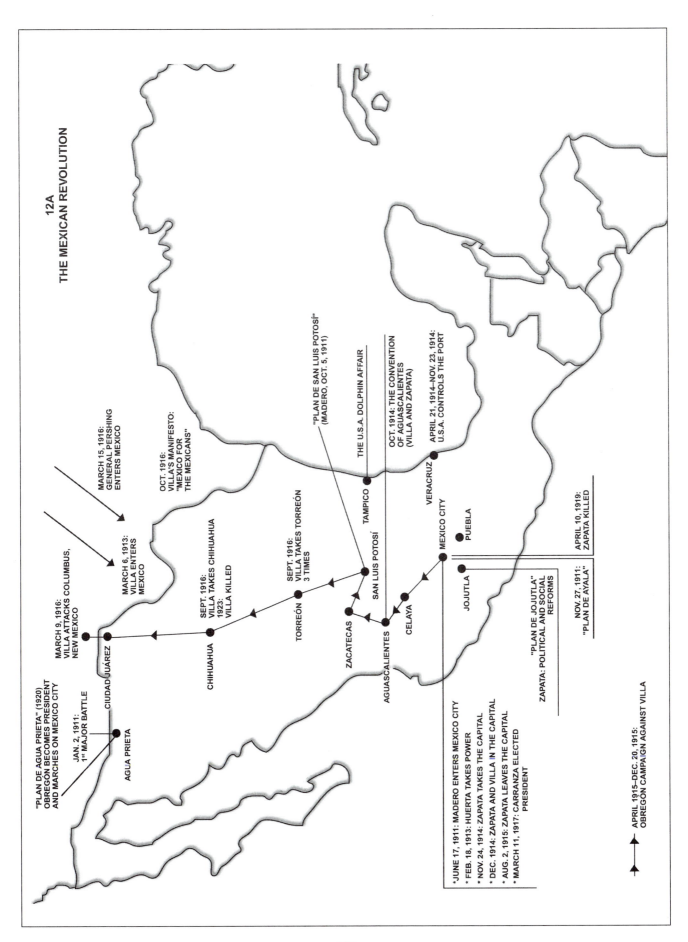

"PLAN DE AGUA PRIETA" (1920)
OBREGÓN BECOMES PRESIDENT
AND MARCHES ON MEXICO CITY

JAN. 2, 1911:
1st MAJOR BATTLE

AGUA PRIETA

MARCH 9, 1916:
VILLA ATTACKS COLUMBUS,
NEW MEXICO

MARCH 15, 1916:
GENERAL PERSHING
ENTERS MEXICO

MARCH 6, 1913:
VILLA ENTERS
MEXICO

OCT. 1916:
VILLA'S MANIFESTO:
"MEXICO FOR
THE MEXICANS"

CIUDAD JUÁREZ

CHIHUAHUA

SEPT. 1916:
VILLA TAKES CHIHUAHUA
1923:
VILLA KILLED

TORREÓN

SEPT. 1916:
VILLA TAKES TORREÓN
3 TIMES

ZACATECAS

AGUASCALIENTES

SAN LUIS POTOSÍ

"PLAN DE SAN LUIS POTOSÍ"
(MADERO, OCT. 5, 1911)

THE U.S.A. DOLPHIN AFFAIR

OCT. 1914: THE CONVENTION
OF AGUASCALIENTES
(VILLA AND ZAPATA)

TAMPICO

APRIL 21, 1914–NOV. 23, 1914:
U.S.A. CONTROLS THE PORT

VERACRUZ

CELAYA

MEXICO CITY

PUEBLA

JOJUTLA

NOV. 27, 1911:
"PLAN DE AYALA"

"PLAN DE JOJUTLA"
ZAPATA: POLITICAL AND SOCIAL
REFORMS

APRIL 10, 1919:
ZAPATA KILLED

*JUNE 17, 1911: MADERO ENTERS MEXICO CITY
* FEB. 18, 1913: HUERTA TAKES POWER
* NOV. 24, 1914: ZAPATA TAKES THE CAPITAL
* DEC. 1914: ZAPATA AND VILLA IN THE CAPITAL
* AUG. 2, 1915: ZAPATA LEAVES THE CAPITAL
* MARCH 11, 1917: CARRANZA ELECTED
            PRESIDENT

APRIL 1915–DEC. 20, 1915:
OBREGÓN CAMPAIGN AGAINST VILLA

12B

Bolivia and Guatemala: The Early 1950s

A secondary wave of revolutionary struggles spread through Latin America in the mid-twentieth century, the result of a combination of factors including: the emergence of populism, import-substituting economics, modernization, rural-urban migration, and a rising tide of unfulfilled expectations. These struggles were most clearly seen in Bolivia in the early 1950s and in Guatemala at about the same time period. The Cuban Revolution (1959) is outlined in the following chapter.

In Bolivia and Guatemala, the central concern involved an almost feudal land tenure system, the exploitation of workers in the most significant sectors of the export economy (tin in the case of Bolivia, agricultural products in Guatemala), and changes in government that favored workers while challenging outside mining and agricultural interests conducting business in Latin America. The stakes were high for all parties involved, and the United States tended to brand nationalist reformers in Latin America as troublemakers—or worse, communists.

Both revolutionary processes involved the nationalization of key components of the economies' export sectors. In April 1952, Bolivia's Víctor Paz Estenssoro created a governing body known as the MNR (National Revolutionary Movement); he had won, a year earlier, the presidential elections in a plurality and thus held a legitimate claim to the office of the presidency. Paz's goals included nationalization of the tin industry, but he convinced worried leaders in Washington that he was neither communist nor pro–Soviet Union. However, the nationalization of three important tin mines and land reforms directed to benefit the poor sent a contradictory message to key Washington policymakers. The mine owners were the famous "tin magnates," millionaire Bolivians who lived outside the country, mostly in Europe. Confused between Paz's words and actions but willing to tolerate him, the United States adopted a policy of "constructive engagement," making grants, loans, and technical assistance available to Bolivia as a way to encourage moderate reformers rather than more militant revolutionaries within the MNR. Although the United States would remain the largest export market for Bolivian tin, it had very little to lose in Bolivia's nationalization of key industries like tin because investment in Bolivia was minimal compared to other countries within the region.

In Guatemala, the situation was completely different. There, U.S. investment was vast and centered on the holdings of the United Fruit Company (UFCO, or *la frutera*). United Fruit operated as an enclave economy in Guatemala and in other Latin American nations including Honduras and Colombia. The same year that Paz assumed power in Bolivia, Guatemalan president Jacobo Arbenz (1950–1954) implemented a sweeping agrarian reform program designed to bring modernity to his country. The reform inevitably affected UFCO, which held more than half a million acres in the country. About 100,000 poor, landless families received land between 1952 and 1954 in a state-sponsored redistribution effort. Unlike Bolivia, where the nationalization efforts were tolerated, the Arbenz government in Guatemala threatened the sovereignty and land holdings of a powerful U.S. company. U.S. president Dwight D. Eisenhower decided to remove Arbenz, after pressure was applied by lobbyists and lawyers from UFCO. (The director of the CIA, Allen Dulles, and his brother, Secretary of State John Foster Dulles, had both worked for a New York law firm that represented UFCO.)

"Operation Success"—the code name for the plan to overthrow Arbenz—went into effect in May 1954, beginning with the dropping of pamphlets over the capital, Guatemala City. The second phase of Operation Success involved moving in a hand-picked successor, Carlos Castillo Armas, from Honduras with a hastily trained army to put pressure on the Arbenz government. Arbenz resigned rather than face a bloody battle in the streets of Guatemala City.

Though the Bolivian and Guatemalan "revolutions" occurred within a two-year period, there are fundamental differences between the movements, their eventual outcomes, the long-term effects on their respective societies, and relations with the United States. In Bolivia, U.S. presence and investment were minimal, and the Eisenhower government sought to "engage" the moderate Paz and his followers. After recognizing Paz, the United States lavished his regime with favorable trade agreements and military-economic aid. In Guatemala, where U.S. economic interests ran much deeper, Arbenz's relatively mild land reform plan frightened individuals at the top ranks of government in the United States. They took action, preferring to overthrow the reformist, nationalist Arbenz; land reform in Central America—where U.S. corporations had traditionally found a way to express their will—would not be tolerated, especially in the tense Cold War era. When Castillo Armas came to power in Guatemala in 1954, he immediately rounded up followers of the former president, murdered them, and annulled the 1952 land reform.

The secondary reformist-revolutionary wave in Latin America, most notably expressed by the nationalization of key components of the economies of Bolivia and Guatemala and the subsequent reactions of Latin American elites and the U.S. government, can be seen as a dress rehearsal for the larger, truly transformative revolution that would occur in Havana in 1959.

BIBLIOGRAPHY

Blasier, Cole. 1986. *The Hovering Giant: U.S. Responses to Revolutionary Change in Latin America, 1910–1985.* Pittsburgh: University of Pittsburgh Press.

Langley, Lester D. 1989. *America and the Americas: The United States in the Western Hemisphere.* Athens: University of Georgia Press.

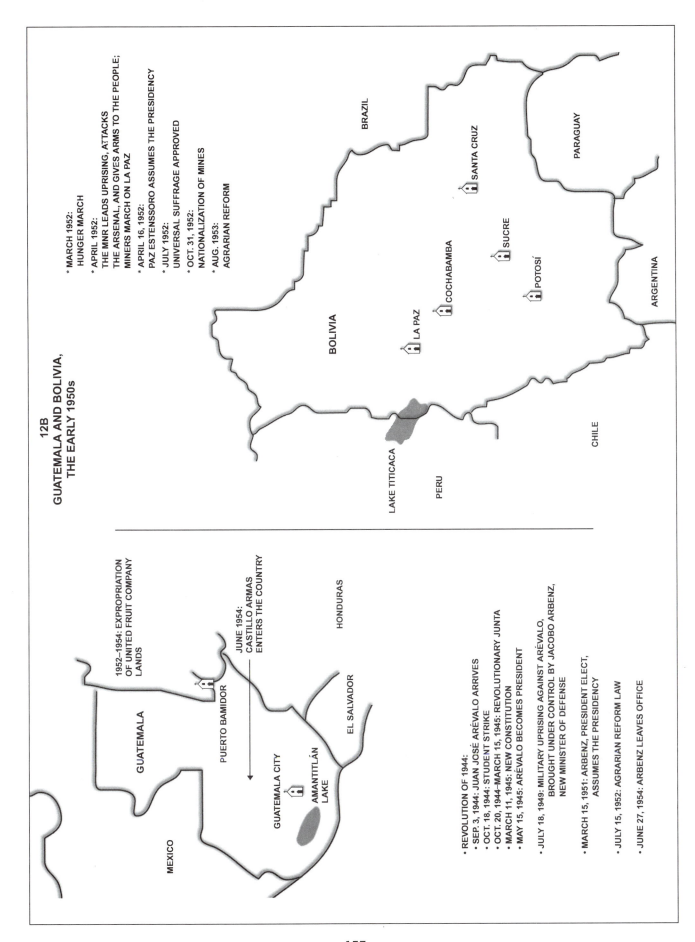

12B
GUATEMALA AND BOLIVIA, THE EARLY 1950s

BRAZIL

PARAGUAY

* MARCH 1952:
HUNGER MARCH

* APRIL 1952:
THE MNR LEADS UPRISING, ATTACKS
THE ARSENAL, AND GIVES ARMS TO THE PEOPLE;
MINERS MARCH ON LA PAZ

* APRIL 16, 1952:
PAZ ESTENSSORO ASSUMES THE PRESIDENCY

* JULY 1952:
UNIVERSAL SUFFRAGE APPROVED

* OCT. 31, 1952:
NATIONALIZATION OF MINES

* AUG. 1953:
AGRARIAN REFORM

SANTA CRUZ

COCHABAMBA

SUCRE

POTOSÍ

BOLIVIA

LA PAZ

ARGENTINA

LAKE TITICACA

PERU

CHILE

1952–1954: EXPROPRIATION
OF UNITED FRUIT COMPANY
LANDS

JUNE 1954:
CASTILLO ARMAS
ENTERS THE COUNTRY

MEXICO

GUATEMALA

PUERTO BAMIDOR

HONDURAS

EL SALVADOR

GUATEMALA CITY

AMANTITLÁN
LAKE

• REVOLUTION OF 1944:
  • SEP. 3, 1944: JUAN JOSÉ ARÉVALO ARRIVES
  • OCT. 18, 1944: STUDENT STRIKE
  • OCT. 20, 1944–MARCH 15, 1945: REVOLUTIONARY JUNTA
  • MARCH 11, 1945: NEW CONSTITUTION
  • MAY 15, 1945: ARÉVALO BECOMES PRESIDENT

• JULY 18, 1949: MILITARY UPRISING AGAINST ARÉVALO,
  BROUGHT UNDER CONTROL BY JACOBO ARBENZ,
  NEW MINISTER OF DEFENSE

• MARCH 15, 1951: ARBENZ, PRESIDENT ELECT,
  ASSUMES THE PRESIDENCY

• JULY 15, 1952: AGRARIAN REFORM LAW

• JUNE 27, 1954: ARBENZ LEAVES OFFICE

12c

Cuba, 1959

The Bolivian and Guatemalan revolutionary struggles of the early 1950s foreshadowed a more significant revolution, which occurred on the island of Cuba in 1959. The Cuban Revolution created deep structural changes and led to the termination of diplomatic relations between the United States and Cuba. The Latin American left enthusiastically embraced the Cuban Revolution, and leaders across the region vowed to imitate the tactics and rhetoric of the Cuban leader, Fidel Castro Ruíz.

That the United States would clash with Castro in the period after 1959 is not surprising given the strange historic relationship between Cuba and the United States. In both 1848 and 1854, the United States had attempted to purchase Cuba from Spain for 100 million dollars and 130 million dollars respectively. Unable to purchase the island outright, the United States undertook a new policy focused on investment in the country. U.S. investment in Cuba increased significantly after the First War of Cuban Independence (1868–1878), and by the mid-1880s, U.S. investment on the island totaled about 50 million dollars.

The nineteenth-century Cuban patriot, intellectual, and military strategist José Martí knew intimately how Cuban and U.S. interests intersected, and warned that a Cuba free of Spanish rule would face political and economic pressures from the emerging power to the north. Martí asked forebodingly, shortly before he was killed by the Spaniards in 1895, "Once the United States is in Cuba, who will get her out?" When the United States entered the Second War of Cuban Independence (1895–1898) and defeated Spain, ostensibly for the "liberation" of Cuba, it quickly became apparent that a war for Cuban independence had in fact become a war of American occupation and conquest, just as Martí had predicted. In 1901, the United States Congress passed the Platt Amendment, which dictated the terms of Cuban independence; the amendment allowed the United States to intervene militarily and politically in Cuban affairs and insisted that Cuban treaties with other sovereign nations be approved by Washington.

In addition to the subjugation of Cuban sovereignty with the passing of the Platt Amendment, world price fluctuations of sugar dramatically affected Cuba. The limitations to Cuban social and economic development became apparent, especially during the 1920s, when the price of sugar reached a high of 22.5 cents per pound before falling to .72 cents per pound after the U.S. stock market crash of 1929. Fulgencio Batista rose to power in the early 1930s, promising to return stability and order to Cuba. He would rule the country as a dictator until Castro's rise to power in 1959.

Cubans noted, particularly during the period from 1930 to the late 1950s, their precarious position in history—and geography. Proximity to the United States meant easy access to U.S. markets for Cuban sugar and a price subsidy to ensure that the price of Cuban sugar could compete with sugar prices from other regions of the world. However, Cubans were also aware that, while the average wage on the island was twice as high as the average wage in Latin America, Cubans earned about five times less than the average worker in the United States. Thus, a "revolution of rising expectations" ensued on the island. This, combined with a growing and dissatisfied middle-professional class and the increasingly arbitrary, violent rule of Batista, created a political crisis on the island in the 1950s. The door was now open for a revolutionary hero to emerge. A young, charismatic, upper-middle-class student named Fidel Castro pointed out the contradictory nature of Cuban history, and went so far as to suggest that the island had, in fact, never enjoyed legitimate "independence."

Batista, openly disdainful of dissenters, ordered Castro sent to prison and then into exile in Mexico. Castro returned to his home in 1956 on a boat called the *Granma*. Many in the landing party were captured or killed by Batista's forces, but Fidel and eleven others, including his brother Raúl and the Argentine physician Ernesto "Che" Guevara, escaped to the Sierra Maestra mountain range. From there, they waged a slow yet effective insurgency. Batista claimed that all of the insurgents had been killed, but when the American journalist Herbert Matthews published an interview with Fidel in 1957 on the front page of the *New York Times,* the world knew that Fidel and his men were alive and well.

Castro and *los barbudos* (the "bearded ones") marched triumphantly into Havana on January 6, 1959; they were greeted as heroes by cheering mobs of students, workers, and the urban middle class. The landed elite were less enthusiastic and many began to leave the island seeking refuge in nearby Florida. When Castro began nationalizing key sectors of the economy, including important national businesses and foreign-owned businesses and estates, the United States reacted with anger and apprehension. In fact, one of President Eisenhower's final acts as president in early 1961 was to cut off diplomatic relations with Havana. U.S.-Cuban relations remain, as of this writing, in a state reminiscent of the Cold War era. And though political freedoms and democratic elections do not really exist in Castro's Cuba, the revolution has improved social conditions and educational opportunities for the vast majority of citizens on the island.

BIBLIOGRAPHY

Matthews, Herbert L. 1961. *The Cuban Story.* New York: George Braziller.
Pérez, Louis A., Jr. 1995. *Cuba: Between Reform and Revolution.* 2d ed. New York: Oxford University Press.

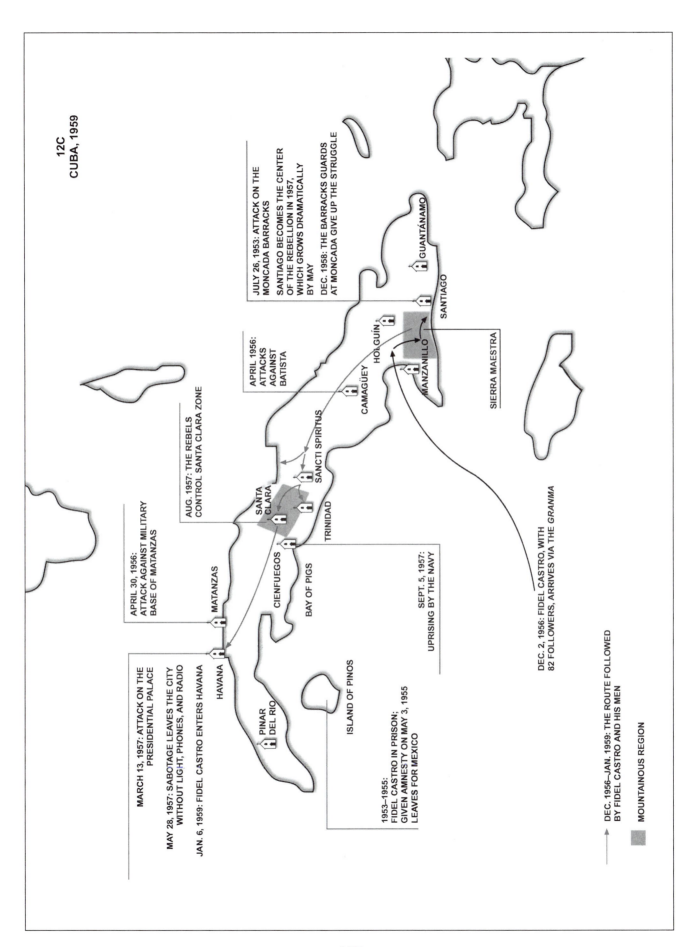

**12C
CUBA, 1959**

MARCH 13, 1957: ATTACK ON THE
PRESIDENTIAL PALACE

MAY 28, 1957: SABOTAGE LEAVES THE CITY
WITHOUT LIGHT, PHONES, AND RADIO

JAN. 6, 1959: FIDEL CASTRO ENTERS HAVANA

APRIL 30, 1956:
ATTACK AGAINST MILITARY
BASE OF MATANZAS

AUG. 1957: THE REBELS
CONTROL SANTA CLARA ZONE

APRIL 1956:
ATTACKS
AGAINST
BATISTA

JULY 26, 1953: ATTACK ON THE
MONCADA BARRACKS

SANTIAGO BECOMES THE CENTER
OF THE REBELLION IN 1957,
WHICH GROWS DRAMATICALLY
BY MAY

DEC. 1958: THE BARRACKS GUARDS
AT MONCADA GIVE UP THE STRUGGLE

GUANTÁNAMO

SANTIAGO

SIERRA MAESTRA

SANTA
CLARA

SANCTI SPIRITUS

CAMAGÜEY

HOLGUÍN

MANZANILLO

TRINIDAD

CIENFUEGOS

BAY OF PIGS

MATANZAS

HAVANA

PINAR
DEL RIO

ISLAND OF PINOS

SEPT. 5, 1957:
UPRISING BY THE NAVY

DEC. 2, 1956: FIDEL CASTRO, WITH
82 FOLLOWERS, ARRIVES VIA THE *GRANMA*

1953–1955:
FIDEL CASTRO IN PRISON;
GIVEN AMNESTY ON MAY 3, 1955
LEAVES FOR MEXICO

DEC. 1956–JAN. 1959: THE ROUTE FOLLOWED
BY FIDEL CASTRO AND HIS MEN

MOUNTAINOUS REGION

Guerrilla Movements: Che and Colombia

Fidel Castro's Cuban Revolution was met with euphoria in some places and terror elsewhere. The revolutionaries in Cuba believed that other Latin American regions were ripe for the revolutionary process, and plans were made to "export" the revolution. However, the Cuban revolutionaries and their Latin American allies never imagined the tenacity of the region's essentially conservative sociocultural structure, which stressed obedience and deference to figures of authority, and they miscalculated the extent to which the United States would support almost any and all counterrevolutionary measures in the region.

One of the twelve disciples of the Cuban Revolution was an Argentine physician named Ernesto "Che" Guevara. Guevara was transformed by his travels in South America in the early 1950s, witnessing the poverty, desperation, and humiliation of millions of Latin Americans who toiled in foreign-owned mines and on the plantations of traditional oligarchs. The poor passed their poverty and debt on to their children and never seemed able to break out of a perpetual cycle of misery. Guevara worked closely with the revolutionary government in Cuba for a time, but the Cuban Revolution was not large enough for the competing egos of Fidel and Che, prompting the latter to leave on a mission of exporting the revolution based on the *foci* theory. Heading for Bolivia, Guevara was convinced that revolutions could be "generated" based on the hard work and commitment of small groups of revolutionaries (the foci) planted and organized around the continent. From these foci, revolutionary ideas would flow out to the periphery, encouraging regional and national support among the people. Bolivia, though, was not Cuba. Certainly labor exploitation, racism, and neocolonialism prevailed in Bolivia, but Che Guevara, an Argentine physician-revolutionary with no real practical experience living among poor indigenous Aymara-speaking peoples, never developed a strong following there. The CIA, working closely with the Bolivian government, trained and equipped the elite counterinsurgency force (the Bolivian Rangers) that captured and killed Che in 1967.

While some Latin Americans viewed Che as a hopeless, out-of-touch romantic who died tragically and led many young Latin Americans to their deaths, others viewed him in a vastly different light—as a hero who died fighting for a noble cause. Che's legacy, and the revolutionary message, lived on in the region long after his death, and one place where this revolutionary sentiment took root was Colombia.

In 1962, the ELN (National Liberation Army) formed in Colombia. Today this group still operates in that country and is based primarily in the state of Santander, north of the capital city. And, while it has never operated on the national level, the revolutionaries did garner significant support among young Colombians, particularly during the 1960s. The ELN formed for reasons unique to Colombia's history, though certainly the movement was inspired by Fidel Castro's successful revolution in Havana.

Colombian elites, in the late 1950s, designed a "power sharing" arrangement that allowed the two main political parties (the Liberals and Conservatives) to alternate power every four years for a total period of twenty years. This arrangement displeased many Colombians, because it essentially eliminated or shut out any and all dissenting political opinions. And nowhere was this displeasure more discernable than among students in the universities. In protest of the elitist power-sharing plan, some students in Bogotá took to the mountains in support of a more equitable political arrangement.

The most famous recruit of the ELN was the Roman Catholic priest, Camilo Torres Restrepo, who joined the organization in October 1965 and was killed in combat against the Colombian army on February 15, 1966. Whereas some Colombians viewed him as a naïve opportunist, many saw "Padre Camilo" as a martyred hero who was willing to die in order to create a more inclusive, democratic, and just Colombia.

Later, in 1966, another revolutionary movement, the FARC (Revolutionary Armed Forces of Colombia), organized and still operates in Colombia today, with an estimated 12,000 insurgents in the field. The group has never officially "taken" power in the country; rather it has always chosen to function as an insurgency, fighting from within the borders of Colombia's complex geography. Throughout its existence, the FARC has been primarily an agrarian movement, growing out of the failed agrarian struggles of the 1930s and 1940s. These conflicts culminated in a decade-long undeclared civil war (of the 1950s) known simply as *la violencia*—The Violence. *La violencia* took the lives of 200,000 citizens—mostly peasants—and altered the course of Colombia's twentieth-century history; it suggested that state power might yield to armed vigilante groups who exerted local "justice" on a stage the size of the Colombian nation. Today, the FARC is widely discredited in Colombia. The group has lost most of its support from urban intellectuals, and its ideology seems to have shrunk to the collection of profit through extortion, kidnapping, and protection of the illegal cultivation of coca and other crops.

The road from Fidel's revolution to the revolutionary processes of the 1960s passed through many regions of Latin America. Revolutionaries were met with severe repression by national governments, and achieved national success in one Latin American country, Nicaragua in 1979.

BIBLIOGRAPHY

Bergquist, Charles, Ricardo Peñaranda, and Gonzalo Sánchez G. 2001. *Violence in Colombia: 1990–2000.* Wilmington, DE: SR Books.

Pérez, Louis A., Jr. 1988. *Cuba: Between Reform and Revolution.* 2d ed. New York: Oxford University Press.

Safford, Frank, and Marco Palacios. 2002. *Colombia: Fragmented Land, Divided Society.* New York: Oxford University Press.

12D
GUERRILLA MOVEMENTS
IN LATIN AMERICA
AND FOUNDING DATES

EJÉRCITO
REVOLUCIONARIO
POPULAR
1996

AGRUPACIÓN POLÍTICA 14 DE JUNIO 1959

MACHETEROS
1978

EGP
(EJERCITO GUERRILLERO
DE LOS POBRES) 1970s
URNG
(UNIDAD REVOLUCIONARIA
NACIONAL DE GUATEMALA) 1982

FSLN
(FRENTE SANDINISTA PARA
LA LIBERACION NACIONAL) 1961

FALN
(FUERZAS ARMADAS
DE LIBERACIÓN NACIONAL) 1962

FMLN
(FRENTE FARABUNDO MARTÍ PARA LA
LIBERACIÓN NACIÓNAL) 1980

ELN
(EJÉRCITO DE LIBERACIÓN NACIONAL) 1962
EPL
(EJÉRCITO POPULAR DE LIBERACIÓN) 1966
FARC
(FUERZAS ARMADAS REVOLUCIONARIAS
DE COLOMBIA) 1966
M-19
(MOVIMIENTO 19 DE ABRIL) 1974

ALFARO VIVE CARAJO! 1984

ACÃO LIBERTADORA NACIONAL
(NATIONAL LIBERATION ACTION) 1968

MRTA
(MOVIMIENTO REVOLUCIONARIO TUPAC AMARU) 1968

MIR
(MOVIMIENTO DE IZQUIERDA REVOLICIONARIA) 1965

TUPAMAROS 1960s

MONTONEROS
1968

157

The Sandinista Revolution and Central America

El Salvador, Guatemala, and Nicaragua experienced similar revolutionary struggles during the twentieth century (struggles that grew intense after about 1960), but Nicaragua stands with Cuba as the only country where armed revolution succeeded.

In El Salvador, a small clique of fourteen families owned most of the country's farm land and industry. Landless peasants who sought a greater share of profits and resources were dealt with brutally. The poor organized in the early 1930s against the large landowning families, especially after the international price for El Salvador's primary export, coffee, collapsed. In 1932, between 20,000 and 30,000 peasants were systematically executed by the Salvadoran armed forces in what became known as "La Matanza" (The Massacre). It was also during this time that General Maximiliano Hernández Martínez consolidated his power, which he gained a year earlier via a coup. He ruled until 1944. Struggles broke out some three decades later, during the 1970s and 1980s, pitting government forces and right-wing death squads (responsible for the murder of the archbishop of San Salvador, Oscar Romero, on March 24, 1980) against a powerful, unified insurgent organization called the FMLN (Frente Farabundo Martí para la Liberación Nacional). The insurgents never took power, but did control many rural zones during the long struggle. In 1992, peace accords were signed in El Salvador, after a war that had cost billions of dollars, left about 75,000 dead, and sent more than half a million citizens abroad in search of a new home. The vast majority of the killings in El Salvador were committed by the Salvadoran army and the right-wing death squads.

Guatemala suffered a similar fate. After reform attempts between 1952 and 1954 were thwarted by wealthy landowners, the Catholic Church, and the United Fruit Company and its U.S. allies, Guatemala spiraled into a seemingly unstoppable civil war that left perhaps as many as 250,000 dead. The Guatemalan government squared off against poor people, the landless, and many urban intellectuals. The civil war, characterized by acts of genocide, was especially brutal during the early 1980s under the government of Efraín Rios Montt. His government targeted indigenous peoples and was responsible for the complete destruction of many indigenous villages. Just as in El Salvador, the insurgents never officially took power and were rendered somewhat powerless by massive infusions of U.S. military and economic aid that continually poured into Guatemala throughout the duration of the bloody conflict. Peace accords were finally signed in 1996 in Guatemala, after thirty-six years of incessant conflict. Rigoberta Menchú Tum received the 1992 Nobel Peace Prize for publishing her testimony of this period, and she continues to work for improved relations between indigenous peoples and people of European descent in her native Guatemala.

The one place, besides Cuba, where revolutionary forces succeeded—at least for a while—is Nicaragua. In 1979, a revolutionary group, the Sandinistas, took power in that country; they derived their name from the early twentieth-century insurgent leader, Augusto César Sandino, who fought a long, bloody war against U.S. intervention in the late 1920s and early 1930s. Sandino was executed in 1934 by Anastasio Somoza García, who consolidated power as director of the newly formed Nicaraguan National Guard, created with U.S. funding to help ensure order and stability in that country once U.S. Marines left (their departure was intended as a gesture of cooperation under Franklin D. Roosevelt's "Good Neighbor Policy"). The Somoza family ruled in Nicaragua for more than four decades and their abuses were legendary: in 1973 when an earthquake struck, a great deal of international relief was stolen by Somoza and the National Guard. This crime, together with the harassment and murder of journalists and Somoza family holdings estimated at one-quarter to one-third of all agricultural production in the country (by the late 1970s), helped turn the tide in favor of the insurgents by 1979.

The Sandinistas, greeted as heroes when they marched into the capital city of Managua in July 1979, put together an eclectic government comprised of economists, revolutionaries who had fought in the streets, and two Roman Catholic priests—Father Miguel D'Escoto, who became foreign minister, and Father Ernesto Cardenal, the minister of culture. The new government adopted a mixed economic plan that combined capitalism, expropriations, and Marxist social science approaches. However, the Sandinista's overall fortunes changed in 1980 when Ronald Reagan was elected president of the United States. Reagan defeated President Jimmy Carter by connecting the Democrat from Georgia to a "weak" foreign policy; he suggested that the triumph of Marxism in Nicaragua was Carter's fault. Once in office, Reagan became obsessed with defeating the Sandinistas, and the United States began channeling—first with the consent of Congress, and later illegally—funds to the *contras,* or counterrevolutionary fighters who worked to overthrow the government. The U.S. president named these mercenaries "freedom fighters" and managed to convince citizens of the United States that ending the Sandinista rule was vital to maintaining U.S. national security.

By 1990, after ten years of war and tens of thousands of deaths, the Sandinistas called elections and lost to Violeta Chamorro, the widow of slain journalist Pedro Joaquín Chamorro, who was killed by Somoza forces in January 1978. This election effectively ended the Sandinista Revolution.

BIBLIOGRAPHY

Keen, Benjamin, and Keith Haynes. 2004. *A History of Latin America.* 7th ed. Boston: Houghton Mifflin.
LaFeber, Walter. 1983. *Inevitable Revolutions.* New York: W.W. Norton.
Woodward, Ralph Lee, Jr. 1999. *Central America: A Nation Divided.* 3d ed. New York: Oxford University Press.

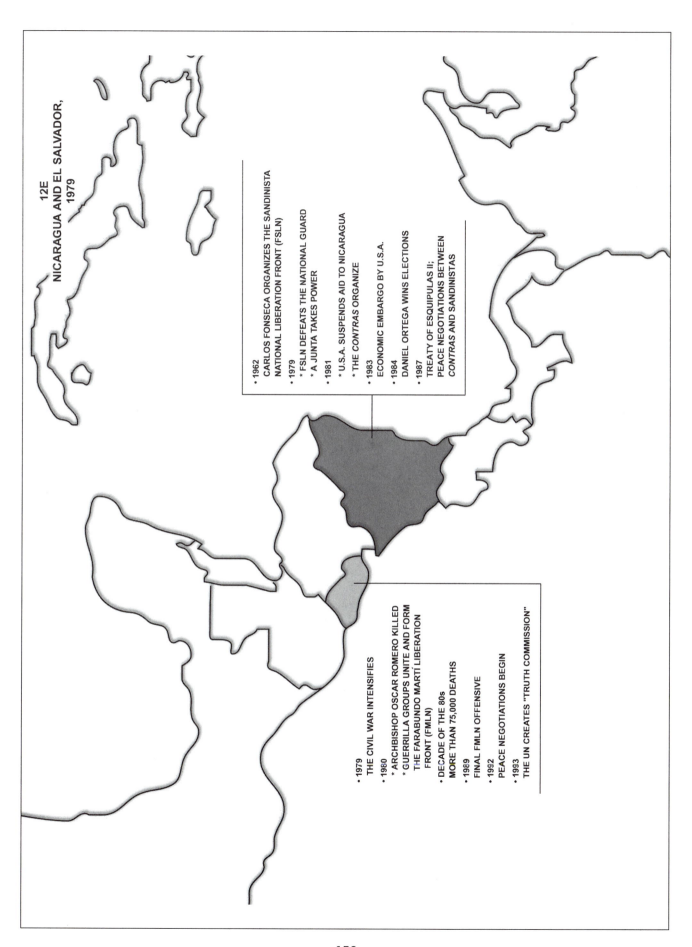

12E
NICARAGUA AND EL SALVADOR, 1979

• 1962
CARLOS FONSECA ORGANIZES THE SANDINISTA
NATIONAL LIBERATION FRONT (FSLN)
• 1979
* FSLN DEFEATS THE NATIONAL GUARD
* A JUNTA TAKES POWER
• 1981
* U.S.A. SUSPENDS AID TO NICARAGUA
* THE CONTRAS ORGANIZE
• 1983
ECONOMIC EMBARGO BY U.S.A.
• 1984
DANIEL ORTEGA WINS ELECTIONS
• 1987
TREATY OF ESQUIPULAS II;
PEACE NEGOTIATIONS BETWEEN
CONTRAS AND SANDINISTAS

• 1979
THE CIVIL WAR INTENSIFIES
• 1980
* ARCHBISHOP OSCAR ROMERO KILLED
* GUERRILLA GROUPS UNITE AND FORM
THE FARABUNDO MARTÍ LIBERATION
FRONT (FMLN)
• DECADE OF THE 80s
MORE THAN 75,000 DEATHS
• 1989
FINAL FMLN OFFENSIVE
• 1992
PEACE NEGOTIATIONS BEGIN
• 1993
THE UN CREATES "TRUTH COMMISSION"

12F

New Indigenous Movements: Peru's Sendero Luminoso, Mexico's EZLN, and Brazil's MST

Revolutionary tactics in Latin America have changed dramatically since the 1970s. The failure of the Sandinistas to realign Nicaragua demonstrated the difficulties and challenges of "administering" once in power. Revolutionary groups in Peru, Mexico, and Brazil organized during the 1980s and 1990s: they challenged their respective states and fought on behalf of the poor and marginalized, much like many of their predecessors. However, these groups distinguished themselves by developing new tactics that frightened citizens in Latin America and policymakers in Washington. The most radical of these groups, Peru's Shining Path (Sendero Luminoso)—influenced by Mao Zedong's rural revolution in China—called for the complete elimination of all Western influences in Peru. The group hoped to return Peru to its pre-Columbian Inca roots, and its emergence in the poor, indigenous southwest state of Ayacucho had a dramatic influence on Peruvian politics, economics, and society during the 1980s and 1990s. Mexico's EZLN (Zapatista Army of National Liberation) emerged on the world scene on January 1, 1994—the same day that the North American Free Trade Agreement went into effect—and Brazil's MST (Landless People's Movement—Movimento Sem Terra) continues to challenge the Brazilian state in defense of poor people's rights to land and work in rural Brazil.

The Shining Path, led by Peruvian philosophy professor Abimaél Guzmán, reacted to grinding poverty in the Ayacucho region and its relative isolation from the capital city, Lima, to advance a radical agenda. The militants who integrated into this organization envisioned a return to an idealized, utopian state, free of outside influences, Western political ideology, and economic exploitation. They hoped to create a sort of *pachacuti,* or complete reordering of society, and their tactics were ruthless. With the support of the United States military, the Peruvian military eventually gained control over the insurgents; the military locked down segments of Ayacucho and instituted its own form of state-sponsored repression. By the time the war ended with the capture of Guzmán in September 1992, between 65,000 and 70,000 Peruvians had been killed, the majority of whom were poor peasants in remote areas of the country. Despite their influence in Ayacucho, the Shining Path never attained political power, to the relief of most Peruvians, who were fearful of the group's radical agenda and tactics. However, the realities of generational poverty, isolation, and racism—factors that fueled the first Sendero struggle in Peru—have contributed to the reemergence of Sendero in rural areas of the country.

On January 1, 1994, the world learned of a "new" revolutionary group in Mexico called the EZLN, which took control of several municipalities in the southern state of Chiapas, a locale long ignored by political and economic elites in the capital city far to the north. The "Zapatistas," as they came to be known, took their name from the iconoclastic folk hero of the Mexican Revolution, Emiliano Zapata, a revolutionary who never succumbed to the temptations of political power or wealth while fighting for the rights of landless peasants in the southern state of Morelos. Zapata's cry of *tierra y libertad* (land and freedom) became the rallying cry for the Zapatistas, and they staged their uprising to coincide with the implementation of NAFTA—the North American Free Trade Agreement. Would NAFTA bring benefits to the poorest of the poor in Mexico, or would it merely advance the interests of capitalists and the professional sector of society?

The EZLN never intended to "take over" Mexican society, and in this sense, they differ dramatically from previous revolutionary groups in Latin America, including the Shining Path. They did, however, manage—via extraordinarily effective communications tactics, including use of the Internet—to convey their message to the world.

In Brazil, during the 1990s, a new revolutionary movement took shape to champion the interests of some 5 million Brazilian rural families who did not own land. The MST has mobilized across that country. Through relatively peaceful tactics such as land invasions, the MST has helped focus attention on the glaring disparities in the structure of Brazilian land tenure in a country where about half the population lives in poverty. In response to this movement, the Brazilian government initiated a moderate program of land distribution in 1994 under President Fernando Henrique Cardoso, which benefited tens of thousands of rural residents through transfer of fallow lands, with adequate compensation to owners. However, the limited nature of these reforms has barely affected the widening gap between the country's haves and have-nots.

The Shining Path of Peru, Mexico's EZLN, and the MST in Brazil represent local responses to poverty, repression, and a confusing array of neoliberal trade and economic policies that seem to ignore the plight of the poor, undereducated, and landless. The fact that all three movements still exist points to fundamental structural problems that are nearly impossible to redress via the polite rhetoric of modern, liberal governments in Latin America.

BIBLIOGRAPHY

Palmer, David Scott, ed. 1994. *Shining Path of Peru.* 2d ed. New York: St. Martin's.
Womack, John. 1999. *Rebellion in Chiapas.* New York: The New Press.
Salgado, Sebastião. 1997. *Terra: Struggle of the Landless.* London: Phaidon.

12F
NEW INDIGENOUS MOVEMENTS

• EPR
(POPULAR
REVOLUTIONARY ARMY)
• EZLN
(ZAPATISTA NATIONAL
LIBERATION ARMY)
• INDIGENOUS MOVEMENT OF
THE PEOPLE OF ANAHUAC
* CNI
(NATIONAL INDIGENOUS CONGRESS)

* COMMUNITARIAN
MISKITO NATION

* QUINTIN LAME
* ONIC
(NATIONAL INDIGENOUS ORGANIZATION OF COLOMBIA)
* CRIC
(REGIONAL INDIGENOUS COUNCIL OF CAUCA)

* COPMAGUA
(COORDINATION OF ORGANIZATIONS
OF THE MAYA PEOPLE OF GUATEMALA)

* CONIVE
(NATIONAL INDIAN COUNCIL
OF VENEZUELA)

* NATIONAL SALVADORAN INDIGENOUS ASSOCIATION

* COPINH
(CIVIC COUNCIL OF POPULAR AND
INDIGENOUS ORGANIZATIONS OF HONDURAS)

* COICA
(COORDINATION OF
INDIGENOUS ORGANIZATION
OF THE CUENCA AMAZONICA)

* NATIONAL INDIGENOUS TABLE OF COSTA RICA

* GENERAL KUNA CONGRESS OF PANAMA

* CONAINE
(CONFEDERATION OF INDIGENOUS NATIONALITIES OF ECUADOR)

* CAPOIB
(COORDINATING COUNCIL OF
INDIGENOUS PEOPLES AND
ORGANIZATIONS OF BRAZIL)

• TUPAC
KATARI
GUERRILLA
ARMY
1991

• MST
(LANDLESS PEOPLE'S
MOVEMENT)

• SHINING PATH
* ALDESEP
(INTERETHNIC ASSOCIATION OF DEVELOPMENT OF THE PERUVIAN JUNGLE)

* CONFEDERATION OF INDIGENOUS
PEOPLES OF BOLIVIA

* NATIVE LEAGUE
FOR AUTONOMY
JUSTICE, AND
ETHICS

* CTLTM
(COUNCIL OF ALL THE MAPUCHE LANDS)

* AIRA
(INDIGENOUS
ASSOCIATION
OF THE
REPUBLIC OF
ARGENTINA)

• ARMED MOVEMENT

* NONARMED MOVEMENT
(INDIGENOUS ORGANIZATION)

INDEX

Michael J. LaRosa is associate professor of history at Rhodes College in Memphis. LaRosa has been a Fulbright scholar in Colombia and has published six books, including a co-edited collection (with Germán R. Mejía) titled *The United States Discovers Panama* (2004).

Germán R. Mejía is professor of history at the Pontificia Universidad Javeriana, Bogotá, Colombia. He is the author of *Los años del cambio: Historia urbana de Bogotá, 1820–1910* (2000). Mejía is editor of the Colombian journal *Memoria y Sociedad* and was named, in April 2004, founding director of the Archivo de Bogotá.